THE INFLUENCE OF EZRA POUND

K. L. GOODWIN

THE INFLUENCE OF
EZRA POUND

London
OXFORD UNIVERSITY PRESS
NEW YORK   TORONTO

Oxford University Press, Ely House, London W.1

GLASGOW   NEW YORK   TORONTO   MELBOURNE   WELLINGTON
CAPE TOWN   SALISBURY   IBADAN   NAIROBI   LUSAKA   ADDIS ABABA
BOMBAY   CALCUTTA   MADRAS   KARACHI   LAHORE   DACCA
KUALA LUMPUR   HONG KONG   TOKYO

First published 1966
Reprinted 1968

Printed Photolitho in Great Britain by
Ebenezer Baylis & Son Limited,
The Trinity Press, Worcester, and London

PREFACE

To PROFIT from advice, to heed warnings, and to know the true value of encouragement are not easy lessons for an author to learn. The least he can do is be grateful to those who have patiently tried to teach him. My thanks are due in various ways to Mr. Wesley Milgate, Mr. A. L. French, Professor G. A. Wilkes, Professor A. C. Cawley, Mr. C. H. Hadgraft, Professor K. G. Hamilton, and Professor John Holloway, from whose help I should have profited more.

The staffs of the state and university libraries of Australia have been tireless in locating and lending material, and a number of university libraries in the U.S.A. have kindly supplied microfilm copies with great promptness. My special thanks are due to Mr. S. J. Routh, whose help and resourcefulness as Reference Librarian in the University of Queensland were unfailing.

For the use of copyright material within the text the following acknowledgements are gratefully made:

CONRAD AIKEN: Extracts from *Ushant: An Essay* reprinted by permission of the author, W. H. Allen and Co., and The World Publishing Company (Meridian Books).

RICHARD ALDINGTON: Lines from *Collected Poems* reprinted by permission of Catherine Guillaume, Alister Kershaw, and the publishers, George Allen and Unwin Ltd. An extract from 'Farewell to Europe' reprinted by permission of Catherine Guillaume, Alister Kershaw, and *The Atlantic Monthly*; copyright © 1940 by The Atlantic Monthly Company, Boston, Mass.

JOHN PEALE BISHOP: Lines from *The Collected Poems of John Peale Bishop* and *Selected Poems* reprinted by permission of the respective publishers, Charles Scribner's Sons and Chatto and Windus Ltd.

PHYLLIS BOTTOME: An extract from *From the Life* reprinted by permission of the Estate of Phyllis Bottome and the publishers, Faber and Faber Ltd.

MALCOLM COWLEY: An extract from *Exile's Return: A Literary Odyssey of the 1920's* reprinted by permission of The Viking Press Inc., The Bodley Head Ltd., and Laurence Pollinger Ltd.

HART CRANE: Lines from *The Collected Poems, Selected Letters and Prose of Hart Crane* reprinted by permission of Liveright, Publishers, New York; copyright © 1966 by Liveright Publishing Corp.

E. E. CUMMINGS: Lines from *Poems: 1923–1954* (from 'Portraits' and *VV(ViVa)*) reprinted by permission of the publishers, Harcourt, Brace and World, Inc.

H.D.: Lines from *Collected Poems of H.D.* (published by Liveright Publishing Corp.) reprinted by permission of Norman Holmes Pearson (copyright 1925) and Grove Press, Inc. Lines from *H.D.: Selected Poems* reprinted by permission of Norman Holmes Pearson (copyright © 1957) and the publishers, Grove Press, Inc.

EDWARD DORN: 'Vaquero' reprinted by permission of the author.

T. S. ELIOT: Lines from *Collected Poems: 1909–1962* reprinted by permission of the publishers, Faber and Faber Ltd. and Harcourt, Brace and World, Inc. (copyright 1936); copyright © 1963 by T. S. Eliot. Lines from *Murder in the Cathedral* and extracts from *Selected Essays* reprinted by permission of Faber and Faber Ltd. and Harcourt, Brace and World, Inc. An extract from *The Sacred Wood* reprinted by permission of Methuen and Co. Ltd. and Barnes and Noble, Inc. Extracts from *On Poetry and Poets* reprinted by permission of the publishers, Faber and Faber Ltd., and Farrar, Straus and Giroux, Inc. An extract from the essay, 'Ezra Pound', which appeared in *An Examination of Ezra Pound*, edited by Peter Russell, reprinted by permission of the publishers, New Directions, New York; all rights reserved.

DONALD FINKEL: Lines from 'An Esthetic of Imitation' reprinted by permission of *The Paris Review* (where it appeared in No. 15, Winter 1957).

R. D. FITZGERALD: Lines from 'Heemskerck Shoals' reprinted by permission of the author.

FORD MADOX FORD: Extracts from *It was the Nightingale* and from 'On Heaven' reprinted by permission of Miss Janice Biala.

DONALD HALL: Lines from *The Dark Houses* reprinted by permission of The Viking Press Inc. and Curtis Brown Ltd.

GLENN HUGHES: An extract from *Imagism and the Imagists* reprinted by permission of Humanities Press Inc.

T. E. HULME: 'Autumn' reprinted from *Speculations* by permission of the publishers, Routledge and Kegan Paul Ltd. and Harcourt, Brace and World, Inc.

ROBINSON JEFFERS: Lines from *Roan Stallion, Tamar, and Other Poems* reprinted by permission of the publishers, Random House, Inc. and The Hogarth Press Ltd.; copyright 1924 by Peter G. Boyle, 1925 by Boni and Liveright, Inc., 1933, 1937 by Random House, Inc.

JAMES JOYCE: Extracts from *Letters of James Joyce*, edited by Stuart Gilbert, reprinted by permission of Faber and Faber Ltd. and The Viking Press Inc.

KENNETH KOCH: Lines from *Thank You and Other Poems* reprinted by permission of the author and the publishers, Grove Press, Inc.; copyright © 1962 by Kenneth Koch.

PHILIP LARKIN: Lines from *The Whitsun Weddings* reprinted by permission of the publishers, Faber and Faber Ltd.

WYNDHAM LEWIS: Extracts from *Time and Western Man* reprinted by permission of Methuen and Co. Ltd.

AMY LOWELL: 'The Pond' and lines from 'In a Garden' reprinted by permission of the publishers, Houghton Mifflin Co.

ROBERT LOWELL: Lines from *Poems: 1938–1949* reprinted by permission of the publishers, Faber and Faber Ltd. and Harcourt, Brace and World, Inc.

RONALD MCCUAIG: Lines from *Quod Ronald McCuaig* reprinted by permission of the author and Angus and Robertson Ltd.

HUGH MACDIARMID: Lines from *In Memoriam James Joyce* reprinted by permission of the author (Christopher Murray Grieve). An extract from *Lucky Poet* reprinted by permission of Methuen and Co. Ltd.

ARCHIBALD MACLEISH: Lines from *The Collected Poems of Archibald MacLeish* reprinted by permission of Houghton Mifflin Co.; all rights reserved. Lines from 'Pole Star for this Year' (from *Public Speech*) reprinted by permission of Holt, Rinehart and Winston, Inc., Publishers, New York; copyright 1936, © 1964 by Archibald MacLeish. Lines from 'Tricked by eternity the heart' reprinted by permission of Random House, Inc.; all rights reserved.

W. S. MERWIN: Lines from *Green with Beasts* reprinted by permission of Rupert Hart-Davis Ltd. and Alfred A. Knopf, Inc.

CHRISTOPHER MIDDLETON: Lines from 'Edward Lear in February' reprinted by permission of the author.

MARIANNE MOORE: Lines from *Collected Poems* reprinted by permission of Faber and Faber Ltd. and The Macmillan Company ('The Fish', 'The Frigate Pelican', 'A Grave', and 'Poetry' copyright 1935 by Marianne Moore, renewed 1963 by Marianne Moore and T. S. Eliot; 'Melancthon' copyright 1951 by Marianne Moore).

EDWIN MUIR: Lines from *Collected Poems: 1921–1958* reprinted by permission of Faber and Faber Ltd.

CHARLES NORMAN: An extract from *The Magic-Maker: E. E. Cummings* reprinted by permission of The Macmillan Company; copyright 1958, 1964 by Charles Norman.

CHARLES OLSON: Lines from *The Distances* reprinted by permission of the author and the publishers, Grove Press, Inc.; copyright © 1950, 1951, 1953, 1960 by Charles Olson.

GEORGE OPPEN: Lines of verse reprinted by permission of the author.

EZRA POUND: Extracts from *Personae: Collected Shorter Poems, Cantos,*

ginative Literature of 1870–1930 reprinted by permission of the publishers, Charles Scribner's Sons.

W. B. YEATS: Lines from *The Collected Poems of W. B. Yeats* reprinted by permission of Mr. M. B. Yeats, Macmillan and Co. Ltd., A. P. Watt and Son, and The Macmillan Company (*In the Seven Woods* copyright 1903 by The Macmillan Company, renewed 1931 by William Butler Yeats; *Poems* copyright 1906 by The Macmillan Company, renewed 1934 by William Butler Yeats; *The Green Helmet and Other Poems* copyright 1912 by The Macmillan Company, renewed 1940 by Bertha Georgie Yeats; *Responsibilities* copyright 1916 by The Macmillan Company, renewed 1946 by Bertha Georgie Yeats; *The Wild Swans at Coole* copyright 1919 by The Macmillan Company, renewed 1946 by Bertha Georgie Yeats). Lines from *The Collected Plays of W. B. Yeats* reprinted by permission of Mr. M. B. Yeats, Macmillan and Co. Ltd., A. P. Watt and Son, and The Macmillan Company (*The Poetical Works of William B. Yeats*, vol. II, Dramatical Poems copyright 1907 by The Macmillan Company, renewed 1935 by William Butler Yeats; *Four Plays for Dancers* copyright 1921 by The Macmillan Company, renewed 1949 by Bertha Georgie Yeats). Extracts from *Autobiographies* and from *Essays and Introductions* reprinted by permission of Mr. M. B. Yeats, Macmillan and Co. Ltd., A. P. Watt and Son, and The Macmillan Company (*Autobiographies* copyright 1916, 1936 by The Macmillan Company, 1944 by Bertha Georgie Yeats; *Essays and Introductions* copyright © 1961 by Mrs. W. B. Yeats). Extracts from *The Letters of W. B. Yeats*, edited by Allan Wade, reprinted by permission of Rupert Hart-Davis Ltd. and The Macmillan Company; copyright 1953, 1954 by Anne Butler Yeats.

I am also grateful for permission to reprint from a note in *Notes and Queries*.

My thanks are due to the people and companies who helped me trace the owners of copyright. Any errors in or omissions from the acknowledgements are, however, my responsibility, and I should be glad to learn of them.

CONTENTS

INTRODUCTION

'*TOUTE étude de la poésie américaine moderne,*' wrote René Taupin in 1930, '*doit commencer par une étude des œuvres critiques et poétiques d'Ezra Pound.*'[1] The belief that Pound has been the chief influence on American poetry this century, and one of the chief influences on British poetry, is widely held. It is a belief that receives support from the testimony of some of the greatest poets of the century. W. B. Yeats acknowledged that Pound 'helps me to get back to the definite and concrete, away from modern abstractions, to talk over a poem with him is like getting [Lady Gregory] to put a sentence into dialect. All becomes clear and natural.'[2] T. S. Eliot wrote that

He has enabled a few persons, including myself, to improve their verse sense; so that he has improved poetry through other men as well as by himself. I cannot think of any one writing verse, of our generation and the next, whose verse (if any good) has not been improved by the study of Pound's.[3]

Pound has been acclaimed not just as a critic of contemporary verse, but as a critic of the poetic tradition, one whose insights, notably into Dante, Shakespeare, Milton, Guido Cavalcanti, and Arnaut Daniel, have been major contributions to literary criticism. His kindness to young writers, his concern for their physical as well as their literary well-being, has been praised even by his detractors. He has been credited with achieving publication for James Joyce, and providing the conditions under which *Ulysses* and *Finnegans Wake* could be written. He has been, throughout his long and energetic life, an inveterate maker of acquaintances, writer of letters, and giver of advice; he has known personally most of the important poets and critics of the twentieth century—and those whom he has not met have had some knowledge of his work; he has interested himself not only in literature but also in sculpture, in music, in

[1] 'La poésie d'Ezra Pound', *Revue Anglo-Américaine*, VIII (1930–1), p. 221 n.
[2] Quoted by Joseph Hone, *W. B. Yeats: 1865–1939*, 2nd ed. (London: Macmillan, 1962), p. 272.
[3] 'Isolated Superiority', review of *Collected Poems* by Ezra Pound, *The Dial*, LXXXIV (January 1928), p. 5.

economics, and in politics, with the result that opinions about his work in one of these fields tend to be carried over by those who hold them into some or all of the other fields; he and his works have created implacable enemies, and equally implacable defenders; and his poetry remains an occult scripture, more commented on than read.

He has obviously had a multitude of opportunities to exert influence. That he has effectively used these opportunities is more often assumed than investigated. The most easily ascertainable facts —facts about his relations with publishers, and about the spread of terms that he made fashionable—are generally the least interesting, not merely because they are obvious and indisputable, but also because they concern the accomplishment of deeds or the transfer of qualities that are superficial or unimportant. The transfer of fundamental attitudes, beliefs, interests, and techniques is more interesting, but less easily demonstrated; more significant, but also more conjectural.

There are two obvious ways of investigating Pound's influence, one through a chronological study of his interests and friends, the other through a study of textual or literary evidence. Both are adopted in this book. Part I is a study of Pound's interests and friends, divided chronologically into four chapters. Part II applies a combined chronological and textual method of study to the two great poets whose lives came into contact with Pound's in conditions almost ideal for influence. Part III is a textual study of other poets who were influenced.

PART I. INTERESTS AND FRIENDS

1. TO 1914

THE earliest literary influence by Pound of which there is any record occurred during his student days at the University of Pennsylvania, in the early years of the twentieth century. There he met one of his lifelong friends, William Carlos Williams, who was studying medicine at the same time as Pound was studying Latin, English, and American history. They were in the same dormitory, and met late in 1902 or early in 1903, during Williams's first term. Williams has always acknowledged Pound's friendliness to him, but minimized (and possibly underestimated) any direct influence:

I wish it to be clearly understood that I am deeply indebted to him for much of my early knowledge of the problems faced by a writer. . . . What have you read? is still his attack upon me. That has been the beginning and the end of his whole poetic dynamization.[1]

All of Williams's printed reminiscences support this attitude. In his autobiography[2] he reports that at the outset of his university career in medicine he carefully considered each of the arts before deciding that he would give what time he had to literature. This 'preliminary skirmish', he says, ended with the spontaneous writing of a poem:

> A black, black cloud
> flew over the sun
> driven by fierce flying
> rain.[3]

The first important thing to be noted about this poem is that it

[1] Preface to *Poetry: The Australian International Quarterly of Verse*, No. 25 (10 December 1947), p. 8.
[2] *The Autobiography of William Carlos Williams* (New York: Random House, 1951).
[3] Ibid., p. 47.

I

does not differ in style from a great many poems written much later by Williams, poems like 'The Term' or the opening of 'To a Poor Old Woman'.[1] Secondly, it is very like many 'imagist' poems, though Imagism as a movement was not inaugurated until 1908. Thirdly, Williams in his autobiography deliberately suggests that it was written before he knew Pound, and he reinforces this impression by statements elsewhere, such as this, from his *Selected Essays*: 'There was a group of young men and women centering about Ezra Pound in those days who were important to me. At the same time my mind was tough and not easily carried away by the opinions of others.'[2] The evidence indicates, then, that Pound's influence on Williams was not, as it might seem at first sight, in the direction of imagism, and that it did not occur in the early days of their friendship. I suggest that influence occurred much later, when Williams was writing *Paterson*, and that it occurred largely as a result of the one source of influence that Williams admits, namely advice about his reading.

The letters that Williams wrote during his student days present a reasonably detached description of Pound's personality, a description that is remarkably similar to the one given by Wyndham Lewis of Pound as he knew him some ten or fifteen years later.[3] In one letter Williams comments on Pound's optimism, assurance, affectation, adoption of poses, essential tenderness and kindness, and loquacity.[4] These early responses to Pound's personality are set down in a more systematic way (and without the distortion that often comes from hindsight) in Williams's autobiography, where he sums Pound up as being 'often brilliant but an ass'.[5] In this work he comments on Pound's sublime self-confidence; the serious professional attitude he had towards his literary career; and his infinite capacity for taking pains, both with his own work, and with the work of others. He notes in addition Pound's 'often painful self-consciousness'[6] (a quality that Pound's influence has helped to make

---

[1] See *The Collected Earlier Poems of William Carlos Williams* (Norfolk, Conn.: New Directions, 1951), pp. 99, 409.

[2] *Selected Essays of William Carlos Williams* (New York: Random House, 1954), pp. xi–xii.

[3] See *Time and Western Man* (London: Chatto & Windus, 1927).

[4] A letter to his mother, written 30 March 1904; *The Selected Letters of William Carlos Williams*, ed. with introduction by John C. Thirlwall (New York: McDowell, Obolensky, 1957), p. 6.

[5] Williams, *Autobiography*, p. 58.   [6] Ibid.

a prominent feature of twentieth-century verse), and the posturing that went with it (a quality that must have had an effect on Pound's doctrine of the 'persona').

These qualities, possessed by Pound throughout his life, go part of the way towards explaining the extent of his influence, or at least towards explaining the large numbers of people who think they have been influenced by him. Another student at the University of Pennsylvania, Phyllis Bottome, has testified that 'Ezra gave me the first unbiased and objective literary criticism I had ever known. I still listen to this criticism, and that it has increased in value with every year of my growth, says something perhaps for its young creator.'[1] Unlike Williams, Miss Bottome gives a brief account of the content of this criticism. According to her, it was chiefly advice to concentrate on the image, to avoid superfluities, and to 'live' what she wanted to write. This advice, she says, was given when she met Pound in London at a literary tea-party given by May Sinclair. It seems likely from other remarks in *From the Life* that she must have met Pound fairly soon after his arrival in London. Now it is well known from other sources that by 1908—that is, on his arrival in London, or shortly afterwards—Pound held views similar to those mentioned by Miss Bottome. This is apparent from his letters;[2] and from his magazine articles. In his article, 'A Few Don'ts by an Imagiste', for instance, he wrote:

An 'Image' is that which presents an intellectual and emotional complex in an instant of time . . . .

It is better to present one Image in a lifetime than to produce voluminous works.

Use no superfluous word, no adjective which does not reveal something.[3]

If the advice given to Williams was based on the same precepts as

---

[1] *From the Life* (London: Faber & Faber, 1944), p. 72.
[2] See, for instance, the letter to William Carlos Williams, 21 October 1908; *The Letters of Ezra Pound: 1907–1941*, ed. D. D. Paige (London: Faber & Faber, 1951), pp. 39–40.
[3] *Poetry*, I, 6 (March 1913), pp. 200–201; reprinted in *Literary Essays of Ezra Pound*, ed. T. S. Eliot (London: Faber & Faber, 1954), p. 4.

Pound espoused in 1908, he would have to be considered as one of the originators of Imagist doctrines, and would have to share some of the credit accorded to T. E. Hulme and F. M. Hueffer in the standard accounts of the movement.

When Pound settled in London towards the end of 1908 there was a great deal more literary ferment there than in any American city. As Pound said, having made many contacts with writers and their ideas in his first few months, 'London, deah old Lundon, is the place for poesy.'[1] By contrast, Williams, Harriet Monroe, H.D., John Gould Fletcher, Amy Lowell, and many other young American poets were at this time struggling in a dissatisfied way with their existing ideas without being able to find a direction for new ideas: almost all of them (including Williams, who was very nationalistic in his beliefs about literature) lost little time in making a pilgrimage to London, some of them prompted by Pound's enthusiasm.

Pound's first important acquaintance seems to have been Elkin Mathews, the printer and publisher. In December, Mathews published half the copies of Pound's first London volume, *A Quinzaine for this Yule*,[2] and later published a number of books for Pound and for his friends. Pound's next important contact was with T. E. Hulme and with what he himself afterwards christened 'Imagisme'. The meeting with Hulme seems to have taken place at one of Hulme's Thursday evening gatherings in a Soho restaurant, on 22 April 1909. This is an important date in the history of Pound's contribution to Imagism; by this time a number of imagist poems had been published by people in Hulme's circle independently of any influence by Pound; after this time, the same people are possible objects for his influence.

The earliest poems claimed by Pound as 'imagistic' were apparently written not only independently of Pound's influence, but even possibly a year or so before Pound stated some of the principles of imagism to Phyllis Bottome. The evidence occurs in a verse letter from Allen Upward:

---

[1] Letter to William Carlos Williams, 3 February 1909; *Letters*, p. 41.
[2] There were two hundred copies, the first hundred published by the printer of all the copies, Pollock & Co., the second hundred by Elkin Mathews. Mathews's publication in April 1909 of Pound's next volume of verse, *Personae*, served to make Pound fairly well known in London literary circles.

THE DISCARDED IMAGIST

To the Editor, *The Egoist.*

.   .   .   .

In the year nineteen hundred a poet named Cranmer Byng
    brought to my attic in Whitehall Gardens a book of
    Chinese Gems by Professor Giles,
Eastern butterflies coming into my attic there beside
    the Stygian Thames,
And read me one of them—willows, forsaken young wife,
    spring.

Immediately my soul kissed the soul of immemorial China:
I perceived that all we in the West were indeed barbarians
    and foreign devils,
And that we knew scarcely anything about poetry.

I set to work and wrote little poems
Some of which I read to a scientific friend
Who said,—'After all, what do they prove?'

Then I hid them away for ten or twelve years,
Scented leaves in a Chinese jar,
While I went on composing the poem of life.

I withstood the savages of the Niger with a revolver:
I withstood the savages of the Thames with a printing-press:
Byng and I we set up as publishers in Fleet Street, and
    produced the 'Odes of Confucius,' and the 'Sayings.'

My own poems I did not produce:
They were sent back to me by the *Spectator* and the
    English Review.
I secretly grudged them to the Western devils.

After many years I sent them to Chicago, and they were
    printed by Harriet Monroe. (They were also printed
    in *The Egoist.*)
Thereupon Ezra Pound the generous rose up and called
    me an Imagist. (I had no idea what he meant.)
And he included me in an anthology of Imagists.[1]

---

[1] *Des Imagistes: An Anthology*, ed. Ezra Pound (London: Poetry Bookshop; New York:
A. & C. Boni, 1914).

This was a very great honour.
But I was left out of the next anthology.[1]
This was a very great shame.

And now I have read in a history of Imagism
That the movement was started in nineteen hundred and
    eight
By Edward Storer and T. E. Hulme.

.   .   .   .

ALLEN UPWARD.[2]

The 'history of Imagism' referred to by Upward was F. S. Flint's 'A History of Imagism'.[3] It is this article that provides the evidence for what appears to have been Pound's first meeting with Hulme. Speaking of Hulme's weekly gatherings, Flint records that 'On April 22, 1909, Ezra Pound, whose book, "Personae," had been published on the previous Friday, joined the group, introduced, I believe, by Miss Farr and my friend T. D. FitzGerald.'[4] Had Hulme already known Pound, he, as leader of the group, would no doubt have introduced him; what actually happened is, fairly obviously, that Pound was introduced to Hulme on this occasion.

Now by this time, as Flint records, a number of imagist poems had been published by various people known to Hulme. The Poets' Club,[5] from which Hulme and his group had broken away, had already published two of the five poems by Hulme which Pound later printed at the end of his *Ripostes* and claimed as imagistic. This publication occurred in the small pamphlet, *For Christmas MDCCCCVIII.*[6] In November, Edward Storer, who was one of the inaugural members when Hulme's Thursday night group first

---

[1] *Some Imagist Poets: An Anthology*, ed. Amy Lowell (Boston and New York: Houghton Mifflin; London: Constable, 1915). This volume was published after Pound and Amy Lowell had disagreed about the principles of, and the publishing policy desirable for, the Imagists, and Pound had withdrawn from the publishing venture. In *Catholic Anthology*, which he edited later in the same year, some of Upward's work was included.

[2] *The Egoist*, II, 6 (1 June 1915), p. 98.

[3] *The Egoist*, II, 5 (1 May 1915), pp. 70–1.   [4] Ibid., p. 71.

[5] So called by Flint in this article. The same group is referred to as 'the Poetry Club' by Stanley K. Coffman, Jr., in his *Imagism: A Chapter for the History of Modern Poetry* (Norman, Oklahoma: University of Oklahoma Press, 1951).

[6] *For Christmas MDCCCCVIII*: New Poems by Selwyn Image, Lady Margaret Sackville, Henry Simpson, Marion Cran, F. W. Tancred, T. E. Hulme and Dermot Freyer (Piccadilly, London: Women's Printing Society, January 1909).

met in 1909, had his *Mirrors of Influence* published. I have not seen a copy of this book, but according to Flint it was

the first book of 'Imagist' poems, with an essay at the end attacking poetic conventions. The first poem in the book was called 'Image,' here it is:

Forsaken lover,
Burning to a chaste white moon,
Upon strange pyres of loneliness and drought.[1]

So far, then, it is obvious that at least two fairly independent starting points for imagism, or for something akin to imagism, can be found in the work of Upward, and in the work of Hulme and a few friends of Hulme, perhaps influenced by his theories and practice. A third claim for originality has been made by Ford Madox Hueffer (later Ford), a novelist and critic who seems to have spent a good deal of his life making claims for having influenced the history of English poetry and of the English novel in a major, but so far unacknowledged, way. According to Hueffer:

I do not suppose that I have led a movement, though I dare say I have. There isn't, you know, any knowing in these matters. Supposing that I should say that my young friends the Imagists were children of my teaching, I expect that, with one accord, they would get up and say that they had never heard of me. The world is like that. But still, unceasingly, in season and out, for a quarter of a century I have preached the doctrine that my young friends now inscribe on the banner of their movement. . . .
What, then, is this doctrine? Simply that the rendering of the material facts of life, without comment and in exact language, is poetry and that poetry is the only important thing in life.[2]

Hueffer's claim embraces practice as well as theory with the same rather suspicious retrospectivity. In a volume of memoirs he asserted that he had adopted a modern kind of verse by 1898. The example quoted is 'The Great View', which he takes to illustrate the virtues of dealing with everyday life, using the diction of prose, giving a 'marmoreal' treatment to the subject, avoiding unnecessary thought dictated by a rhyme-scheme, and subduing metre to 'the personal cadence of the writer's mind or the pressure of the recorded emotion'.[3]

---

[1] F. S. Flint, loc. cit., p. 70.
[2] F. M. Hueffer, 'A Jubilee', *The Outlook*, XXXVI (1915), p. 46.
[3] See his *Thus to Revisit: Some Reminiscences* (London: Chapman & Hall, 1921), pp. 206–7.

Pound accepted some of Hueffer's verse as being 'written in the "twentieth-century fashion" ', and having ' "the modern cadence " ',[1] and this opinion apparently extended to verse printed in Hueffer's *Songs from London* (London: E. Mathews, 1910), much of which, he said, 'hangs in my memory'.[2] Now *Songs from London* contained the verses that Hueffer had written since the publication of his previous volume of verse, *The Face of the Night*, in 1904; many had appeared in periodicals before Hueffer knew Pound. There can be little doubt, then, that Hueffer had arrived at something like Imagism before meeting Pound. Pound, at any rate, would admit that this was so, and would even admit to being influenced by Hueffer. He often acknowledged Hueffer's primacy in insisting on the avoidance of 'literary' expressions and on keeping to the simplicity of speech:

It should be realized that Ford Madox Ford had been hammering this point of view into me from the time I first met him (1908 or 1909) and that I owe him anything that I don't owe myself for having saved me from the academic influences then raging in London.[3]

So far we have isolated what appear to be three independent starting points for Imagism apart from Pound: Upward, Hulme, and Hueffer. Now it is possible that these starting points are not entirely independent—possible, for instance, that both Upward and Hulme unconsciously drew their ideas from Hueffer's frequent periodical articles, or from discussions with him. This particular possibility (which is the most likely one) exists only if (i) Hueffer's arrival at Imagistic principles took place about 1898, as he asserts, or at least before about 1906; (ii) these principles found their way into his articles and reviews, and into his spoken discussions; (iii) Upward and Hulme were acquainted either with him or with his work. The least likely of these conditions is the third. The fact that during the fifteen months he was editor of *The English Review* (December 1908 to February 1910; Vol. I, No. 1 to Vol. IV, No. 3) Hueffer printed no work by either of them, though both were gaining publication elsewhere, suggests that he was not a close friend of

[1] Ezra Pound, 'The Prose Tradition in Verse', *Poetry* (1914); reprinted in *Literary Essays*, pp. 373, 374.
[2] Ibid., p. 375.
[3] Note signed 'E.P. January, 1937' in Harriet Monroe, *A Poet's Life: Seventy Years in a Changing World* (New York: Macmillan, 1938), p. 267.

theirs. It is true that his neglect of their work may not have been reciprocated, but in view of the cliquishness that prevailed in London literary circles it seems likely that it was.

It may be asked whether Pound should be considered as an independent starting point for Imagism. His admission that he had learnt from Hueffer might suggest a lack of independence, but if Miss Bottome is right in indicating that he held the basic ideas of Imagism in 1902 or 1903 he must obviously have arrived at them independently of Hueffer, whose work he did not know until his arrival in England.

It would seem, in any case, that Pound was not the sole originator of either the theory or practice of Imagism. There are at least three others whose work, published before he knew them, he has accepted as being imagistic. William Carlos Williams is a possible fourth, if we accept his account of the composition of his early poems. And if one merely looks for independence in adopting imagistic principles, irrespective of priority in time, one would have to take account of H.D., Richard Aldington, and T. S. Eliot. Pound's influence on Imagism was chiefly as an organizer and publicist. The first printed mention of Imagism as a school was made by Pound in the Prefatory Note to 'The Complete Poetical Works of T. E. Hulme', published at the end of Pound's *Ripostes* in October 1912. In it he refers to 'The "School of Images", which may or may not have existed', and, again, to 'the forgotten school of 1909'.[1] These appear to be references to the group meeting under Hulme's tutelage on Thursday evenings in 1909. This group was small, and did not seek publicity. It did not leave any published monuments to itself. But in 1912 Pound revived, and perhaps systematized, the ideas current in 1909. In the Prefatory Note referred to, one can discern the first shot of a publicity offensive on typical Poundian lines. It is the apparently objective, slightly mystifying, and purposely self-advertising announcement that 'As for the future, *Les Imagistes*, the descendants of the forgotten school of 1909, have that in their keeping.'[2]

It is perhaps unfair to speak of Pound as 'self-advertising' in this

---

[1] Reprinted in *Personae: Collected Shorter Poems of Ezra Pound* (London: Faber & Faber, 1952), p. 259.
[2] Ibid.

example. His motives for the revival of Imagism were largely altruistic and didactic. He wrote that 'The name was invented to launch H.D. [Hilda Doolittle] and Richard [Aldington] before either had enough stuff for a volume. Also to establish a critical demarcation long since knocked to hell.'[1] H.D. had known Pound quite well when he was at the University of Pennsylvania, and had met him again during his stay in America from the summer of 1910 until February 1911. Perhaps because of Pound's urging, she decided in 1911 to visit London, where she met, and later married, Aldington. Aldington has left an account of Pound's announcement of the movement to its inaugural members:

the Imagist movement was born in a teashop—in the Royal Borough of Kensington. For some time Ezra had been butting in on our studies and poetic productions, with alternate encouragements and the reverse, according to his mood. H.D. produced some poems which I thought excellent, and she either handed or mailed them to Ezra. Presently each of us received a ukase to attend the Kensington bunshop. Ezra was so much worked up by these poems of H.D.'s that he removed his pince-nez and informed us that we were Imagists.[2]

Pound's enthusiasm was conveyed in a letter to Harriet Monroe enclosing H.D.'s poems for publication in *Poetry* (Chicago). The letter makes it clear that Pound took no credit for having influenced H.D.'s work. He tells Miss Monroe that H.D.'s subjects were ones that she had 'lived with . . . since childhood'; and her treatment of them, being so exact an exemplification of his own principles of objectivity and directness, obviously caused him as much astonishment as delight. He summed up the treatment by saying that it was 'modern, . . . in the laconic speech of the Imagistes'.[3] It is doubtful whether Harriet Monroe knew at this stage what an 'Imagiste' was supposed to be, but she introduced the term to America with the reference to Aldington as 'one of the Imagistes' in the Notes to Vol. I, No. 2 (November 1912), and with the printing of H.D.'s poems in Vol. I, No. 4 (January 1913) as by 'H.D., Imagiste'. In the same issue as H.D.'s poems was an article by Pound, 'Status Rerum' (pp. 123—127), in which he referred to the Imagistes as a

[1] Letter from Ezra Pound to Glenn Hughes, 26 September 1927; *Letters*, p. 288.
[2] 'Farewell to Europe', *The Atlantic Monthly*, CLXVI (1940), pp. 526–7.
[3] October 1912; *Letters*, p. 45.

live literary group in London, but did not mention his connexion with them. Two months later, Imagism became as plain to readers of *Poetry* as Pound was ever able to make it with an article, 'Imagisme', by F. S. Flint (pp. 198–200), which was a report of an interview with Pound, and Pound's own 'A Few Don'ts by an Imagiste' (pp. 200–206). In Flint's article occurred what Pound was later[1] to call 'the first manifesto'. It consisted of the principles that Pound had announced to Aldington and H.D.:

1. Direct treatment of the 'thing,' whether subjective or objective.
2. To use absolutely no word that did not contribute to the presentation.
3. As regarding rhythm: to compose in the sequence of the musical phrase, not in sequence of a metronome.[2]

1913 was a very busy year for Pound. In the first few months he worked indefatigably as foreign correspondent for *Poetry*, securing work from Robert Frost, Rabindranath Tagore, and D. H. Lawrence. As a result of the publication of his own work in *Poetry*, Amy Lowell, the Judas of Imagism according to Pound's view, came to London and announced her conversion to the movement. By November at the latest Pound was contemplating an anthology of Imagism, and inviting Miss Lowell to appear in it. His desire for an anthology seems to have sprung, in part at least, from a dissatisfaction with *Poetry*. Pound wanted to see the best work of the Imagists printed together, unadulterated by their own inferior work or by the work of others. As editor of *Poetry*, Miss Monroe was almost always willing to print the material Pound sent her, but she reserved the right to include what Pound considered 'rot'. There was, thus, a dilution of Imagism at the level of publication, and Pound wanted a medium in which he would be the sole arbiter of taste. It was fear of the same dilution that caused him to withdraw later from Amy Lowell's publishing ventures on behalf of the Imagists. Pound's temporary resignation from *Poetry* in November 1913[3] may well have been influenced by the prospect of a purer medium for periodical publication in *The New Freewoman*, the first issue of which had appeared in London on 15 June. It was not long before Pound's main energies were diverted from *Poetry* to this

---

[1] See letter to Glenn Hughes, 26 September 1927; *Letters*, p. 288.
[2] *Poetry*, I, 6 (March 1913), p. 199.   [3] See *Letters*, pp. 64, 67.

magazine. Vol. I, No. 5 had a laudatory article on 'Imagisme' by Rebecca West (pp. 86–87) which reported the material that had appeared in the March issue of *Poetry*. This was followed by seven poems under the heading, 'The Contemporania of Ezra Pound' (pp. 87–88). In the following issue, Vol. I, No. 6 (September 1913), there was a small anthology of imagistic poems by Aldington, H.D., Amy Lowell, Skipwith Cannéll, F. S. Flint, and William Carlos Williams, under the heading 'The Newer School' (p. 114). About this time, Pound seems to have had control of the literary side of *The New Freewoman*,[1] and he was certainly mainly responsible for having its title changed with the first issue of 1914; the title chosen, probably by the nominal editor throughout the history of the magazine, Dora Marsden, was *The Egoist*. The final major occupation of the year for Pound was his visit to Coleman's Hatch in Sussex to spend the winter with Yeats 'as a duty to posterity'.[2]

The anthology, *Des Imagistes*, was published in March 1914. It might have been considered a definitive practical guide to what Imagism is but for the fact that Aldington, one of the practitioners that the movement was intended to publicize, would disagree. In a review which he wrote for *The Egoist*, he said that 'There are poems by five authors in this anthology, which I do not consider to be Imagiste. They are those by Mr. Cournos, Mr. Upward, Mr. Hueffer, Mr. Joyce and Mr. Cannéll.'[3] The inclusion of Joyce was due, in part, to Yeats, who, during the winter of 1913/1914, introduced Pound to Joyce's work and career. Pound probably included a poem from *Chamber Music* partly because he liked it, and partly because he felt the publicity might help Joyce to secure further publication. After all, Imagism was established as a movement primarily to secure publication of good work by Aldington and H.D., and only secondarily to illustrate a critical manifesto. Pound was by no means rigorous in limiting the movement to poems written in accordance with the manifesto. On the other hand, he did actually describe Upward, Hueffer, and Cannéll as Imagists at one time or another, as well as publishing their work in Imagist anthologies. The conclusion to be drawn is that Pound was not very rigorous or

---

[1] See *Letters*, pp. 59, 67.   [2] Letter to his mother; *Letters*, p. 63.
[3] 'Modern Poetry and the Imagists', *The Egoist*, I, 11 (1 June 1914), p. 202. The remaining poets were Aldington, H.D., F. S. Flint, Amy Lowell, William Carlos Williams, and Pound.

systematic as a theorist about Imagism (or, in fact, about most other things). Aldington's statements are generally far more enlightening. In the review mentioned, the first of several statements about Imagism by Aldington, he presents

the fundamental doctrines of the group. You will see that they are all practically stylistic.

1. Direct treatment of the subject. This I consider very important. We convey an emotion by presenting the object and circumstance of that emotion without comment. For example, we do not say 'O how I admire that exquisite, that beautiful, that—25 more adjectives woman, you are cosmic, let us spoon for ever,' but we present that woman, we make an 'Image' of her, we make the scene convey the emotion. Thus, Mr. Pound does not say 'His Muse was wanton, though his life was chaste,' but he says that he and his songs went out into the 4 a.m. of the world composing albas.[1]

2. As few adjectives as possible.

3. A hardness, as of cut stone. . . .

4. Individuality of rhythm . . . .

5. A whole lot of don'ts, which are mostly technical, which are boresome to anyone except those writing poetry, and which have been already published in Poetry.

6. The exact word. . . .[2]

The only one of these points that cannot positively be said to have come from Pound is the third. The quality of 'hardness, as of cut stone' is one that was primary for H.D., and, indeed, it has been often noticed in her work. But apart from this one exception, all the points in Aldington's summary are expressions of Pound's opinions, and seem to have come to Aldington from him. This is a significant conclusion, not least because the first point is almost indistinguishable in Aldington's formulation from Eliot's doctrine of the objective correlative.

After 1914 Pound lost interest in Imagism. Amy Lowell returned to London in the summer of 1914, full of criticism of Pound's handling of Imagism in regard to publication. She persuaded Aldington, H.D., and F. S. Flint to join her in a new anthology, and later asked D. H. Lawrence and John Gould Fletcher to contribute. Pound objected to the democratic method of selection proposed, and to Miss Lowell's failure to observe what he now considered to

---

[1] The reference is to Pound's poem, 'Ancora', reprinted in *Personae*, p. 114.

[2] Richard Aldington, loc. cit.

be the chief point of his original Imagist manifesto, the point about avoiding any superfluity of words.[1] He considered that the movement had been converted into 'Amygism'.

Pound's letters at this time show a good deal of annoyance, and a good deal of criticism of Miss Lowell. They do not, however, reveal much of his inner feelings. It must have come as a shock to Pound to have the movement taken out of his hands, and to find that his protégés were willing to desert him for his intellectual and creative inferior, Amy Lowell. In a letter explaining to her his reluctance that the name of the movement should appear on her anthology, he wrote of his own plans and ambitions: 'I have little enough time for my own work as it is. And all things converge to leave me all too little for the part I should like to give to actual creation, rather than to criticism, journalism etc.'[2]

The shock of the Imagists' defection seems to have made Pound somewhat disgruntled about his campaigns to help young writers, and to have suggested to him that he might devote more time to his own 'actual creation'. The declaration of war in August 1914 probably strengthened this attitude, for it helped to break up the literary coteries of young writers in London, and it opened up many avenues of publication for poets in the armed forces. In any case, whether these were the causes or not, Pound himself felt that 1914 marked a change in his relations with other writers. In 1927 he wrote that

If at the present moment I were asked to spend a sum of money on literature or the arts I should have to pause and make enquiries. From 1908 to 1914 I could have 'placed' amounts of any size, from two dollars upwards; for I then knew and *believed in* a certain number of people whose work has since been recognized as having value, people who were then frequently worried by perfectly simple eliminatable causes.[3]

Pound still continued his interest in his new discoveries of 1914 (Eliot, and John Rodker, for instance), but he lost interest in some of his earlier discoveries, and did not in the future make so many new contacts.

With this rather tenuous background to the period, it may be possible to review Pound's contributions to, and influence on, literature from 1908 to 1914. I think it is true to say that the fact of

[1] See letter to Glenn Hughes; *Letters*, p. 288.   [2] *Letters*, p. 78.
[3] 'Mr. Pound on Prizes', *Poetry*, XXXI, 3 (December 1927), p. 158.

Pound's residence in London was responsible for no changes in anyone's poetry but his own. There were so many potential influences for any poet in London that Pound was reduced to the status of 'a small but persistent volcano in the dim levels of London literary society'.[1] W. B. Yeats, who will be dealt with in a later chapter, may be thought an exception, but Pound's influence on Yeats was effected chiefly through his periods of residence with him in Sussex. Amy Lowell may be thought another exception, but it should be remembered that she became a convert to Imagism from afar, through reading the work of Pound and H.D. in *Poetry*. She did sit at Pound's feet for a few months after her arrival in England in 1913, but personal contact probably hastened her defection from the cause. There can be little doubt, I think, that Pound's influence on her produced an improvement in her verse. In any case, Pound was deceived in his original enthusiastic judgement of her work. Perhaps he was flattered by her discipleship, swayed by the letter of introduction she brought from Harriet Monroe, or impressed by her affluence and her appearance of authority and efficiency. The verses of hers that he printed in *The New Freewoman*, *The Egoist*, and *Des Imagistes* are non-imagistic, garrulous, and 'poetic' in diction and in syntax. It is almost incredible that Pound could ever have selected lines like these for publication:

> Damp smell the ferns in tunnels of stone,
> Where trickle and plash the fountains,
> Marble fountains, yellowed with much water.[2]

Upward, Hulme, Aldington, H.D., and Flint all came into Pound's orbit because he found their work interesting and 'imagistic'. He did not pretend to dictate how they should write. Aldington was only eighteen when Pound met him, but already he had set ideas of his own; as Pound admits, 'Upon many points of taste and of predilection we differed.'[3] The others were older, and Hulme, at any rate, had more literary prestige than Pound. Pound did voice his opinions about H.D.'s early poems, but apparently said little more than that he did not like them:

[1] Richard Aldington, 'Farewell to Europe', *The Atlantic Monthly*, CLXVI (1940), p. 519
[2] 'In a Garden', *The New Freewoman*, I, 6 (1 September 1913), p. 114.
[3] *Pavannes and Divisions* (1918); reprinted in *Literary Essays*, p. 3.

Ezra Pound was very kind and used to bring me (literally) armfuls of books to read. . . . I did a few poems that I don't think Ezra liked. . . . but later he was beautiful about my first authentic verses, 'Hermes' and 'Spare Us from Loveliness,' and 'Acon' (a transposition from that Renaissance Latin book) and sent my poems in for me to Miss Monroe.[1]

Pound must have had virtually no influence on the content of H.D.'s work, for her latest published work is identical in style and in the type of subject chosen to her earliest, whereas it is only on her earliest published work that Pound is ever supposed to have had an influence.

Rabindranath Tagore was not discovered by Pound. Yeats, who did the introduction to Tagore's first volume of verse in English (1913), probably drew Pound's attention to him. In any case, Pound admitted that without any effort by him Tagore's poems 'are going to be THE sensation of the winter'.[2] Pound's energies were directed to seeing that *Poetry* was the first American magazine to print Tagore. Yeats seems to have suggested to Tagore that Pound would look over his English and correct it, though Pound does not seem to have relished the prospect. He wrote to Harriet Monroe: 'God knows *I* didn't ask for the job of correcting Tagore. He asked me to.'[3] It is obvious from the same letter that Pound had little sympathy with the content of Tagore's writings, and it is doubtful whether Tagore allowed him to alter much.

Pound had a larger share in bringing Robert Frost to notice. In March 1913 he was writing to Alice Corbin Henderson, Harriet Monroe's assistant: 'Have just discovered another Amur'kn. *VURRY* Amur'k'n, with, I think, the seeds of grace.'[4] Pound wrote the review of Frost's book *A Boy's Will* appearing in *Poetry* in May. He used an advance copy, and the notice was certainly the first to appear in America. In June, Pound was writing to his father: 'I'll try to get you a copy of Frost. I'm using mine at present to boom him and get his name stuck about.'[5] According to Pound, writing two years later:

He [Frost] came to my room before his first book *A Boy's Will* was pub-

[1] Letter from H.D. to Glenn Hughes; printed in Hughes, *Imagism and the Imagists: A Study in Modern Poetry* (Stanford University, California: Stanford University Press, 1931), pp. 110–11.
[2] Letter to Harriet Monroe, [24] December 1912; *Letters*, p. 44.   [3] *Letters*, p. 55.
[4] Ibid., pp. 49–50.   [5] Ibid., p. 57.

lished. I reviewed that book in two places[1] and drew it to other reviewers' attention by personal letters. I hammered his stuff into *Poetry* . . . .[2]

It is not easy to say how much longer Frost would have required for recognition had not Pound been so enthusiastic. It is doubtful whether he would have been reviewed at all in America, for even Harriet Monroe was not impressed by the work that Pound showed her.[3] But Pound's effort on Frost's behalf ends with publicity. Pound 'would have refashioned both the man and his verse had not Frost rebelled and fled London', according to Richard Ellmann, who cites an interview he had with Frost in 1947 as evidence.[4]

On Imagism Pound had a more decisive and lasting influence. Without him it is almost certain that Imagism would never have become a movement. He provided the energy that got the creative works and the critical principles published; he gave the movement a name; and his publicity secured for it a degree of fame or notoriety. Now most of the valuable part of this activity would have happened in any case. Hulme and Hueffer probably had sufficient status as critics to nurture poetry of the type demanded by Pound's manifesto, and there can be no doubt that this type of poetry would have been written without Pound. The process would have been slower, and it might never have made much impression on American literary circles, but it would have taken place. Pound himself mentioned the time lag that would have occurred without his contribution in a letter to Amy Lowell, where he referred to

my machinery for gathering stray good poems and presenting them to the public in more or less permanent form and of discovering new talent . . . or poems which could not be presented to the public in other ways, poems that would be lost in magazines. As for example 'H.D.'s' would have been, for some years at least.[5]

I have suggested that without Pound the principles of Imagism might have had little success in America. It is also true to say, I think, that they would have had far less influence on the history of poetry after, perhaps, 1920; they would have been far less firmly

[1] One was *Poetry*. The other was *The New Freewoman*, I, 6 (1 September 1913), p. 113.
[2] Letter to the Editor, Boston *Transcript*, August 1915; *Letters*, p. 107.
[3] See *Letters*, p. 165.
[4] *James Joyce* (New York: Oxford University Press, 1959), p. 362.
[5] *Letters*, pp. 77–8.

C

based in the twentieth-century poetic and critical traditions. A good deal of their permanence comes from Pound's reputation as a craftsman and teacher, qualities that are admitted even by those who detest his poetry. On the other hand, Hulme and Hueffer, who, presumably, would have been the chief proponents of Imagist ideas but for Pound, have little critical status today. Hulme has been recently compared in importance with Colin Wilson;[1] and Hueffer is quite forgotten as a periodical essayist and reviewer and still rather neglected as a novelist. Without Pound's propaganda, the *Georgian Poetry* or *Wheels* type of verse might have completely overshadowed the *Des Imagistes* and *Catholic Anthology* type.

This is, of course, essentially a conjecture. In view of what has been said about Pound's lack of influence on what was actually being written in England at the time of the Imagist anthologies, it might seem a wild conjecture. A little further positive evidence will be presented in some of the ensuing chapters, but it is possible to see one or two suggestions of the strength and perseverance of Imagist ideas even in the early period. These must be looked for not in Britain but in America, where Imagism aroused more attention and was far more hotly debated. In the words of Conrad Aiken, at first a vigorous critic of Imagism, 'The Imagist movement was from the outset international in character, and remained so, with London and Boston as its two centers.'[2]

The reason for the success of Imagism in America seems to have been basically the lack of any alternative. Whereas in Britain London was the acknowledged centre for poets, in America the main literary circles were in Chicago, Boston, and New York, and there were many other cities with literary pretensions. As a result, poets did not travel to other cities in order to join in discussions. Literary coteries were small, and lacked the vitality given by opposition. Imagism offered a ready-made programme that had greater authority and more adherents than any local movement could have.

---

[1] 'University Presses in the Field', *The Times Literary Supplement*, 4 March 1960, p. 147.
[2] *Ushart: An Essay* (New York: Duell, Sloan & Pearce; Boston: Brown, 1952), p. 216. Boston is named presumably because Amy Lowell lived there, because the anthologies entitled *Some Imagist Poets* were published there, and because a number of literary coteries were established there. Chicago was, however, the real publishing centre, for it was the home of *Poetry*, and of *The Little Review*.

Even those who were initially sceptical or antipathetic were generally won over. Aiken was an exception. He vehemently opposed the prominence given by Harriet Monroe to the work of the Imagists, and was only temporarily placated during his visit to London in 1914. Not being able to find a publisher for Eliot's 'Prufrock', he gave the manuscript to Pound,[1] and was responsible for Eliot's meeting Pound.[2] Pound seems to have treated Aiken as a loyal member of his coterie, at least until he failed to arrive at the *Blast* dinner to which Pound had invited him. He was certainly drawn into Pound's circle to some extent, for he had

tea with Rabbi Ben Ezra, . . . and [made] the expeditions, from Rabbi Ben Ezra's triangular flat, and his Gaudier-Brzeskas, on the uniformly unsuccessful visits, whether to Yeats or Ford Madox Hueffer, for they were never, never in . . . .[3]

But Pound, according to Aiken, 'if a good teacher, was also something of a tyrant',[4] and the connexion was broken when Aiken returned to America. Yet despite a certain amount of jealousy of both Pound and Eliot, Aiken did derive a few phrases and mannerisms from them both, notably in *The Jig of Forslin*, which echoes a few lines from *Prufrock*. On returning to America, Aiken continued his attack on Imagism, drawing attention to the factitious nature of the Imagists' published eulogies of each other, the lack of emotional force in their work, and the presence of the decoration that they professed to eschew.[5]

Lesser poets than Aiken were fairly easily won over to Imagism, especially if they remained in America. George Sterling wrote to Harriet Monroe at the beginning of 1913: 'I like *Poetry* more and more with each number. It seems to me more readable than its twin over in England. I see both periodicals have incurred Ezra Pound.'[6] By 1915 he was obviously more familiar with Pound's work, and somewhat more favourably disposed towards it: 'By the way, what do you think of Schauffler's whack at Ezra? I confess the latter isn't one of my enthusiasms, but on the other hand we *are* for the most

[1] See letter from Aiken, *The Times Literary Supplement*, 3 June 1960, p. 353.
[2] See letter from Eliot, *The Times Literary Supplement*, 23 August 1957, p. 507.
[3] Aiken, *Ushant*, p. 205.   [4] Ibid., p. 215.
[5] See, for instance, Aiken, 'The Place of Imagism', *The New Republic*, III (1915), pp. 75–6.
[6] Harriet Monroe, *A Poet's Life*, p. 225.

part a "mass of dolts." '[1] In 1926 he was admitting to Harriet Monroe: 'You were right and I was wrong, and I have been dropping little things from my style ever since *Poetry* began.'[2]

Two other poets who illustrate this trend are Robert Sanborn and Carl Sandburg. The lesser poet of the two, Sanborn, accepts Pound at his own estimation as a tireless labourer in the field of poetry. His statement bears a curious resemblance to some of Pound's own (and to the statements of later critics favourably disposed to Pound such as Hugh Kenner and William Fleming):

> I take back most of what I have said to you and others, and thought to myself, about Ezra Pound. . . . I begin to like Pound very much; what's more to the point I begin to learn from him—or perhaps, having been learning from him through the months of my distaste, I am at last burning with a fanaticism to shout the admission from the house-top.
>
> .   .   .   .
>
> In all the years I have been humming pretty tunes to myself and calling them poetry, he has been making a dust and getting dirty and sweating in old tombs, delving out stuff that never stales, and not caring at all how stained his copy is. Why should he, when the effect is provocative of agitation in the languid ranks of American poets?[3]

Carl Sandburg was saying the same sort of thing in a more restrained way. In a long article on 'The Work of Ezra Pound' he began:

> If I were driven to name one individual who, in the English language, by means of his own examples of creative art in poetry, has done most of living men to incite new impulses in poetry, the chances are I would name Ezra Pound.
>
> This statement is made reservedly, out of knowing the work of Pound and being somewhat close to it three years or so.[4]

It was in America, then, that Pound's ideas gained most attention. To some extent this was due to Harriet Monroe, who provided more opportunities for young poets in *Poetry* than any magazine in England. Even *The Egoist*, which was perhaps more under Pound's domination than *Poetry*, did not give a great deal of space to poetry, though it gave more space to criticism. *Poetry* provided a forum for

---

[1] Harriet Monroe, *A Poet's Life*, p. 376.   [2] Ibid., p. 225.
[3] Letter from Robert A. Sanborn, *Poetry*, VII, 3 (December 1915), pp. 158-60.
[4] *Poetry*, VII, 5 (February 1916), p. 249.

the discussion of Pound's ideas both in theory and practice in a far
more single-minded way than any English journal. No alternative
doctrine of comparable status presented itself, and there were no
demands on space from other forms of literature. There was every
incentive for enthusiastic young poets to offer imagistic work to an
editor sympathetic to the aims of the movement, and a great many
of them did.

2. THE WAR YEARS

SHORTLY after the publication of *Des Imagistes*, Pound lost interest in the Imagist movement, and decided to spend less time nurturing *'les jeunes'* and more time writing in a creative way. As a result, in the period 1914 to 1922 his published books appeared more frequently than in the earlier period: the peaks occurred in 1916 and 1920, in each of which years he had three books published. It was also about 1914 that he met a number of people who were doing work that he admired very greatly, and who were not too old or too well-established to resent his interest and willingness to help. They have been described by Wyndham Lewis as 'the men of 1914': Lewis, Joyce, and Eliot, to whom might be added Gaudier-Brzeska.

It is interesting to note that not all of these men were poets: Wyndham Lewis was a prose writer and artist; Joyce was primarily a prose writer; and Gaudier-Brzeska was a sculptor. Wyndham Lewis has an explanation of a trait in Pound's character that may have caused him to immerse himself in matters removed from his own original interests: 'It is *disturbance* that Pound requires; that is the form his parasitism takes. He is never happy if he is not sniffing the dust and glitter of action kicked up by other, more natively "active" men.'[1] This search for activity led Pound into an interest in several arts. In addition to his connexion with the visual arts through Lewis and Gaudier-Brzeska, Pound during this period maintained his interest in music, becoming very friendly with Edmund Dulac and Arnold Dolmetsch.

Two other newly acquired interests that serve to mark off 1914 in Pound's life are his marriage, and his work on the manuscripts left by Ernest Fenollosa. In 1914 Pound married Dorothy Shakespear, the daughter of Yeats's friend, Olivia Shakespear. In the previous year, the widow of Ernest Fenollosa, having read some of Pound's work, sent to him her late husband's manuscripts, with the request that Pound should act as literary executor. For several years Pound devoted himself to editing and publishing Fenollosa's prose

---

[1] *Time and Western Man*, pp. 56–7.

translations of Japanese plays and to assimilating and eventually publishing Fenollosa's essay on 'The Chinese Written Character'.

Finally, 1914 marks a transition period in Pound's development as a poet. His work up till then is full of romance, of the style of the nineties, and of the troubadours. It is juvenilia, in the sense that it shows constant experimentation, uncertainty, and painful self-consciousness. *Lustra* (1915), however, prepares the way for the mature Pound of *Mauberley*, *Propertius*, and the Cantos. Its poems tend to be more serious and sophisticated; frequently they substitute self-critical irony for the self-conscious guffaws found in the early poems.

Despite his other interests, Pound still spent a good deal of time 'attending to other people's affairs, weaning young poetettes from obscurity into the glowing pages of divers rotten publications, etc. . . . Conducting a literary kindergarten for the aspiring, etc. etc.'[1] Of the young writers that he helped after 1914 the most devoted and most grateful was Iris Barry, whose work he first saw in 1916.[2] But by this time Pound was more irascible with requests for comment from unpromising writers, probably feeling that they ought first to read his printed instructions, such as 'A Few Don'ts'. His activities became more concentrated on the best artists that he knew. With the notable exception of Eliot, they were generally not prepared to listen to detailed criticism by Pound, and so he directed his energies towards being an entrepreneur: acting as literary agent, securing jobs, and looking after their material welfare.

The pivot for his manifold activities was his lodgings in Kensington, at 5 Holland Place Chambers, near St. Mary Abbots Church. There was a standing invitation to all Pound's friends to assemble there on Thursday evenings at eight o'clock. During the war years, Pound and his wife frequently welcomed Aldington and H.D., Eliot, Henry James, Ford Madox Hueffer, F. S. Flint, Arthur Waley, Harriet Shaw Weaver (the editor of *The Egoist*), and, among somewhat lesser-known names, Edmund Dulac, John Cournos, May Sinclair, Violet Hunt, Anthony Ludovici, Edgar Jepson, Iris Barry, and Paul Selver. Wyndham Lewis called when he was on leave, and there were occasional visits from Yeats, Florence Farr, Arthur Symons, W. W. Gibson, and Arturo del Re.

---

[1] Letter to his mother, November 1913; *Letters*, p. 63.   [2] See *Letters*, pp. 124 ff.

In the field of employment, *The Egoist*, which was kept going by donations from Miss Weaver and others, provided a source of income for some of Pound's friends. The rates for contributors were low, but there were a few paid positions on the staff. Pound had been running the literary side of *The New Freewoman* in August 1913,[1] but he apparently resigned this job in favour of Aldington, of whom he wrote in December, 'Richard is now running the *N.F.* which is now to appear as *The Egoist*.'[2] In May 1916, H.D. joined Aldington as an Assistant Editor, and when he was called up for military service towards the end of the year, she was left with most of the editorial work—this was, no doubt, a contributing factor in the non-appearance of an issue for March 1917. With the June 1917 issue (Vol. IV, No. 5), T. S. Eliot was appointed Assistant Editor, again apparently on Pound's recommendation, and he remained in that position until the demise of *The Egoist* at the end of 1919. It is noticeable that with Vol. V (1918) *The Egoist* changes to a more regular arrangement of material, with 'departments' on French writing, English writing, and new books, as well as the familiar philosophical department contributed by Dora Marsden, the original editor. In the history of literary periodicals, the format of this volume of *The Egoist* marks a transitional phase between the early numbers of *The English Review* (when it was edited by Hueffer) and the sophisticated, permanent-looking periodicals of the early 1920's, such as *The Dial* and Eliot's own magazine, *The Criterion*. Pound has always praised very highly the early numbers of *The English Review*—and rightly, for the first issue (December 1908), which was not untypical, printed work by Hardy, James, Galsworthy, Tolstoy, and Wells. It seems quite likely that Eliot, who as Assistant Editor of *The Egoist* was more amenable to Pound's suggestions than Aldington had been, had taken the trouble to look at the early numbers of *The English Review* and had borrowed some ideas from them.

Eliot profited from Pound's connexion with *The Egoist* in one other way. *The Egoist* ceased publication ostensibly so that there could be more concentration on the issuing of books from The Egoist Press. But this press had already published one volume for

[1] See letter to Harriet Monroe, 13 August 1913; *Letters*, p. 58.
[2] Letter to W. C. Williams, 19 December 1913; *Letters*, p. 65. See also *Letters*, p. 161.

Eliot, *Prufrock and Other Observations* (1917), after Pound had secured publication for most of the contents in *Poetry*, *Others*, and *Blast* in 1915.

The Egoist was also used by Pound to draw attention to the plight of James Joyce. Pound's article, 'A Curious History',[1] related the abnormal difficulties Joyce had had over a period of several years in getting *Dubliners* published. Joyce later wrote that:

Ten years of my life have been consumed in correspondence and litigation about my book *Dubliners*. It was rejected by 40 publishers; three times set up, and once burnt. It cost me about 3,000 francs in postage, fees, train and boat fare, for I was in correspondence with 110 newspapers, 7 solicitors, 3 societies, 40 publishers and several men of letters about it. All refused to aid me, except Mr Ezra Pound. In the end it was published, in 1914, word for word as I wrote it in 1905.[2]

Publication was not due to Pound's efforts, though the publisher, Grant Richards, who was at this time reconsidering the matter, may have been swayed by Pound's article in *The Egoist*. Pound was, however, responsible, with B. W. Huebsch, for persuading H. L. Mencken to print two of the stories from *Dubliners* in the May 1915 issue of *The Smart Set*.

Pound was very impressed by the first chapter of *A Portrait of the Artist as a Young Man*, which Joyce sent to him. He showed it to Harriet Shaw Weaver, at that time business manager of *The Egoist*, but later (in July) to become its editor. They arranged for serial publication to begin in the issue of 2 February 1914 (Vol. I, No. 3). Pound devoted himself to the task of interesting others in the work, and he was tireless in thrusting copies of *The Egoist* into the hands of people who might be willing to review the instalments, to help Joyce financially, or to publish the complete work.

Book-publication could not be considered until the last instalment was to hand, in July or August 1915. Then Pound and Miss Weaver submitted the script to publisher after publisher in England. Faced with so many refusals, Miss Weaver contemplated having it published by *The Egoist*, a venture which would have been

---

[1] *The Egoist*, I, 2 (15 January 1914), pp. 26–7.
[2] Letter to John Quinn, 10 July 1917; *Letters of James Joyce*, ed. S. Gilbert (London: Faber & Faber, 1957), p. 105. Padraic Colum has recorded that he recommended Joyce to see Pound: Mary and Padraic Colum, *Our Friend James Joyce* (London: Gollancz, 1959), p. 99.

both novel and risky for the magazine. But investigations along these lines were hindered by the refusal of a succession of printers, fearing prosecution for obscenity, to set up the book. Pound then thought of an ingenious scheme whereby the objectionable passages would not be set up in type, but would have blanks left for them. The book would be copyrighted and published in this form, but the excisions would be type-written and pasted into the blank spaces.[1] While waiting for Joyce's response to this suggestion, Pound thought of the possibility of publishing the book in America. He had a book of his own, *This Generation*, placed with John Marshall of New York, and he wrote to Marshall advising him that if he could not publish two books, he ought to give preference to Joyce's.[2] But in the end Marshall published neither book. Miss Weaver, however, did induce B. W. Huebsch to publish Joyce's. Huebsch had wanted to publish *Dubliners*, but had been hindered by a lack of finance. With the *Portrait*, Miss Weaver promised to take 750 copies for publication in England, and Huebsch was able to go ahead.

Pound obtained various sums of money as donations for Joyce over a period of some years. The most substantial sums came from official sources. The first of these was made possible by Joyce's move in June 1915 from Trieste, which was in enemy territory, to Zürich, which was neutral. At this stage, Pound persuaded Yeats to approach the Royal Literary Fund for a grant. The approach was made through Edmund Gosse, but both Yeats and Pound were asked to send letters of recommendation to the secretary of the Fund. As a result, a grant of £75 was made. In the following year, Pound decided to see if he could secure for Joyce a Civil List grant, which Yeats told him it was the prerogative of the Prime Minister to award. Pound asked Lady Cunard to lend Joyce's books to Edward Marsh, the Prime Minister's secretary. Marsh wrote to Yeats and George Moore to ask their opinion, and subsequently a grant of £100 was made. Joyce wrote to those who had helped, ending his letter to Yeats with the words:

I have every reason to be grateful to the many friends who have helped me since I came here and I can never thank you enough for having brought

---

[1] See *Letters of Ezra Pound*, pp. 74-5.
[2] See *Letters*, p. 124.

me into relations with your friend Ezra Pound who is indeed a wonder worker.[1]

In 1917, Joyce was corresponding with both Pound and Miss Weaver about the possibility of publishing *Ulysses* in serial form. Both were enthusiastic, the more so when Joyce sent the first chapter in December. As it happened, Miss Weaver had considerable difficulty in finding a printer willing to set up the work, and it was only in 1919 that she found one willing to do some of the chapters. This was effected through Pound's foreign editorship of *The Little Review*, edited by Margaret Anderson and Jane Heap. Early in 1917 Pound had made clear to Margaret Anderson his requirements if he were to work for *The Little Review*:

I want an 'official organ' (vile phrase). I mean I want a place where I and T. S. Eliot can appear once a month (or once an 'issue') and where Joyce can appear when he likes, and where Wyndham Lewis can appear if he comes back from the war.[2]

Pound, true to his role of entrepreneur and literary agent, refused to allow direct correspondence between the magazine and Joyce (just as he had refused to allow correspondence between *Poetry* and Eliot a few years before).[3] Joyce was to send the episodes to him, and he would send them on to *The Little Review*. This arrangement had some effect on the printed product, for Pound was not averse to acting as editor. In April he was writing to John Quinn, the New York lawyer who later handled the obscenity charge over *Ulysses*, and who supplied Pound with money for various writers from time to time: 'I may say that I rec'd the fourth chapter some days ago, and deleted about twenty lines before sending it off to N.Y.; and also wrote Joyce my reasons for thinking the said lines excessive.'[4] It is impossible to determine which these lines were, though Patricia Hutchins believes that they were probably in the 'Hades' episode, because 'a comparison with the book form shows considerable extension by Joyce in places'.[5] It may be remarked that Pound's concern with the excision of the otiose amounted almost to an

---

[1] *Letters of James Joyce*, p. 95. [2] *Letters of Ezra Pound*, pp. 160–1.
[3] See Richard Ellmann, *James Joyce*, p. 434; and Pound, *Letters*, p. 85.
[4] *Letters*, p. 192.
[5] Patricia Hutchins, *James Joyce's World* (London: Methuen, 1947), p. 240.

obsession, and constitutes possibly his greatest contribution to practical criticism and the critical tradition.

Towards the end of 1919, Joyce returned with his family from Zürich to Trieste, but because of Pound's intervention he did not stay there long. In the summer, Pound and his wife, who was ill, were in Italy, and Pound asked Joyce to meet him at Sirmione, in the Alpine district. Joyce raised many difficulties, but Pound was insistent that they ought to meet:

Mr. Pound wrote to me so urgently from Sirmione (lake or Garda) that in spite of my dread of thunderstorms and detestation of travelling I went there bringing my son with me to act as a lightning conductor. I remained two days there and it was arranged when I explained my general position and wishes that I would follow him on to Paris . . . .[1]

Pound's object in wishing Joyce to follow him to Paris was that together they might make arrangements for a French translation of *A Portrait of the Artist*, and perhaps one of *Dubliners*. Joyce intended to stay only a week or two in Paris to complete the business, and then go on to London and Ireland, as had been planning before Pound intervened. By the time Joyce arrived with his family in Paris, Pound had secured temporary accommodation, made tentative arrangements for a translation of *A Portrait*, and prepared a large number of literary people for the arrival of a brilliant writer. Pound had, in fact, arranged so many contacts that it was not long before Joyce was established permanently. In the early stages at least, Pound did a good deal to see that Joyce was supplied with money.[2]

The influence of Paris on Joyce was almost entirely favourable. In time he came to regard it as 'the last of the human cities'.[3] It provided him with the material to write about, and the means to live by. And but for Pound's work, Joyce would never have gone there.

Pound's influence on the material details of Wyndham Lewis's life was less extensive. The two men became associated about the time when Pound was losing interest in Imagism. Indeed, one of the reasons for this loss of interest was his attachment to the group centring on Lewis, mainly composed of artists. According to Lewis:

[1] *Letters of James Joyce*, p. 142.   [2] See, for example, *Letters of James Joyce*, p. 143.
[3] Ellmann, op. cit., p. 523.

Ezra Pound attached himself to the Blast Group. That group was composed of people all very 'extremist' in their views. In the matter of fine art, as distinct from literature, it was their policy to admit no artist disposed to technical compromise, as they regarded it. What struck them principally about Pound was that his fire-eating propagandist utterances were not accompanied by any very experimental efforts in his particular medium. . . .[1]

Lewis is at a loss to understand what similarity in content there was between the views of the Blast group, which were based on opposition to the 'futurist' doctrines of Marinetti, and Pound's antiquarian outlook on poetry. There was, in fact, probably none, at least at this time; though the Blast group may have had some influence on Pound's modernization of his poetic style about this time. The explanation of Pound's attachment to the group is probably to be found in his disgust with Amy Lowell's effect on Imagism, and his attraction by the vitality of Lewis. Yet it should be realized that Pound himself thought that there was some connexion between his own beliefs and those of the Blast group. It was he who gave the name Vorticism to Lewis's movement. In explaining Lewis's particular excellence to John Quinn (who bought a good many of Lewis's works), he wrote:

It is not merely knowledge of technique, or skill, it is intelligence and knowledge of life, of the whole of it, beauty, heaven, hell, sarcasm, every kind of whirlwind of force and emotion. Vortex. That is the right word, if I did find it myself.[2]

And in a way that would probably be quite spurious if both Imagism and Vorticism were confined to their most likely meanings, he included his own movement in Lewis's:

The image is not an idea. It is a radiant node or cluster; it is what I can, and must perforce, call a VORTEX, from which, and through which, and into which ideas are constantly rushing. In decency one can only call it a VORTEX. And from this necessity came the name 'vorticism'.[3]

To some Imagists it seemed as if Pound was perverting the original dogma of his school by making the image purely visual. There is certainly a difference between his definition of the Image

---

[1] Lewis, op. cit., p. 55.
[2] *Letters*, p. 122. In a previous letter, written at the end of 1913, Pound had referred to London literary life as 'The Vortex'; *Letters*, p. 65.
[3] 'Vorticism', *The Fortnightly Review*, XCVI, n.s. (1914), pp. 469–70.

in 'A Few Don'ts', written in 1913, and the implied definition in
'The Rev. G. Crabbe, Ll.B.', written in 1917. In 1913 he wrote that
'An "Image" is that which presents an intellectual and emotional
complex in an instant of time.'[1] In 1917 he wrote that Wordsworth
'was a silly old sheep with a genius, an unquestionable genius, for
imagisme, for a presentation of natural detail, wild-fowl bathing in a
hole in the ice, etc. . . .'[2] This visual interpretation of the image
may, in fact, be a more honest description of what the Imagists did
in their poetry, but it is certainly not identical with the original
formulation agreed on by Aldington and H.D. It would seem likely
that the change in Pound's thinking came about through contact
with Wyndham Lewis. The 'external' quality of Lewis's graphic
art has often been commented on, and it is precisely this quality
that Pound seems to have taken over into his Imagist-Vorticist
theory of poetry. Whether the transition partly caused or partly
resulted from the defection of the Imagists from Pound, or whether
it was quite independent of that defection will probably never be
known.

Although he may not have understood or agreed with what Lewis
was trying to do, Pound had no hesitation in subscribing his name
to the manifesto that appeared in the first issue of *Blast: Review of
the Great English Vortex*, edited by Wyndham Lewis. Aldington
(whose signature was probably secured by Pound) and Gaudier-
Brzeska were among the others listed as signatories. According to
Lewis:

Pound supplied the Chinese Crackers, and a trayful of mild jokes, for our
paper; also much ingenious support in the english and american press;
and, of course, some nice quiet little poems—at least calculated to vex
Signor Marinetti with their fine passéiste flavour.[3]

The poems were not perfectly nice and quiet, for three lines in one
of them had to be blacked out by hand before publication. The jokes
are certainly mild. What the 'Chinese Crackers' are I do not know,
unless Lewis is referring to the strident typographic lay-out of
Blast. The shock-tactics of the lay-out do suggest some of the more
sub-adult of Pound's letters. The 'ingenious support' is typified
by Pound's article, 'Wyndham Lewis', which appeared in *The
Egoist* five days before the publication of *Blast*; it begins: 'Mr.

---

[1] *Literary Essays*, p. 4.   [2] Ibid., p. 277.   [3] Op. cit., pp. 55-6.

Wyndham Lewis is one of the greatest masters of design yet born in the occident.'[1]

While Lewis was at the war, Pound seems to have acted as his literary agent. A letter to Lewis dated 25 August 1917 indicates that Pound had sent *Tarr* by registered post to an American publisher, and had received a cheque for an Egyptian drawing by Lewis.[2] During the war period, Pound saw that *Tarr* was serialized in *The Egoist* and ultimately published by The Egoist Press. *The Caliph's Design* was later published by the same press. Lewis's short stories were being printed in *The Egoist*, and also sent to *The Little Review*; one of them, in fact, *Cantleman's Spring Mate*, apparently led to the suppression of *The Little Review*.[3]

After the war, Pound could be of little help to Lewis, though Lewis has recorded that

Once towards the end of my long period of seclusion and work, hard-pressed, I turned to him for help, and found the same generous and graceful person there that I had always known; for a kinder heart never lurked beneath a portentous exterior than is to be found in Ezra Pound.[4]

Pound's own development during this period as a critic (which by no means runs parallel to his development as a poet) is chiefly explained by his enthusiasm for the ideas of three men: Wyndham Lewis, Ernest Fenollosa, and Major C. H. Douglas. Of these three, Fenollosa, who had died in 1908 in America, was the only one he did not know personally. Pound knew nothing of his work until late in 1913 when his widow asked Pound to become his literary executor. The first product of Pound's labours on the Fenollosa manuscripts was the abstracting of a Japanese play, *Nishikigi*, translated by Fenollosa. Pound's opinion of the work, and the extent of his editorial labours are conveyed in a letter to Harriet Monroe; in it he asks her to suppress his name, believing that the work will have a better chance of being accepted as the first successful attempt to re-create Japanese literature in English if it is ascribed solely to Fenollosa.[5]

In a pseudonymous review of the issue of *Poetry* containing *Nishikigi*, Pound displayed his usual talents as a publicist and instigator of convenient rumours. The issue, he wrote, 'contains the

[1] *The Egoist*, I, 12 (15 June 1914), p. 233.   [2] *Letters*, pp. 173-5.
[3] See *Literary Essays*, p. 81.   [4] Lewis, op. cit., p. 54.   [5] *Letters*, p. 69.

first of the Fenollosa translations from the Japanese "Noh." It is beginning to be whispered that Ernest Fenollosa was one of the most important men of his time . . . .'[1]

The most significant effect of Pound's interest in 'Noh' was probably the transmission of this interest to Yeats, with whom Pound stayed during the winters 1913/1914, 1914/1915, and 1915/1916. There was also, because of Pound's advocacy, a quickening of interest in literary circles. As Pound pointed out in the letter to Harriet Monroe mentioned above, there had been earlier attempts to translate Noh into English, but they had, on the whole, been dismal failures, and had not succeeded in attracting much attention to the form. Pound helped to direct new interest to the form by his publication of material from the Fenollosa papers; by his personal advocacy; by his critical writing; and by his fostering of those who were practitioners of the form. The magazine publications from the Fenollosa papers were collected in a small volume, *Certain Noble Plays of Japan* with a preface by Yeats (Churchtown, Dundrum: The Cuala Press, 1916). A more substantial volume was *'Noh' or Accomplishment: A Study of the Classical Stage of Japan*, including translations of fifteen plays by Ernest Fenollosa and Ezra Pound (London: Macmillan, 1916). Pound's personal advocacy interested Yeats, Arthur Waley, Edmund Dulac, and others, who discussed Noh at Pound's rooms, and elsewhere. His interest in practitioners is indicated by his discovery of the penurious Japanese dancer, Michio Ito, who was persuaded to play in Yeats's *At the Hawk's Well*. Another Japanese, Yone Noguchi, was invited, apparently by Pound, to contribute 'The Everlasting Sorrow: A Japanese Noh Play', and later an article, 'The Japanese Noh Play', to *The Egoist*.[2] Pound's sponsorship was probably responsible for Noguchi's having some of his *hokku* published in *The Egoist* and in *Poetry*, and possibly responsible for the publication of Jun Fujita's *tanka* in the same number of *Poetry*.[3]

Waley, Yeats, and Pound were as much interested in Fenollosa's insight into Chinese poetry as in his insight into Japanese Noh

---

[1] *The Egoist*, I, 11 (1 June 1914), p. 215. The review is signed 'Bastien von Helmholtz'.
[2] *The Egoist*, IV, 9 (October 1917), pp. 141–3; V, 7 (August 1918), p. 99.
[3] *The Egoist*, III, 11 (November 1916), p. 175; *Poetry*, XV, 2 (November 1919), pp. 67–9.

drama. Pound himself had already become interested in Chinese poetry, possibly through friendship with T. E. Hulme and F. S. Flint. His 'Contemporania', published in 1913,[1] could be considered to have a Chinese clarity and immediacy of image; they were, at any rate, what brought him to Mrs. Fenollosa's notice. The first published result of his interest in the new insight provided by Fenollosa seems to have been 'Exile's Letter', which appeared in *Poetry*,[2] and was later included in Pound's volume *Cathay*. The publication of this free translation in *Poetry* opened the way for the publication of translations by Amy Lowell, Arthur Waley, and Florence Ayscough.[3]

At this time Pound apparently had no knowledge of either Chinese or Japanese. His work on Fenollosa's manuscripts led to the beginnings of his attempts to acquire both languages, attempts that have left a deep impression on the Cantos. Pound's interest seems to have been stimulated by Fenollosa's notes on what he (not entirely accurately) supposed to be the nature of Chinese characters. These notes were published as 'An Essay on the Chinese Written Character' in Pound's volume, *Instigations* (New York: Boni & Liveright, 1920).[4]

Fenollosa's explanation of the ideogram was adapted by Pound into his current theories of the image and the vortex. At the time when he was first studying Fenollosa's explanation, Pound was, as I have already suggested, modifying his concept of the image. In one direction it was becoming visual, to accord with Wyndham Lewis's theories about art. In another direction it was losing its stillness, and becoming a vortex, 'from which, and through which, and into which ideas are constantly rushing'. Now this second change is due partly to the influence of Wyndham Lewis, and partly to the influence of Fenollosa. It is true to say, I think, that the concept of motion came from Lewis (though there may possibly have been

---

[1] *Poetry*, II, 1 (April 1913), pp. 1–12; *The New Freewoman*, I, 5 (15 August 1913), pp. 87–8.

[2] V, 6 (March 1915), pp. 258–61.

[3] See, for instance, Amy Lowell, 'Lacquer Prints', *Poetry*, IX, 6 (March 1917), pp. 302–7; Arthur Waley, 'Chinese Poems', *Poetry*, XI, 4, 5 (January, February 1918), pp. 198–200, 252–4; Florence Ayscough, 'Chinese Written Wall Pictures', *Poetry*, XIII, 5 (February 1919), pp. 233–42.

[4] An abridged version appeared in *The Little Review*: see *The Little Review Anthology*, ed. Margaret Anderson (New York: Hermitage House, 1953), pp. 190–206.

D

some influence from Yeats's concept of the gyres); and the concept of the content of the elements that were in motion came from Fenollosa. These elements were, in Pound's terminology, superimposed images. In his popularization of the theory in his *A B C of Reading* he wrote that 'Chinese Ideogram . . . is still the picture of a thing; of a thing in a given position or relation, or of a combination of things.'[1]

He [the Chinaman] is to define red. How can he do it in a picture that isn't painted in red paint? He puts (or his ancestor put) together the abbreviated pictures of

ROSE	CHERRY
IRON RUST	FLAMINGO[2]

This method seemed to Fenollosa and Pound to be both scientific and poetic; it was both of these because it abjured philosophical abstractions and concentrated on individual examples. It fitted in very well with what Pound had already proclaimed in the first point of the original Imagist manifesto, and in his principle from 'A Few Don'ts': 'Go in fear of abstractions.'

This refined doctrine of the image had a great effect on the composition of Pound's later poetry. It was now possible for him to go beyond the short imagistic poems where an image often took up no more than a single line. It was now possible to use a narrative as an image. This was what Pound did in the Cantos, and what W. C. Williams, Hart Crane, Archibald MacLeish, and Louis Zukofsky, for instance, did in their long poems. I am not suggesting that these other poets necessarily understood or believed in Pound's theory, but there is a good deal of evidence that they were following Pound's successful practice. The refined doctrine of the image had a second advantage in that it was no longer necessary for a poem to confine itself to two images; any number of images could participate in the ideogram or vortex, and mutually illuminate each other. Longer poems like the Cantos were theoretically made possible, and the theory justified a construction that was pictorial rather than logical or entirely narrative. This construction, which is similar in both theory and result to that justified by the analogy often drawn between poetry and music, has been widely used by Pound and by

---

[1] *A B C of Reading* (London: Routledge, 1934), p. 5.   [2] Ibid., p. 6.

other poets. Once again it is true that Pound's influence on poets has been more through example than precept.

The influence of Fenollosa on Pound was, in general, salutary. The same cannot be said about the influence of Major C. H. Douglas, whom Pound met in 1917. Pound had always been interested in the practical job of enabling writers to live, and it seems likely that he was first attracted to Douglas's economic theories by the hope that they would result in a utopian state where writers would not have to struggle to exist. Under Douglas's influence he began to study economics, and arrived at Douglasite conclusions which he has held ever since. He accepted Douglas's abhorrence of 'usury' and of the 'jews' who were alleged to be its main practitioners. 'Usury' and the 'international jew' form the subject of many of the Cantos, some of them being rather hysterical in tone and, I would think, dispensable. But even if Pound's own use of these ideas in poetry were unobjectionable, the same cannot be said for the use made of them by his friends. William Carlos Williams imported usury into Parts II and IV of *Paterson* to the detriment of the poem; and one or two of Eliot's references to the 'jew' seem rather gratuitous.

Most of the ill effects of Pound's absorption in Douglas Credit came after the period of his residence in London. During that period, however, he managed to implicate his friends in his current enthusiasms. His enthusiasm for Fenollosa is a good example of this. But the files of *The New Freewoman* and *The Egoist* show the results of Pound's constant recommending of books to his friends. One of Pound's major enthusiasms during the period was Rémy de Gourmont. *The New Freewoman*, the literary side of which was directed by Pound, published a translation by Cécile Sartoris of Gourmont's novel, *The Horses of Diomedes*. Then in *The Egoist*, which was still very much under Pound's domination at the time, Richard Aldington reviewed Gourmont's *Promenades Littéraires*, Ve. Série,[1] and a little later wrote a major article on Gourmont,[2] the material of which found its way into his *Literary Studies and Reviews* (London: Allen & Unwin, 1924). It was probably Pound who directed Aldington's attention to Gourmont in the first place, for Aldington

---

[1] *The Egoist*, I, 4 (16 February 1914), p. 66.
[2] 'Le Latin Mystique', *The Egoist*, I, 6 (16 March 1914), pp. 101–2.

showed no interest in him before the articles in *The Egoist* appeared. An even more likely case of Pound's transfer of enthusiasm occurred with Gaudier-Brzeska. Before *Blast* appeared, Pound was lauding the work of his new discovery in a long article in *The Egoist*, accompanied by reproductions of two statues and a drawing.[1] By the following year Pound had apparently converted the poet John Cournos, one of '*les jeunes*' represented in *Des Imagistes*, to an appreciation of Gaudier, for Cournos has two articles in *The Egoist*, one being a record of Gaudier's death, the other an appreciation of his work.[2]

Pound's own assessments of the work he did for other writers and artists during the period 1914 to 1921 can be accepted almost at their face value. In 1918 he made the claim:

I have had to write, or at least I have written a good deal about art, sculpture, painting and poetry. I have seen what seemed to me the best of contemporary work reviled and obstructed. Can any one write prose of permanent or durable interest when he is merely saying for one year what nearly every one will say at the end of three or four years? I have been battistrada for a sculptor, a painter, a novelist, several poets. I wrote also of certain French writers in *The New Age* in nineteen twelve or eleven.[3]

The sculptor was, of course, Henri Gaudier-Brzeska, whose early death in the war gave Pound the self-imposed task of preserving his work. The painter was Wyndham Lewis, for whom Pound acted as artistic and literary agent during the war, having a notable success in interesting John Quinn in his work. The novelist was Joyce, whose causes for gratitude to Pound have already been mentioned. The 'several poets' would include Frost, H.D., Aldington, William Carlos Williams, Skipwith Cannéll, and Eliot. Yeats hardly comes into this category, but Pound's influence on him, which will be the subject of a later chapter, is one of the most interesting and significant elements of Pound's career during this period. Pound's claim about the articles on French writers is not worthy of much attention, as F. S. Flint, who was at the time publishing articles on

---

[1] 'The New Sculpture', *The Egoist*, I, 4 (16 February 1914), pp. 67–8; reproductions p. 80.
[2] II, 8 (2 August 1915), p. 121; 'Gaudier-Brzeska's Art', II, 9 (1 September 1915), pp. 137–8.
[3] *Pavannes and Divisions* (1918); reprinted in *Literary Essays*, p. 13.

French writers, records that in 1909 Pound 'could not be made to believe that there was any French poetry after Ronsard'.[1]

Pound also makes a claim to having begun an interest in 'modern' poetry in the United States. This was a claim that was resisted by American poets who had spent most of their lives in America and who looked on Pound as something of an un-American renegade. In *Make It New*, Pound replied to their criticism:

> I think there is only one largish current error of this sort, namely that in America, the stay-at-home, local congeries did ANYTHING toward the *stil'nuovo* or the awakening. Robinson is still old style, Lindsey [Vachel Lindsay] did have a rayon of his own, the rest trundled along AFTER the hypodermic injection had been effected via London. Even Frost the prize autochthonous specimen made his début in London, and was forced into the local New England bucolic recognition from Kensington, W.8. The *pièces justificatives* are the back files of *Poetry* and the *Egoist* from October 1912 onward. The *Little Review*, 1917–19, as monthly, with the later quarterly issues.[2]

The evidence is, as Pound says, in the files of these magazines, not only in his own critical articles, but also, with the early issues of *Poetry*, in the articles and letters opposing Pound's critical pronouncements. This kind of evidence is worth comparing with the critical atmosphere of contemporary periodicals that did not have connexions with Pound. A fair example of such a 'control group' is *The Dial*, published, like *Poetry*, in Chicago. It was less biased and conservative than most literary magazines, for it actually welcomed *Poetry* in an editorial note at a time when most magazines were sneering that it was a refuge for minor poets.[3] But at the same time *The Dial*'s reviews in its regular feature, 'Recent Poetry', showed little awareness of any new movements in poetry. Established writers like Swinburne, Hardy, Yeats, Masefield, and Kipling were not overlooked, but a typical issue could review quite seriously *Horizons and Landmarks* by Sydney Royse Lysaght, *The Lost Vocation* by Marion Fox, *The Voice of the Infinite and Other Poems* by N. D. Anderson, *Youth, and Other Poems* by Charles Hanson Towne, and *Little Grey Songs from St Joseph's* by Grace Fallow

---

[1] 'A History of Imagism', *The Egoist*, II, 5 (1 May 1915), p. 71. Pound's articles, 'The Approach to Paris', in seven parts, actually appeared in *The New Age* during September and October 1913. See also his *Letters*, p. 175.

[2] Reprinted in *Literary Essays*, p. 80.   [3] *The Dial*, LIII (1912) p. 478.

Norton.[1] Imagist and other 'modern' poets received no acknow-
ledgement in the pages of *The Dial* until the poetry reviews were
taken over in the middle of 1915 by Raymond M. Alden.

Alden was a competent critic who reversed the existing policy of
reviewing only volumes of poetry that could receive the critic's
comfortable approbation. In his first article he reviewed and damned
Some Imagist Poets, Irradiations: Sand and Spray by John Gould
Fletcher, and *Spoon River Anthology* by Edgar Lee Masters.[2] In
subsequent reviews Alden sometimes referred to the Imagists and
to *Spoon River Anthology* in order to praise more conventional
poems by contrast, but all of his reviews offered explicit and detailed
criticism. *The Dial* was not favourably disposed towards the modern
movement in poetry until it changed hands in 1920, but from 1915
onwards it did give consideration to the more substantial works produced by this movement. But by June 1915 Pound had been waging
his campaign in *Poetry* for over two and a half years. And *The Dial*
did acknowledge what it regarded as the dubious distinction of
Pound's precedence, as in the review of Kreymborg's second *Others*
anthology: 'Who it was that started the current fad for curio-col-
lecting is a question not hard to answer: Ezra Pound is the man, let
the Imagists and others deny it as loudly as they will.'[3]

It is fairly obvious, then, that even a somewhat reactionary regular periodical could follow Pound's lead in the attention it gave to
modern poetry. Of the fugitive periodicals, the only one with any
claim to precedence in time over Pound's publicity campaign
would be Kreymborg's *The Glebe*, which was published from September 1913, probably to November 1914. But Kreymborg himself
indicates that his interest in modern tendencies was awakened by
the work of Pound, and that Pound was responsible for sending a
packet containing work by Pound, Joyce, Allen Upward, Hueffer,
H.D., Aldington, Flint, Cannéll, Amy Lowell, and William Carlos
Williams.[4]

Pound's claim to have inspired and led critical interest in modern
poetry in the United States can, then, be substantiated. Its importance is probably equal to his other major claim for this period, the

---

[1] LII (1912), pp. 281–5.   [2] LIX (1915), pp. 26–30.   [3] LXIV (1918), p. 111.
[4] See Alfred Kreymborg, *Troubadour: An Autobiography* (New York: Boni & Liveright,
1925), pp. 199–205.

claim to have organized the publication and guided the critical assessment of writers like Joyce, Wyndham Lewis, and Eliot.

Towards the end of the period under review, Pound's activities in the cause of literature decreased, as he gave more time to his studies of economics. Iris Barry dates the end of 'the Ezra Pound period' in 1919, and it is true that from then until 1921, when he left London permanently, he had little effect on the English literary scene. This was partly because he was on the Continent for some of this time; during the war his movements had been restricted, and he was now taking the opportunity to revisit Italy and France. The main reasons for his leaving London permanently seem to have been disgust with the policy of the British Government and disgust with the policy of British publishing houses. He may have wanted to continue his patronage of Joyce, whom he had persuaded to live in Paris. There are also rumours of a dispute with Middleton Murry which lost Pound an assistant editorship on *The Athenaeum*, worth five pounds a week, and of a projected duel with Lascelles Abercrombie. In any case, it was with some relief that Pound turned his back on London.

3. PARIS

'FOR the post-war years up till 1924 or 1925 the activity of both America and England was perhaps more apparent in Paris than anywhere else.'[1] Pound's comment refers, of course, mainly to the literary activity of America and England. Americans made up the majority of English-speaking writers in Paris after the war, though there were major British writers such as Joyce and Ford Madox Ford (formerly Hueffer) there, and Wyndham Lewis made frequent visits. The cost of living and the cost of printing were both low. *Avant-garde* magazines constantly sprang up, bloomed for a short time, then withered when money or enthusiasm ran out. Small American publishers sometimes had their books printed in France to save money, and at least one magazine—Margaret Anderson's *The Little Review*—changed its home from New York to Paris for the same reason. The erosion of American isolationism during the war had something to do with the migration of American writers afterwards, but there were probably more positive reasons, such as the mercenary atmosphere and the corrupt administrations in America.

Because of the concentration of talent in Paris during his three and a half years there, Pound was able to meet or to renew acquaintance with, and very frequently to help, people like Joyce, Hemingway, William Carlos Williams, Gertrude Stein, Ford Madox Ford, Robert McAlmon, Malcolm Cowley, George Antheil the composer, and Constantin Brancusi the sculptor. The last two were very important in Pound's life, for his stay in Paris was his most intense period of sculpting and composing. His literary activities fall under much the same headings as before: he looked after the material welfare of writers; gave advice about manuscripts; edited a series of books by his friends; associated himself with magazines; acted as a guide to the *salons* for Americans; and proceeded with his own work, especially the Cantos. His activities as an entrepreneur seem more crowded at the beginning of the period; towards the end he seems

[1] *Make It New*; reprinted in *Literary Essays*, p. 82.

to have experienced something of the same *malaise* that affected him towards the end of his stay in London.

On arrival in Paris Pound was largely occupied with helping Joyce, Eliot, and Hemingway; and learning from and publicizing the work of Brancusi and Antheil. The necessity to see Joyce through the litigation over the publication of instalments of *Ulysses* in *The Little Review* had helped to preserve Pound's connexion with that magazine. John Quinn, the lawyer who handled the case for the defence (and who was Joyce's agent in America), did not get on well with the editors, Margaret Anderson and Jane Heap. Pound managed to keep them on speaking terms by writing frequent letters to them. In 1921, however, the case had been concluded, so Pound severed his connexion with *The Little Review*, and began a somewhat looser connexion with *The Dial*. During most of his stay in Paris he wrote the regular 'Paris Letter' feature for *The Dial*, and sent a good deal of other copy.

The first edition of *Ulysses* was a limited one, published mainly by subscription. Pound was one of those who interested themselves in securing subscriptions. Because of his large number of friends, he had a good many successes, including W. B. Yeats. When Sylvia Beach, the principal of Shakespeare and Company, which was bringing out the edition, received a good-natured refusal from George Bernard Shaw, Pound badgered him by private letter and in print[1] in an unsuccessful attempt to make him change his mind. When the book appeared, Pound's reviews of it were probably the first to appear in an American or a French journal.[2]

Pound's solicitude for Joyce's material circumstances showed itself in his supplying him with money from time to time, and in his anxiety about his eyesight. Despite considerable grants from various sources (including Harriet Shaw Weaver), Joyce's expenditure was chronically in excess of his income. Pound, whose income was a good deal less than Joyce's, but who lived with less extravagance, frequently gave Joyce small sums from his own pocket, and encouraged wealthier friends to do the same. When John Quinn

---

[1] See, for instance, his 'Paris Letter' to *The Dial*, LXXII, 6 (June 1922), p. 627; reprinted in *Literary Essays*, p. 407.

[2] 'Paris Letter', *The Dial*, LXXII, 6 (June 1922), pp. 623–9; 'James Joyce et Pécuchet', *Mercure de France*, CLVI, No. 575 (1 June 1922), pp. 307–20. The 'Paris Letter' is reprinted in *Literary Essays*, pp. 403–9.

arrived in Paris in October 1923, Pound carefully stage-managed his first meeting with Joyce in the hope of securing further patronage.[1] Joyce was not pleased by Quinn's attitude, but refrained from showing his annoyance. As it happened, Quinn died in the following year, without having helped Joyce very much.

Joyce's eyesight was a constant source of trouble to him. While Pound was in Paris, Joyce had several operations on his eyes. Pound seems to have taken a paternal interest in Joyce's health, on one occasion sending him to see a visiting New York doctor.[2] It is also possible that Pound persuaded Joyce's friends to visit him while he was recovering from the operations. This would be in keeping with Pound's nature, and it is given some support by the fact that when Joyce had an operation shortly after Pound had gone to live in Rapallo, his wife complained that 'though Joyce was supposed to be surrounded by admirers, she and he had sat there together, the two of them like a couple of old hens, for hours on end without a visitor'.[3]

Pound was also worried about Eliot's health. *The Waste Land* had been written mainly in Switzerland during a convalescence from illness. In January 1922 Pound gave advice to Eliot, who had returned to work in his London bank, about many details of the poem. By March, when the final draft had been completed, Eliot was again physically ill. At this stage, Pound started what he called 'Bel Esprit', a scheme designed to solicit from writers subscriptions that could be applied to promising writers one by one, in order to release them from the obligation to earn a living and give them time to write. Eliot was to be the first recipient. Pound enlisted the help of Robert McAlmon and William Carlos Williams to promote the scheme in the United States, and of Richard Aldington to promote it in England. Pound himself and Hemingway promoted it in Paris. How successful the appeal was is not certain. Not all of Pound's acquaintances responded with donations; one reports that after Pound had explained the purpose of the fund he was uncertain whether a donation was expected or not, so 'to be on the safe side, I nodded sympathetically and a few moments later took my leave'.[4]

---

[1] See Richard Ellmann, *James Joyce*, p. 569.   [2] See ibid., p. 550.
[3] Ibid., p. 581. The operation was performed in the middle of April 1925. Pound had left for Rapallo earlier in the year.
[4] Paul Selver, *Orage and the 'New Age' Circle*, p. 44.

One large contribution to the cause, if not exactly to the 'Bel Esprit' fund, was the awarding by *The Dial* of its initial prize for poetry to Eliot; this was worth $2,000. The award, announced at the beginning of 1923, together with financial support for *The Criterion*, made the continuation of 'Bel Esprit', at least for Eliot, unnecessary, and Pound seems to have lost interest in the scheme.

Pound's early relationship with Ernest Hemingway in Paris was similar to his early relationship with Eliot in London. When Hemingway arrived in Paris in 1921 he was in his early twenties. He soon became the protégé of Gertrude Stein, but although she tended to disparage Pound and Joyce, Hemingway became friendly with them both. He seems to have enjoyed settling the fights that Joyce was always likely to stir up in bars. Pound's profession of athleticism possibly attracted Hemingway, though Pound's standard of attainment was apparently not very high.[1] Pound used to look over Hemingway's early manuscripts, and to return them with suggestions for dispensing with many of the adjectives. Hemingway possibly had the same sort of advice from Gertrude Stein, but almost certainly not with the same intensity. Pound's imagistic dictum to 'Use no superfluous word, no adjective which does not reveal something' was one that he was still applying to both verse and prose. It obviously had some effect in forming Hemingway's characteristic spareness. Hemingway himself has acknowledged Pound as 'the man I liked and trusted the most as a critic then, the man who believed in the *mot juste*—the one and only correct word to use—the man who taught me to distrust adjectives'.[2]

Pound also found employment for Hemingway, and secured the publication of some of his manuscripts. The employment was as Assistant Editor of *The Transatlantic Review*, the magazine with which Pound had the closest connexion while he was in Paris. The first publication secured by Pound for Hemingway occurred about the same time, as a result of Pound's connexion with the Three Mountains Press. This press was owned by the American journalist, William Bird, for whom Pound agreed to supervise a series of books under the collective title of 'The Inquest'. Pound's *Indiscretions* was the first of the series, Hemingway's *In Our Time* the sixth and last.

---

[1] See *The Selected Letters of William Carlos Williams*, p. 210.

[2] Ernest Hemingway, *A Moveable Feast* (London: Cape, 1964), p. 116.

Pound did not remain long as editor of the Three Mountains Press. As with most of his publishing or editing ventures he provided the initial impetus and then gave up his position to one of his friends. In this case it was Robert McAlmon. McAlmon had been associated with William Carlos Williams in the production, in 1920 and 1921 with one final issue in 1923, of a magazine called *Contact*. The name of this magazine was incorporated in the imprint of the books printed by Bird after he had become associated with McAlmon: the imprint became 'Contact Editions, including books printed at the Three Mountains Press'.

Pound has been thought to have had some influence on the ethos of the magazine *Contact*. In a monograph on McAlmon, Robert E. Knoll has drawn attention to a statement made by McAlmon and Williams in 1920:

We seek only contact with the local conditions which confront us. We believe that in the perfection of that contact is the beginning not only of the concept of art among us but the key to the technique also.[1]

Knoll's comment about the statement is: 'This declaration is a re-statement of Pound's basic thesis.'[2] By 'Pound's basic thesis' Knoll presumably understands the first tenet of the original Imagist Manifesto, 'Direct treatment of the "thing" . . .', advice similar to that given to Phyllis Bottome, and, no doubt, to Williams, in their days at the University of Pennsylvania. This directness of Pound's certainly corresponds to the 'contact' of McAlmon and Williams, and from the notion of 'contact' with material McAlmon and Williams went on to state the same sort of corollary as Pound had done in the Imagist Manifesto: that from directness or 'contact' with material should follow a similar directness in technique. 'To use absolutely no word that does not contribute to the presentation' was the second point of the Imagist Manifesto; 'contact is . . . the key to the technique also' was the formulation of McAlmon and Williams. So far, then, Knoll is right in asserting that 'This declaration is a re-statement of Pound's basic thesis.' The similarity to Pound's ideas also helps to explain why Williams was hopeful that T. S. Eliot

---

[1] *Contact*, 1 (December 1920), p. 10; quoted in Robert E. Knoll, *Robert McAlmon: Expatriate Publisher and Writer*, University of Nebraska Studies, New Series, No. 18 (Lincoln: University of Nebraska, 1957), p. 39.
[2] Ibid.

would support him in his move to reform American poetry. It may be, then, that Williams thought he was restating Pound's ideas. But the publication of *The Waste Land*, heralded with such delight by Pound, forced him to the conclusion that there was a fundamental contrariety between Pound's attitude to material and his own. They agreed about 'contact' or directness, but, according to Williams's view, they differed fundamentally about what kind of material this contact should be with. In the *Contact* statement, Williams's position is quite clear: 'contact with the local conditions which confront us' is what he advocates. But *The Waste Land* showed him that Pound and Eliot were practising a quite different approach. With the publication of *The Waste Land*, says Williams,

> Critically Eliot returned us to the classroom just at the moment when I felt that we were on the point of an escape to matters much closer to the essence of a new art form itself—rooted in the locality which should give it fruit. I knew at once that in certain ways I was most defeated.
> Eliot had turned his back on the possibility of reviving my world. And being an accomplished craftsman, better skilled in some ways than I could ever hope to be, I had to watch him carry my world off with him, the fool, to the enemy.[1]

Williams, then, came to believe that Pound and Eliot were using quite different material from himself. They, as he explained some years later, were using 'the forms of the past', which inevitably carried with them an anti-democratic bias, a tendency to regard culture as being transmitted through a succession of great minds, a preference for autocratic demands. Williams preferred to deal with present-day material in his work, to regard culture as 'arising from great movements of the people', and to adopt forms that were generated directly by present-day society.[2] This attitude is present in embryo in the statement quoted from *Contact*, but its opposition to the ideas of Pound and Eliot was apparently not perceived at the time by Williams, nor has it been given due emphasis by Knoll.

McAlmon has already been mentioned as an organizer for 'Bel Esprit'. He was one of Pound's most useful friends in regard to the supply of money for impoverished writers, for in February 1921 he had married 'Miss Winifred Bryher', not knowing that she was in

[1] *The Autobiography of William Carlos Williams*, p. 174.
[2] See Preface to *Poetry: The Australian International Quarterly of Verse*, No. 25 (10 December 1947), p. 10.

fact the only daughter of the enormously wealthy English ship-owner, Sir John Ellerman.

After Pound had given up his position as editor of the Three Mountains Press in favour of McAlmon, his thoughts turned to the editing of a review. As had been the case with *The Egoist* and possibly with *The Criterion*,[1] he did not propose to edit it himself—he was too busy with his sculpture and music—but he did propose to supervise the contents. He assembled piles of manuscript, arranged financial backing, and secured an office and a secretary. The major problem was to find an editor. Pound's plans allowed for Hemingway to be Assistant Editor. Possibly his slight disappointment over Aldington's performance on *The Egoist*[2] prevented his appointing such a young man as Editor, or Hemingway may not have wanted the job. In any case, when Ford Madox Ford arrived in Paris he found that Pound's choice for editorship had, apparently quite recently, settled on him. Ford seems to have resented not only the ready-made arrangements and Pound's intention of supervising the magazine, but also the advance publicity by which Pound had already spread news of the impending venture among the literary people of Paris and announced that Ford would edit it. But Ford overcame his initial aversion as he realized the need for the type of magazine that Pound wanted. He did, however, insist that alterations in the arrangements be made. In order to be free of interference from financial backers he stipulated that he would find 51% of the capital and hold 51% of the shares. There was, of course, always interference from Pound to be reckoned with. After five numbers he was writing from Assisi:

Cher F

April number good. Especially Hem.[ingway] and Djuna [Barnes]. Want more of them and of McAlmon and Mary Butts. May number not so good.

   .   .   .   .

The chap on Palestrina, Cingria, quite intelligent. H.Z.K.T. = *Times*

---

[1] The theory that Pound originally planned *The Criterion* is given some support by an announcement in *Poetry*, XIII, 6 (March 1919), p. 347: 'It is understood that Mr. Pound will issue, in [London], the first number of a new magazine to be called *The Criterion*.'

[2] Pound wrote to Margaret Anderson early in January 1917: 'I got Aldington that job several years ago. He hasn't done quite as well as I expected, BUT he was very young.' *Letters*, p. 161.

Lit. Sup. rubbish. He 'enjoyed articles'[1] = plus his personal biography, touching British delight in landscape—failed to grasp point—ghost of Clutterbrock. (*It adds to the enjoyment of this that H.Z.K.T. and Cingria are one and the same gentleman.* Ed.)

.   .   .   .

Will come back and (?) manage you at close range before you bring out any more numbers.

Yours
Old Glory[2]

It is obvious from this letter that Ford exercised a good deal of initiative in collecting contributions. He had, after all, successfully edited the early numbers of *The English Review* some years before without Pound's help. He was successful in persuading Joyce to let a part of *Finnegans Wake* be printed after Joyce had refused Eliot permission to print any in *The Criterion*, and he was responsible for putting it under the heading 'Work in Progress', which was adopted by Joyce as the interim title for subsequently published parts.[3] On the other hand, Ford deferred a good deal to Pound, printing his verse and musical criticism, and on one occasion devoting a whole page to a letter from Pound announcing in a few lines the importance of Sadakichi Hartmann's *Confucius*.[4] Pound was probably fairly satisfied with the conduct of the magazine, for its pages were filled with good material that might have had difficulty being printed elsewhere, and there were very few poor contributions. Hemingway's editorship of two numbers in Ford's absence was rather irresponsible, and perhaps contributed to Ford's unwillingness to keep the magazine going at the end of its first year; by this time it had run into financial difficulty through the death of John Quinn, one of the backers, and through the failure of American agents to pay for copies. In addition, Pound had already decided to leave Paris, and so there was no attempt made to prolong the life of the magazine.

If *The Transatlantic Review* corresponds in Pound's life to *The Egoist* of an earlier period, and if Hemingway corresponds to Aldington, the sculptor Constantin Brancusi and the musician George

---

[1] These were Pound's articles on harmony.
[2] *The Transatlantic Review*, I, 6 (June 1924), p. 480.
[3] See Richard Ellmann, *James Joyce*, pp. 569, 574.
[4] *The Transatlantic Review*, II, 3 (September 1924), p. 312.

Antheil correspond in various ways to Gaudier-Brzeska, to Wyndham Lewis, to Edmund Dulac, and to Arnold Dolmetsch. Brancusi was regarded by Pound as a kind of neo-Vorticist, carrying on Gaudier's process of eliminating 'rhetoric' from sculpture;[1] Antheil he fitted into theories that he had formulated after discussions with Dolmetsch and Dulac, and perhaps earlier with Florence Farr and Yeats. Apparently for the first time, Pound became while in Paris a practitioner of the art of sculpture. Ford Madox Ford has described his efforts in terms that are not inconsistent with Pound's description of Brancusi's work in the article referred to: 'As sculptor Ezra was of the school of Brancusi. He acquired pieces of stone as nearly egg-shaped as possible, hit them with hammers, and then laid them about on the floor.'[2] Pound had been familiar with music for many more years than he had been with sculpture. It is not surprising, then, that he should at this time have been thinking of entering the field of composition. His aim was to write the music of an opera, using poems by Villon as text. Antheil was giving him some help with this, and in return Pound did a good deal to publicize him. The publicity culminated in the writing of a small book,[3] which purported to explain Antheil's theories, but which, according to Antheil, simply attached his name to Pound's theories.[4]

With the book on Antheil published, and his first book of Cantos ready,[5] Pound wanted a more secluded place than Paris to put the finishing touches on his opera. At the end of 1924 he left Paris, and early in 1925 settled in Rapallo, Italy. As with the move from London to Paris, Pound had been contemplating this move for some time, and had made exploratory visits—a good deal of 1924 was, in fact, spent in Italy. As early as 1923 he had been telling Malcolm Cowley:

Now he was thirty-seven years old and it was time for him to stop doing so much for other men and for literature in general, stop trying to educate the public and simply write. It would take years for him to finish the *Cantos*; he wanted to write an opera and he had other plans. To carry them out it might be best for him to leave Paris and live on the Medi-

---

[1] See Pound's article, 'Brancusi'; reprinted in *Literary Essays*, pp. 441-5.
[2] *It Was the Nightingale* (London: Heinemann, 1934), pp. 275-6.
[3] *Antheil and the Treatise on Harmony* (Paris: Three Mountains Press, 1924).
[4] See Richard Ellmann, op. cit., p. 568.
[5] *A Draft of Sixteen Cantos* (Paris: Three Mountains Press, 1925).

terranean, far from distractions, in a little town he had discovered when he was in villeggiatura.[1]

The ostensible reason for the move, then, was to secure more time for his own creative work, to secure a respite from the young writers who wanted help. There may also have been some thought of a better climate, for Pound had been ill earlier in 1924. It is possible, too, that he was disappointed with his failure to establish a literary and artistic domination over Paris. In this regard he had been no more successful than in London. It is true that Pound and Joyce were the centres of the two main groups of writers,[2] but there were many *salons* with literary interests. Gertrude Stein attracted mainly painters (including Picasso), but had some writers; Natalie Barney, whom Pound greatly admired, kept together the remnants of Rémy de Gourmont's old salon, and attracted men of letters from several countries; there were the two main literary bookshops attracting writers, Sylvia Beach's Shakespeare and Company, and Adrienne Monnier's La Maison des Amis des Livres; and there were the offices of the various fugitive magazines published by literary exiles. In the atmosphere of friendly rivalry that existed, Pound was important, but not so important that he would be greatly missed from Paris.

The period in Paris confirmed Pound's slight withdrawal from '*les jeunes*'; his increasing preoccupation with his own writing; his continuing good nature towards those who needed help; his interest in economics; the maintaining of his interest in reviews; and his decreasing span of interest in any project. In the first half of the period he had completed the chief part of his help to Joyce and to Eliot; Hemingway became his major literary disciple; but he failed to discover any new major poet. His main achievements in publication were with the Three Mountains Press and *The Transatlantic Review*. He was passing through a temporary phase of intense interest in music and sculpture, which he was to carry on for some time at Rapallo. The end of his stay in Paris and his move to Rapallo marked a withdrawal from the day-to-day activities of new writers, in which he had been immersed for so many years. He was probably

---

[1] Malcolm Cowley, *Exile's Return: A Literary Odyssey of the 1920's*, 3rd ed. (New York: The Viking Press, 1951), p. 122.
[2] See Ford, op. cit., p. 183.

E

beginning to feel that he was no longer of the same generation as '*les jeunes*'; he did, for instance, remark to Cowley about his age. By the end of his stay in Paris he had no firm connexion with an American magazine; there was nowhere that he could be sure of publication; and writers in America were beginning to forget him. At the end of 1925 an American reviewer commented:

Not long ago Mr Pound galloped up and down the frontier of criticism like an early American general, cursing the enemy, firing his recruits, and embarrassing the fearless with decorations of praise. The gallant fighter appears to have withdrawn from the hubbub; precocious children now mature in black ignorance, the makers of plaster casts grow rich, uncursed. He devotes his retirement no less than his notoriety to music and verse; the music is composed in forgotten modes, for the flute, and the poems have all been cantos.[1]

[1] Glenway Westcott, 'A Courtly Poet', review of *A Draft of Sixteen Cantos*, *The Dial*, LXXIX (1925), p. 501.

4. RAPALLO AND AFTER

By the end of his residence in Paris, Pound had only tenuous connexions with American little magazines. He had given up the foreign editorship of *Poetry*, and later that of *The Little Review*, and his 'Paris Letters' to *The Dial* had ceased. In England, too, his outlets for occasional publication were few, as *The Egoist* had closed, and even before A. R. Orage had given up the editorship in 1922 *The New Age* was able to accept Pound's contributions only if they were about the relatively uncontroversial subject of music. As Pound concentrated on his own creative work, and withdrew himself to some extent even from those who were writing in the same city as he, the inevitable result was that his work became less familiar to young writers. Paul Selver noted that in the mid-twenties Pound seemed 'slightly subdued'.[1] In 1927 Robert Graves, who had disliked Pound and his theories from his first contact with them, referred to Pound's reputation in Bloomsbury as being currently 'sinking'.[2] In the same year a young American poet, Maurice Lesemann, dissected Pound's reputation at some length in *Poetry*:

Miss Monroe has asked me to express what the younger poets now think of Mr. Pound. So far as I can tell they do not think of him. I find no curiosity about him among young people who read or write poetry. Only here and there one runs across some vague knowledge of him. But he is spoken of without enthusiasm.[3]

Lesemann went on to account for this neglect partly in terms of Pound's absorption in music, but mainly in terms of his concentration on experiment and technique being considered out-of-date by a new poetic generation more interested in subject-matter.

The middle years of the twenties were not good ones for *Poetry*. It was printing the work of Hart Crane and Robinson Jeffers, but not that of John Crowe Ransom or E. E. Cummings. Most of the

[1] *Orage and the 'New Age' Circle*, p. 44.
[2] In a letter to *The Monthly Criterion*, VI, 4 (October 1927), p. 357.
[3] 'Mr. Pound and the Younger Generation', review of *Personae: The Collected Poems of Ezra Pound*, Poetry, XXX, 4 (July 1927), p. 216.

new poets it was printing were nonentities—there was a large number of poetesses among them—and the established poets who were
frequently printed were chiefly of a minor nature—they included
H.D., Alfred Kreymborg, Edward Sapir, and Louis Ginsberg. An
index of the decline of *Poetry* is provided by the names of those
appearing in its lists of awards. These were made each year to the
writers of the best verse appearing in the magazine. The chief
awards in 1922 went to Robert Frost and Alfred Kreymborg; in
1923 to Edwin Arlington Robinson and Lola Ridge; in 1924 to Amy
Lowell and Amanda Hall; in 1925 to Ralph Cheever Dunning and
Leonora Speyer; in 1926 to Mark Turbyfill and Agnes Lee; and in
1927 to Malcolm Cowley and Leo C. Turner. Even allowing for the
fact that no previous recipient was eligible for an award, it can be
seen that the standard of contributions must have declined in the
mid-twenties. To some extent this was due, I feel, to Pound's withdrawal from the magazine. Without his contributions, without the
contributions that he obtained from other writers in Europe, and
without his pungent criticism and paternal interest, Harriet Monroe
was not able to find good material for her magazine. She had relied
on Pound to get contributions from Europe and so had not made
many personal contacts with writers working there; when he ceased
to send material she had to rely on material from America to fill the
magazine and on her own judgement to select it. In the post-war
years, when so many of the best American writers were working in
Europe, the result was a decline in standard.

Pound himself seems to have felt an alienation from American
creative activity, an alienation that was felt by most of the American
'exiles' on the Continent. The magazine that he edited in 1927 and
1928 was called *The Exile*. The first number of this magazine includes some verses by Richard Aldington, humorously commenting
on Pound's withdrawal from the literary scene, called 'Natal Verses
for the Birth of a New Review'. They include the lines:

> Don Ezra,
> Who having secured at the prime of life
> A more than Horatian otium,
> And having obtained more applause by his silence
> Than ever he obtained by his not always negligible speech,

·   ·   ·   ·   ·   ·

And let us regret the fall of this man
For he once had the courage
To be silent for several years.[1]

Other items in the four numbers of the magazine suggest that Pound
was no longer merely an eccentric littérateur of consistently *avant-
garde* prejudices but was by this time devoting a good deal of attention to his peculiar set of non-literary obsessions and becoming
more and more belligerent in his literary judgements. The magazine
had articles on politics and commerce (with a strongly anti-American
bias), and even on prohibition and sex.[2] Some of the poetry shows
a rather blind following in the steps of Pound. The second number
of *The Exile*, for instance, has some poems by Carl Rakosi (pp. 36–39),
who has picked up Pound's tricks of omitting articles, using alliteration for pairs of words, and dispensing with capital letters, but
seems to have understood little of what Pound was trying to do.
His poem 'Characters' begins:

> One of our brassy beefeaters
> in grandstand on the continent
> bares biceps to the gaping millions,
> sinks shaft in market, pockets wheat
> holds cornucopia of cash.[3]

Yet although belligerent in his literary judgements, Pound was by
no means narrow-minded. He seems to have been always able to
appreciate verse written in a different style from the one he was
currently using himself, provided that its style was one that he had
once been attracted to. Like Yeats who, when he had moved away
from Pound's influence in the latter part of his life, returned to the
inversions that Pound had once persuaded him to avoid, Pound
never managed to shake off a certain attraction to his early styles. In
The Exile, for instance, he was willing to print the work of Ralph
Cheever Dunning. In 1925 he had tried to get Dunning's *The Four
Winds* printed,[4] although he was 'aware . . . that the opus is more
or less in the dialect of Swinburne, Rubaiyat, Dowson, etc. . . . . but

---

[1] *The Exile*, No. 1 (Spring 1927), pp. 86–7.
[2] The article 'My Five Husbands' by 'Stella Breen' (the pen-name of George Steele
Seymour) was printed in No. 2 (Autumn 1927), pp. 87–111. It is of a type that one
would expect today to find in a 'cheesecake' magazine.
[3] *The Exile*, No. 2 (Autumn 1927), p. 36.
[4] See letter to H. L. Mencken, Rapallo, February 1925; *Letters*, p. 270.

I don't see that it matters (i.e. in this case)'. In *The Exile* he printed Dunning's 'Threnody in Sapphics', which is very close in style to some of Pound's early poems and in its double caesuras very similar to the handling of Sapphics in Pound's 'Apparuit'. It begins:

> Standest thou importunate? Knowest thou not
> Death, O Spring hath taken her—she that last year
> Crowned and fair, a goddess and maiden, praised thee
> More than all others?[1]

Despite the fewness of his own ventures into Sapphics, Pound seems to have thought that they provided a useful exercise for young poets. In a letter to Mary Barnard written in the thirties he advised her to write and translate Sapphics.[2]

During his early years at Rapallo, Pound seems to have worked very hard on literary matters. The sixteen Cantos published in volume form in 1925 were supplemented by another eleven published in 1928, and a further three in 1930. His translation of the Confucian classic, the *Ta Hsio*, appeared in 1928. His pamphlet on a method of approaching world literature, *How to Read*, was published separately in 1931, having appeared a few years before in the *New York Herald Tribune*.

Pound's attitude to the virtue of isolation was, of course, ambivalent. He settled in Rapallo partly to secure the isolation from disciples, imitators, and literary affairs in general that he could not secure in Paris. Had he not done so he would certainly not have produced so much literary work at the end of the twenties. It is true too that he had a horror of being reduced to conformity by having too many other writers understand and imitate what he was doing. Yet on the other hand he enjoyed telling young poets what they ought to do—especially if they were intelligent and respectful; he enjoyed being the literary oracle that was always available for consultation; and he had an even greater horror of being neglected than of being understood and imitated.

In so far as this ambivalence of attitude results in an alternation of periods of withdrawal and of altruistic activity it is true to say, I think, that the early years spent at Rapallo are characterized by withdrawal, and the early years of the thirties by altruistic activity.

---

[1] *The Exile*, No. 2 (Autumn 1927), p. 31.   [2] *Letters*, pp. 336–7.

This re-engagement in public matters may have been due to several causes. The isolation produced the conditions in which Pound was able to add impressively to the volume of his poetry, and this attracted attention. *The Exile* reminded people that Pound was still about, and so did his gaining of *The Dial* award for 1927. This award had been announced by the editor in a manner suggesting that the activities for which it was gained were matters of history rather than of current events:

Perhaps the only similarity between Mr Pound and Anatole France [wrote Marianne Moore] is that they both encouraged new writers. Where Anatole France encouraged mostly bad ones, it can be said that Mr Pound has never made a mistake. When he was foreign editor of *The Little Review*, *The Little Review* was the most interesting magazine of a quarter century.[1]

The closure of *The Dial* and of *The Little Review* in 1929 may have persuaded Pound that his services were needed more than ever in the task of educating the young. This closure also stopped two of his outlets for periodical publication, and probably made him welcome all the more the return to England of A. R. Orage and the subsequent beginning of a new review to replace *The New Age*. The publication of the new review, *The New English Weekly*, edited by Orage, can only be considered disastrous for Pound, as it gave him scope to present his economic theories at considerable length to the detriment of his poetic production.

The New English Weekly did not, however, appear until 1932. By then the renascence of Pound's direct literary influence had begun. One of the first activities was Pound's patronage of the 'Objectivist' movement. This movement was mainly the work of Louis Zukofsky, who had known and admired Pound for a few years.[2] When Zukofsky was in New York early in 1928, Pound arranged introductions for him to Basil Bunting (another of Pound's protégés) and William Carlos Williams. Williams was impressed; 'I heartily support your judgment of Zukofsky's excellence (in the one poem at least) and he seems worth while personally', he wrote.[3] As a

---

[1] *The Dial*, LXXXIV (1928), p. 89.
[2] See, for instance, his 'Poem Beginning "The" ', *The Exile*, No. 3 (Spring 1928), pp. 9–27.
[3] 16 April 1928; *The Selected Letters of William Carlos Williams*, p. 96.

result of this meeting, a new movement was soon launched. The other original members were Charles Reznikoff, a New York lawyer and writer, and George Oppen. According to Williams, Objectivism was a successor to Imagism. Imagism had been useful in 'ridding the field of verbiage', but it had rapidly degenerated into formless 'free verse'. What needed to be done was to consider the poem as a work of art, as an object. It would be given its form by the social conditions in which it came into being.[1] These fairly simple theories represent a more explicit announcement of those latent in the *Contact* statement of some ten years earlier. For the most part, they owe their origin to Pound. Williams's account of Imagism as being essentially a matter of 'ridding the field of verbiage' and as quickly expending itself can be paralleled in many accounts written by Pound. In the same year as Objectivism was launched, for instance, Pound wrote to Dr. Glenn Hughes that the test of an Imagist lay 'in the second of the three clauses of the first manifesto',[2] that is to say, in the clause that Pound himself summed up in the instruction, 'Use no superfluous word.' Williams's dictum that 'There is no such thing as free verse! Verse is a measure of some sort' reflects the attitude that Pound himself frequently expressed by quoting T. S. Eliot's aphorism: 'No *vers* is *libre* for the man who wants to do a good job.'[3] The Objectivist theory that a poem is an object can also be traced to Pound, who often spoke of a poem as an object analogous to a musical composition, a painting, or a piece of sculpture. The best examples of this attitude are probably those to be found in his article, 'Vorticism'.[4] In this article he also puts forward a theory of organic form that bears some relationship to the Objectivist notion of form being dictated by social conditions. Pound's theory on this matter is, however, a good deal more refined and more plausible than the Objectivist one: Pound regards the form as being dictated by the matter rather than by the social conditions in which the work comes into being.

It would seem, then, that Objectivism represents largely an emphasizing of certain notions that Pound had long held, and that

[1] See *The Autobiography of William Carlos Williams*, pp. 264–5.

[2] *Letters*, p. 288.

[3] See, for instance, 'A Retrospect' (1918), *Literary Essays*, p. 12; or Pound's review of *Prufrock and Other Observations*, *Literary Essays*, p. 421.

[4] *The Fortnightly Review*, XCVI (1914), pp. 461–71.

Williams and Zukofsky must have been familiar with. I am, of course, making the assumption that Williams's account of Objectivism is a reliable one. There is really no way of knowing whether this is so or not, as Zukofsky's formulations of the essentials of the theory are incomprehensible. They were, at any rate, incomprehensible to several readers of the 'Objectivist' number of *Poetry* (February 1931), who expressed themselves in the April issue as being uncertain whether 'Objectivism' was a movement or not, and unable to work out what 'objectification' meant. An examination of Objectivist poems suggests that the movement in practice was no more than a revival of Imagism, without the limitation of length imposed by a strict adherence to Imagist doctrines. Objectivist poems are generally written in free verse containing confident assertions made in a deliberately prosaic style, frequently using 'This is', 'It is', 'There should be', and so on. Their images are intensely visualized, and are set down without explanation.[1]

Objectivism was one of the last named literary movements that Pound was associated with at all closely. But he continued to give help to individual poets. The old problem of finding jobs for them seems not to have worried him very much at this time. He did make several recommendations to the Guggenheim Foundation, but with a uniform lack of success.[2] Most of his effort went into promoting promising young poets: recommending them to editors and publishers, and introducing them to each other. A good indication of the authors in whom he was interested can be gained by listing the contributors to *Active Anthology*, which he edited in 1933: they were William Carlos Williams, Basil Bunting, Louis Zukofsky, Louis Aragon (translated by E. E. Cummings), E. E. Cummings, Ernest Hemingway, Marianne Moore, George Oppen, D. G. Bridson, T. S. Eliot, and Ezra Pound. Early in the following year Pound wrote to T. C. Wilson,[3] a young American poet, stating that if he brought out another edited volume he would include more younger poets, including Wilson himself, some poets from the Cambridge Left (Drummond, Kemp, Goodman, and Madge were

---

[1] For recent editions of Objectivist work, see Louis Zukofsky, *16 Once Published* (Edinburgh: Wild Hawthorn Press, 1962); George Oppen, *The Materials* (New York: New Directions, 1962); Charles Reznikoff, *By the Waters of Manhattan*, with introduction by C. P. Snow (New York: New Directions, 1962).

[2] See *Letters*, pp. 268–70, 345–6.   [3] Rapallo, 7 January 1934; *Letters*, pp. 334–5.

mentioned), and possibly Mary Barnard, Cullis, and Rakosi (who had appeared in *The Exile*). Auden and Ronald Bottrall are also mentioned with approval in this letter. It will be realized at once that if Marianne Moore's assertion that in encouraging young writers Pound had 'never made a mistake' had ever been true, it was certainly not true at this time; the poets he was interesting himself in have, almost without exception, proved to be of very minor importance. Most of them were encouraged, it would seem, because they were respectful imitators of Pound. But it should be noted that Pound was no longer certain of his ability to select promising young poets; his withdrawal from active literary circles had decreased his knowledge of, and possibly his interest in, contemporary young poets. In the letter to T. C. Wilson he admitted that the compilation of an anthology of young poets was something for which he was no longer fitted:

I don't think at my age it is a suitable job. I mean one CAN'T select the next generation as one selects one's own, but it seems almost the only knot hole for new writers to get thru. *Act. Anth.* really clearing off arrears of the past 7 years. Ought to be something younger and fresher.

. . . I do distinctly want guidance from younger man IF I take on the job.[1]

Of all the poets in whom Pound was interested at this time, Basil Bunting was probably the closest friend. This may have been because he was the most enthusiastic of Pound's admirers. He seems to have spent a good deal of time in Rapallo with Pound; he was certainly there in 1933 and 1934.[2] At any rate he made sufficient impression on Pound to gain several brief mentions in the later Cantos.

If the young poets in whom Pound was interested at this time can be divided into the less important and the more important, it is probably true to say that the less important were chiefly influenced by Pound's imagistic technique, and the more important by his handling of colloquial rhythms. This is what one would expect, because the imagistic technique is much more easily learned, but the handling of colloquial rhythms has far more applications. Of the first group, T. C. Wilson may be considered as typical, with his imagistic lines such as

[1] *Letters*, p. 334.
[2] See *Poetry*, XLII, 6 (September 1933), pp. 356–7; XLV, 1 (October 1934), p. 60.

The wind was sharp on our faces,
over our legs—the
ground hard
under the spades. We could feel

winter
unwilling to give. . . .[1]

Even more preciously imagistic are George Oppen's lines:

The evening, water in a glass
Thru which our car runs on a higher road

Over what has the air frozen?[2]

In this example, the treatment of the air as if it were animate may
be derived from Pound's similar treatment in such expressions as
'void air taking pelt' and 'The air burst into leaf.'[3] The second
group—the more important (and more intelligent) of Pound's followers at this time—were more influenced by Pound's colloquial
rhythms. Bunting must be included in this group, and so much
Ronald Bottrall, though Bottrall was probably more influenced by
Eliot than by Pound.

During the 1930s, Pound was very much occupied with the
problems of translation. By this time he had encountered most of
them himself in several languages, and felt that he was competent
to offer advice to other translators, both those who, like Laurence
Binyon and W. H. D. Rouse, were striving to make classics in other
languages available to readers of English, and those who, like Mary
Barnard, were translating as an apprentice exercise for writing
English poetry. Binyon bridges the gap between these two types of
translator, at least on Pound's view, for Pound thought that the
discipline of translating had enabled Binyon to rid himself of the
faults of his earlier original verse. Pound was, in fact, rather surprised by the excellence of Binyon's translation of Dante's *Inferno*.[4]
As he pointed out in his review of it for *The Criterion*, he remembered as far back as 1908 'Binyon's sad youth, poisoned in the cradle

---

[1] 'Spring Morning', *Poetry*, XLII, 5 (August 1933), p. 268.
[2] *Active Anthology*, p. 213.   [3] Cantos II, XXVII; Faber editions, pp. 12, 137.
[4] *Dante's Inferno, with a translation into English Triple Rhyme* by Laurence Binyon
(London: Macmillan, 1933).

by the abominable dogbiscuit of Milton's rhetoric'.[1] In his letter to
Binyon while he was writing the review he had to begin with what
amounted to an apology for the unkind things he had previously
said about him.[2] He went on to offer Binyon the notes he had made
as he went through the book 'syllable by syllable'. Binyon was
sufficiently grateful for Pound's comments at this time to submit
the proofs of his *Purgatorio* to Pound some years later. Pound
worked through them doggedly in April and May 1938 and submitted several pages of suggestions. Apart from pointing out mis-
prints and inaccuracies or infelicities in single words, most of his
comments concerned the possibilities of achieving prose order and
of omitting line-fillers. In the 1934 review of the *Inferno* Pound had
discussed the question of prose order fairly fully. His initial response
to Binyon's inversions of normal prose order had been one of irrita-
tion. While the review was being written he wrote to Binyon saying
that 'I was irritated by the inversions during the first 8 or 10 cantos,
but having finished the book, I think you have in every (almost
every) case chosen the lesser evil in dilemma.'[3] In the review he
carefully explained to his young followers, whom he expected not to
get beyond his own initial response, that inversion could be justified
in translation from a medieval poem:

> A younger generation, or at least a younger American generation, has
> been brought up on a list of acid tests, invented to get rid of the boiled
> oatmeal consistency of the bad verse of 1900, and there is no doubt that
> many young readers seeing Binyon's inversions, etc., will be likely to
> throw down the translation under the impression that it is incompetent.
> The fact that this idiom, which was never spoken on sea or land, is NOT
> fit for use in the new poetry of 1933–4 does not mean that it is unfit for
> use in a translation of a poem finished in 1321.[4]

He still thought, however, that prose order should be kept wherever
possible, and in detailed suggestions in succeeding letters he gave
several examples of the possibility of avoiding inversion.[5] Binyon
emended in most of the places pointed out by Pound, accepting
Pound's alternatives in over half of them.

The second major type of suggestion he made to Binyon was also

[1] 'Hell', *The Criterion*, XIII, No. 52 (April 1934); reprinted in *Literary Essays*, p. 201.
[2] Rapallo, 21 January 1934; *Letters*, pp. 335–6.   [3] Ibid., p. 336.
[4] *Literary Essays*, p. 206.   [5] See *Letters*, pp. 404–8.

one that went back to Imagism and 'A Few Don'ts', namely the avoidance of line-filling decorative words. In this review of the *Inferno* he praised Binyon's spareness and straightforwardness of language:

Working on a decent basis, Binyon has got rid of pseudo-magniloquence, of puffed words, I don't remember a single decorative or rhetorical word in his first ten cantos. There are vast numbers of mono-syllables, little words. Here a hint from the *De Eloquio* may have put him on the trail.[1]

When he wrote to Binyon after receiving the proofs of the *Purgatorio*, he suggested that rhetorical line-fillers might be dropped even at the expense of irregularity in metre: 'Would you feel utterly immoral,' he asked, 'if you used an occasional 8 syllable line, where at present you have used fillers? or even 9 syllable?'[2] In his practical criticism he included suggestions for omitting words like 'does', 'doth', 'did', and 'dost'.[3] As with the suggestions about inversion, Binyon accepted them in more than half the places. His preface to the edition thanks Pound for 'a great number of careful criticisms'.[4]

Pound always had a healthy respect for anyone who had been working on the problems of translating an author for a long period of time. It was his own length of experience, he felt, that gave him the right to make suggestions to others. When W. H. D. Rouse, an even more venerable scholar than Binyon, produced his prose translations of parts of the *Odyssey* under the title *The Adventures of Ulysses*, Pound wrote to him in unusually respectful terms suggesting that Rouse (who, Pound must have realized, had at least fifteen years more experience than he did) could prove useful not only to Binyon but also to Pound himself:

To repeat that about Binyon: do you know him? He needs you. I need yr. criticism more than you do mine. Nobody has taught me anything about writing since Thomas Hardy died. More's the pity.[5]

Pound thought, at least at first, that Rouse's translation had the same feature that had attracted him to Binyon's work. In the same letter he contrasted Rouse's translation with the usual 'adorned' ones, and praised the straightforwardness of his narrative. As he

---

[1] *Literary Essays*, p. 205.   [2] *Letters*, p. 403.   [3] See ibid., pp. 404–5.
[4] *Dante's Purgatorio with a translation into English Triple Rhyme* by Laurence Binyon (London: Macmillan, 1938), p. vii.
[5] Rapallo, 30 December 1934; *Letters*, p. 351.

had done with Binyon, he offered to send Rouse the notes he had made: 'I don't know whether my actual notes on minutiae wd. interest you or not? If so, I can send up the volume. Or summarize, as you like.'[1] Later, as Rouse went on with his translation, Pound became less and less satisfied with the results. In February 1935 he was writing that 'Certain words seem to me "literary," no longer living, no longer *used* in speech as I heard it during my 12 years in England. Never have I heard the word "flight" spoken, though one reads it in detective stories.'[2] In March he began a letter with the words: 'N O NO! Doc: Here you are backslidin' on all your highly respectable principles and slinging in licherary langwidg and putting yer sentences all out of whack.'[3] Later in the same month he was writing to Eliot that 'ole Rouse is getting stubborn, won't pay any attention to Aurora's manicuring or Telemachus' feet. Damn. And he might have been useful stimulus both to Bunt. and Bin.'[4] Yet, in spite of this recalcitrance, Rouse continued to solicit his opinions, and Pound supplied him with a good many detailed suggestions about improving the colloquial tone by substitutions of words and changes of word order. Pound was unable to be as helpful as he had been to Binyon, because he felt that Rouse was going too fast,[5] and that as he was striving for speed and interest in narration it was best not to offer too many detailed comments until the work was finished.[6] But Rouse was not prepared to give the finished narrative the close revision that Pound thought was necessary.

The translations of Binyon and Rouse received more help from Pound than any others during the nineteen-thirties. The help given to them is, in fact, only equalled throughout Pound's career by the help given ten or fifteen years later to Marianne Moore, when she was engaged in translating *Les Fables* of La Fontaine.[7] Pound's contribution to all three consisted in a clear statement of two or three principles which he felt most previous translators had neglected, and in detailed applications of these principles. It is certain that Pound's intervention improved the finished product. Although this intervention could be brought to bear directly on only a small pro-

[1] *Letters*, p. 349.   [2] Ibid., p. 357.
[3] Ibid., p. 359.   [4] Ibid., p. 361.   [5] See ibid., p. 363.
[6] See ibid., pp. 356, 363.
[7] Published as *The Fables of La Fontaine*, translated by Marianne Moore (New York: Viking Press, 1954).

portion of the readings in a translation, his exasperated interest in the work of these translators and his constant admonitions to them must have had their effects on many other readings. It should be noted, though, that Pound became interested in the work of Binyon and Rouse because of the admirable qualities it possessed when it was published, and that his intervention was mainly aimed at keeping up the original standard. It is doubtful whether Pound's campaigns for the necessity of modernity and a colloquial tone in translation had much effect on the intentions of Binyon and Rouse before they began their translations. Rouse, for instance, had been insisting on the need for a modern, colloquial rendition of the classics even before he became headmaster of the Perse School in 1902.

Pound's own major feat of work on a foreign author was coming to an end about the time he began to take an interest in Binyon and Rouse. This was his work on Guido Cavalcanti, which had occupied him since the early years of the century. One of the early results had been an edition of *Sonnets and ballate of Guido Cavalcanti*, with translations of them, and an introduction, by Ezra Pound (London: S. Swift; Boston: Small, Maynard, 1912). The major result, however, was his *Guido Cavalcanti: Rime* (Genoa: Marsano, 1932), an edition with a critical apparatus and notes. About the same time, he finished his major essay on Cavalcanti, subsequently printed in *Make It New* (1934). Having established the text, he then went on to set a good deal of it to music in an opera that has never been performed. By 1934 this must have been almost finished.[1]

About the same time Pound's name began to appear more in *The Criterion* than in *Poetry*. For two or three years before this there had been a renascence of interest in Pound in *Poetry*, probably stimulated by the appearance of his *XXX Cantos* and *How to Read*. Pound wrote a few articles for the magazine; there were several critical notices devoted to his books; and there were numerous references to him as a guide or model in notices of other writers' books. This renascence corresponds roughly with a revival of interest in poetry generally, shown in Britain, for instance, by the attention given to

---

[1] See 'Date Line', *Make It New* (1934), reprinted in *Literary Essays*, p. 85; and letter to Laurence Binyon, Rapallo, 30 August 1934, *Letters*, p. 347.

Auden and others in the group of young poets at the Universities, and in the United States, for instance, by the upsurge of pamphlet publication of poetry.[1] By 1934, F. R. Leavis was able to comment on 'the admission to something like respectability of Ezra Pound', adding that 'at any rate, it is now a thing of course for the *Cantos* to receive respectful attention'.[2]

In 1935, however, it is quite noticeable that Pound figures more prominently in *The Criterion* than in *Poetry*. For this year and succeeding ones *The Criterion* published more of his articles than it had ever done before, and he was referred to more often by other contributors. This change of attention from *Poetry* to *The Criterion* is an indication of Pound's change of primary interest from literary matters to economic ones. He by no means neglected literary matters, but he became more and more obsessed with economics. *Poetry* was not, of course, interested in economics, whereas *The Criterion*, which had several followers of Major Douglas among its contributors, was. The boundary between literature and economics was becoming rather confused for Pound at this time. This is shown most obviously in his fourth and fifth decades of Cantos (published respectively in 1934 and 1937), which have large tracts of pedestrian moralizing about usury. It is also shown, however, in his advice to other poets. In writing to Laurence Binyon about his review of Binyon's *Inferno*, he said that

The one footnote I shall add, when I reprint, is from Lord Bryce, who was more intelligent than either of us and saw that Dante MEANT *plutus*, definitely putting money-power at the root of Evil, and was not merely getting muddled in his mythology. . . .[3]

In enthusing about W. H. D. Rouse's methods of teaching Greek and Latin at the Perse School, he asked:

Along with direct teaching of the language, is there any attempt to teach real history? 'Roman mortgages 6%, in Bithinya 12%.'
I have been for two years in a boil of fury with the dominant usury that impedes every human act, that keeps good books out of print, and pejorates everything.[4]

[1] For a useful listing of some series of pamphlets see T. C. Wilson, 'The Pamphlet Poets', *Poetry*, XLIII, 4 (January 1933), pp. 225–9.

[2] 'English Letter', *Poetry*, XLIV, 3 (June 1934), p. 100.

[3] Rapallo, 6 March 1934; *Letters*, p. 340.

[4] Letter to W. H. D. Rouse, Rapallo, 30 December 1934; *Letters*, p. 349.

This last statement offers a clue about when Pound's overriding obsession with economics began. The 'boil of fury' that had lasted for two years in 1934 was almost certainly fired by A. R. Orage's return to England and his beginning *The New English Weekly*, the first number of which appeared on 21 April 1932. Orage and Pound were both strong supporters of Major Douglas's theories, whereas Eliot, who was interested in economics but who had had the sobering experience of working in a bank, was not. Pound and Eliot had frequent disputes in the pages of *The New English Weekly*, Pound contributing to almost every number.

Towards the end of the thirties Pound was able to express his economic and political theories in several magazines, apart from *The New English Weekly*. *Purpose*, *The Townsman*, and the *British Union Quarterly*, for instance, printed several of his contributions. The editor of *The Townsman*, Ronald Duncan, asked for Pound's advice some time before beginning the magazine. In reply to his introductory letter asking for advice and contributions, Pound asked him: 'How many of the writers whom I read with respect and/or interest are you willing to include?', and informed him that 'Heaven knows there is *work* for a live monthly magazine. And also I wd. be willing to put a good deal of energy into the *right* one.'[1] At least at first, this energy was directed into literary matters rather than political and economic ones. In one letter, he advised that as Duncan and his associates (Auden, Denys Thompson, and Montgomery Butchart) were interested in Wyndham Lewis it would be worth while to investigate *Blast*; that James Laughlin of New Directions ought to be invited to become American editor; and that work by E. E. Cummings and Hilaire Hiler would be as much American literature as the English reading public would bear for the first six months.[2] In another letter, he advised on the finances.[3] In a third, he advocated getting material from Robert McAlmon, Eliot, Zukofsky, Bunting, W. C. Williams, and Jean Cocteau, in some instances offering to write to them himself.[4] Despite his lack of interest in

[1] Rapallo, 27 January 1937; *Letters*, p. 378.
[2] Letter to Duncan, Rapallo, 10 March 1937; *Letters*, p. 382.
[3] Letter to Montgomery Butchart, Rapallo, 11 December 1937; *Letters*, pp. 393-4.
[4] Letter to Montgomery Butchart and Ronald Duncan, Rapallo, 11 December 1937; *Letters*, pp. 394-5.

F

play scripts, Pound even went to the trouble of making some suggestions about Duncan's play, *Pimp, Skunk and Profiteer*.[1]

By this time, Pound's political opinions were almost certainly
making it difficult for him to obtain publication in American
magazines. *Poetry*, for instance, has no work by or articles about
Pound from the beginning of 1939 until the last number of 1940,
when there was a review of some of his publications under the heading of 'The Pound Problem'.[2] A few months later there was an
ominous 'News Note' concerning Pound's broadcasts from Rome
urging the United States to keep out of the war; it ended with the
comment: 'In the onrush of events, Pound may soon find himself
in a very clear-cut and tragic position indeed.'[3] William Carlos
Williams had felt much the same sort of thing when he met Pound
in 1939. This was during Pound's first visit to the United States for
twenty-eight years, and as he arrived with his return ticket already
purchased he felt no obligation to alter his expressed views for the
occasion. Williams wrote to James Laughlin:

The man is sunk, in my opinion, unless he can shake the fog of fascism
out of his brain during the next few years, which I seriously doubt that
he can do. The logicality of fascist rationalization is soon going to kill
him. You can't argue away wanton slaughter of innocent women and
children by the neoscholasticism of a controlled economy program. To
hell with a Hitler who lauds the work of his airmen in Spain and so to hell
with Pound too if he can't stand up and face his questioners on the point.[4]

Pound returned to Rapallo with his wife and parents. The out-
break of war in September 1939 had the effect of stopping his two
main sources of income, namely the royalties from the books he had
published in England and America, and the fees obtained from
articles written for English and American magazines. With his
elderly parents to look after as well as his own family, Pound was
financially embarrassed. He therefore welcomed the invitation to
broadcast for Radio Rome's nightly 'American Hour'. The Jews,
the English, the gold standard, the gunmakers, and Roosevelt were
his main targets for criticism, and his basic exhortation was that

---

[1] See letter to Ronald Duncan, Rapallo, 6 August 1939; *Letters*, pp. 419–20.

[2] J. V. Healy, rev. of *Cantos LII–LXXI*, *Polite Essays*, etc. by Ezra Pound, *Poetry*,
LVII, 3 (December 1940), pp. 200–14.

[3] *Poetry*, LVII, 6 (March 1941), p. 398.

[4] 7 June 1939; *The Selected Letters of William Carlos Williams*, p. 184.

America should stay out of the war. In 1941 he tried to get permission to enter the United States to lecture on Fascism, but he was refused a passage across the Atlantic. At the end of the year, a few days after Pearl Harbour, Germany and Italy declared war on the United States after many months of strained relations. Pound continued to broadcast. In its April issue *Poetry* disowned him in an article headed 'The End of Ezra Pound' written by Eunice Tietjens, a member of the Advisory Committee. The article was as melodramatic as its title would suggest. It began:

The time has come to put a formal end to the countenancing of Ezra Pound. For a number of years, at the beginning of the magazine, he was associated with *Poetry*, and the association was valuable on both sides. Then he quarreled with us, as he has quarreled with everyone, yet continued to use the magazine as an outlet for the publication of his *Cantos* and other poems. Now, so far as we and the rest of the English-speaking world of letters are concerned, he has written *finis* to his long career as inspired *enfant terrible*.

. . . Although never a major poet himself, he probably did more than anyone else in his day to 'incite new impulses in poetry,' as Carl Sandburg once wrote in these pages. Pound served actually as a sort of catalytic agent of other men's ideas and abilities, spurring them on to new accomplishments. And like a catalyst he himself did not change.[1]

The article went on to denounce Pound as a supporter of the enemy, if not a traitor.[2] *Poetry* seems to have imposed a ban on the mention of his name. During the course of the war there were only two or three occasions on which he was mentioned, and in these the reference was a slighting one. Leon Edel, in reviewing *A Treasury of Great Poems*, published by Simon and Schuster, said that 'one wonders at the inclusion of Ezra Pound, for instance, and the absence of James Joyce'.[3] D. S. Savage, in an article on 'Form in Modern Poetry', offered Pound the same sort of position in English poetry as Eunice Tietjens had:

Pound may be taken, indeed, as summing up in himself all the faults and shortcomings of the 'brilliant' second-rate poet who is led, owing to the absence of a fundamental religious seriousness and consequently of a central emotional impulse to his work, into dilettantism, expressed in an

[1] *Poetry*, LX, 1 (April 1942), pp. 38-9.
[2] Similar sentiments had already been expressed in Gilbert Highet's parody-satire, 'Homage to Ezra Pound', *The Nation*, CLIV (21 February 1942), pp. 228-30.
[3] 'Propaganda for Poetry', *Poetry*, LXII, 1 (April 1943), p. 46.

incoherence of subject matter and an exaggerated, self-stultifying pre-occupation with 'technique.'[1]

With Pound unable to contribute to English-speaking magazines and with a conspiracy of silence on the part of some editors against him,[2] the war years mark the nadir of his reputation and influence. Had he died during the war it is doubtful whether present-day scholars and critics would pay him much attention. Any attention they did pay him would probably be for his years in London and in Paris. The years in Rapallo that have been the subject of this chapter would be considered as marking a turning away from literature towards economics and politics. The difficulty of obtaining the texts published in Italy would reinforce the doctrinaire abhorrence of what those texts contained, the result being a complacent neglect.[3]

Yet it should not be forgotten that the composition of the Cantos progressed faster in the 1930s than in any other decade. The first publication of the Cantos in book form was in 1925, when the first sixteen were published. A further fourteen were published in a limited edition in 1930. There had been, therefore, a rate of composition of about three Cantos per year in the 1920s. But by February 1940, a further forty-one Cantos had been published, indicating a rate of composition during the 1930s of four Cantos per year. It is not unreasonable to see evidence of this greater speed in the forty-one Cantos. Didactic narrative, often carried on through long quotations from source material, has a greater part in these Cantos than in others. One often feels that it is a pity Pound does not use notes like Eliot or Marianne Moore, or at least prose insertions like William Carlos Williams; as it is, the notes have been put in as if they were part of the poem.

In the early part of the war, Pound was still thinking about the Cantos. But it would seem that well over a year after finishing Canto LXXI he had still not finished Canto LXXII. The Faber & Faber edition of Cantos LII–LXXI had been published in January 1940. In March Pound was writing to Katue Kitasono about some 'lines from a new Canto—or rather for a new Canto . . . . Lines

[1] *Poetry*, LXV, 1 (October 1944), pp. 39–40.
[2] A conspiracy continued after the war by *Who's Who in America*.
[3] It is rather surprising that the Library of Congress, to judge from its printed records, does not even possess a copy of *Guido Cavalcanti: Rime*. The same is true of the British Museum.

to go into Canto 72 or somewhere'.[1] Canto LXXII and Canto LXXIII were the only products of the war years; neither of them has been published. James Blish reports that 'The two omitted Cantos, which are said to be written in Italian, are concerned, according to Pound, to some extent with living political figures and hence have been withheld pending their death.'[2] The lines quoted in the letter to Kitasono are, however, in English. The reason for the suppression of these Cantos may be the fear of perpetrating defamation, treason, or indecency, or it may be that they are virulent to the point of insanity. Canto LXXIV, the first of the Pisan Cantos, was not written until 1945. Pound was arrested by the United States Army in May 1945 when northern Italy was being occupied. For some weeks he was interned in the Disciplinary Training Center at Pisa, before his health made it necessary to transfer him to the Medical Compound of the Center. The eleven Pisan Cantos were written in his tent in the Medical Compound with writing material supplied by the army and the use of a packing-case, given to him surreptitiously by a Negro prisoner, as a table.

In November, Pound was flown to Washington to stand trial for treason, a charge for which he had been indicted in 1943. A report by four psychiatrists submitting that Pound was 'insane and mentally unfit for trial, and is in need of care in a mental hospital'[3] was accepted by the Federal District Court jury, and Pound was committed, in February 1946, to St. Elizabeths Hospital in Washington, where he was to remain for twelve years.

Some idea of the feeling against Pound even in literary circles can be gained from Bennett Cerf's attitude. Cerf, as head of the publishing firm of Random House, had commissioned Conrad Aiken to edit the American part of *An Anthology of Famous English and American Poetry*. Aiken wanted to include twelve poems by Pound, but Cerf overruled him, and the anthology appeared with a note giving the titles of the poems and stating that their omission

---

[1] Rapallo, 12 March 1941; *Letters*, p. 449.

[2] 'Rituals on Ezra Pound', *The Sewanee Review*, LVIII (Spring 1950), p. 226; quoted in Harvey Gross, 'The Contrived Corridor: A Study in Modern Poetry and the Meaning of History' (unpublished doctoral dissertation University of Michigan, 1954), pp. 43–44 n.

[3] *The Pound Newsletter*, 2 (April 1954), p. 4; *A Casebook on Ezra Pound*, ed. William Van O'Connor and Edward Stone (New York: Thomas Y. Crowell, 1959), p. 25.

was due to the publishers. Cerf gave the reasons for his decision in his column, 'Trade Winds', in *The Saturday Review of Literature* (9 February 1946, p. 26), expressing surprise that anyone should question the wisdom of omitting work by a person with Pound's traitorous ideology. The response by readers was, according to Cerf (16 March 1946, pp. 32 ff.), almost evenly divided between support and opposition. Cerf himself became convinced that the decision to exclude Pound was 'an error in judgment' (p. 32), though his opinions about Pound as a person remained unchanged. He regretted the publicity given to Pound by the incident, and undertook to lift the censorship as soon as possible. Further evidence of hostility was shown in September, when *Poetry* broke its long silence about Pound in order to print part of one of the new Cantos (Canto LXXX) and essays on Pound by Eliot and R. P. Blackmur. George Dillon, the editor, expressed a sense of prematureness in printing Pound's work so soon after the war, as he found it difficult 'to disentangle Pound from the war'. But he considered that 'This new poem is excellent', and that in any case Pound 'would be an important writer if it were only for his influence on Eliot and Yeats'.[1]

Further occasional periodical publication of the new Cantos[2] took place up to the appearance in book form of the whole eleven Cantos in 1948.[3] Violent controversy broke out again when this book was chosen for the first Bollingen Prize for Poetry as being the best book of verse by an American-born or American-naturalized person published in 1948. The committee which made this recommendation to the Bollingen Foundation consisted of The Fellows of the Library of Congress in American Letters, at that time Conrad Aiken, W. H. Auden, Louise Bogan, T. S. Eliot, Paul Green, Robert Lowell, Katherine Anne Porter, Karl Shapiro, Theodore Spencer, Allen Tate, Willard Thorp, and Robert Penn Warren. In a brief announcement accompanying the award, it was stated that

The Fellows are aware that objections may be made to awarding a prize to a man situated as is Mr. Pound. In their view, however, the possibility of such objection did not alter the responsibility assumed by the

---

[1] 'A Note on the Obvious', *Poetry*, LXVIII, 6 (September 1946), pp. 322–5.
[2] As, for example, the publication of Canto LXXVI in *The Sewanee Review*, LV (January 1947), pp. 56–67.
[3] *The Pisan Cantos* (New York: New Directions, 1948).

jury of selection. . . . To permit other considerations than that of
poetic achievement to sway the decision would destroy the significance
of the award and would in principle deny the validity of that objective
perception of value on which any civilized society must rest.[1]

Some of the daily and weekly papers did object to the award on
political grounds, slanting their reports and condemning Pound in
editorials. But this was forgotten in a couple of days. A more serious
attack occurred in an editorial by William Barrett in the April issue
of *Partisan Review*.[2] This objected to the 'vicious and ugly matter'
of the *Pisan Cantos*. The May issue provided a quite neutral battle-
ground for the discussion of the question, the case in favour of the
award being put by Auden and Tate, among others. Further comments from contributors were printed in the June issue, but the
matter seemed to be working itself out quietly. Then *The Saturday
Review of Literature* for 11 June printed the first of two bitter and
hysterical articles by Robert Hillyer.[3] These not only attacked
Pound, but accused some of the Fellows, especially Eliot, of Fascist
sympathies, and suggested that modern poetry and criticism were
often manipulated for political ends. The controversy spread to the
newspapers and to Congress. Eventually the Fellows had to release
a detailed statement dealing with the issues raised; the Library
decided to cancel all its awards, those in music and art as well as
those in literature; and the selection of future Bollingen Prize
winners was entrusted to Yale University.

For Pound, all of this was very good publicity. The following
couple of years, in fact, mark the height of interest in Pound and his
works. 1950 saw the publication in the United States of his letters,
a very early essay, 'Patria Mia', and a new edition of *Personae*; and
in Britain of a collected edition of the Cantos.[4] In the same year
there was published in the United States and Britain a collection of

---

[1] Quoted in *A Casebook on Ezra Pound*, p. 46.

[2] 'A Prize for Ezra Pound', *Partisan Review*, XVI (April 1949), pp. 344-7; reprinted
in *A Casebook on Ezra Pound*, pp. 49-53.

[3] 'Treason's Strange Fruit: The Case of Ezra Pound and the Bollingen Award', *SRL*,
11 June 1949, pp. 9-11, 28; 'Poetry's New Priesthood', *SRL*, 18 June 1949, pp. 7-9, 38.

[4] *The Letters of Ezra Pound, 1907-41*, ed. D. D. Paige (New York: Harcourt, Brace,
1950; London: Faber & Faber, 1951). *Patria Mia* (Chicago: R. F. Seymour, 1950).
Personae: The Collected Poems of Ezra Pound (New York: New Directions, 1950;
London: Faber & Faber, 1952). *Seventy Cantos* (London: Faber & Faber, 1950).

essays by Pound's friends to mark his sixty-fifth birthday.[1] This was edited by Peter Russell, who did a great deal to promote Pound's reputation in Britain at this time. Apart from the editing of this volume, his main activities were the foundation of the Ezra Pound Society of London, the editing of a magazine called *Nine*, and the printing and publishing of works by Pound and others. *Nine* had been started in 1949. Its name was designed to utilize the connotations of the Chinese character for the numeral nine and also to refer to the nine Muses which, according to editorial policy, were all to be represented in the articles published. In these matters, and in its attempt to view English literature in the context of European literature, as well as in its belligerent editorial tone, it came close to Pound's ideas. The last issue of *Nine* was in 1958, but beginning in January 1959 it had a successor in the periodical, *Agenda*, edited by William Cookson. Most of the contributors to *Agenda* have been familiar with and sympathetic to Pound's work: they include Hugh MacDiarmid, Ronald Duncan, William Carlos Williams, Alan Neame, Peter Russell, and Noel Stock. The early issues dabble in economic theories of the type approved by Pound, and contain slogans and uplifting quotations from texts recommended by Pound. Space is also given to contributions with a Christian bias. Noel Stock, a frequent contributor, had himself edited a similar periodical, *The Edge*, eight issues of which were published in Melbourne in 1956–7. *The Edge* had the same range of interests, with the addition of Chinese poetry in translation.

Nine was the prototype of these periodicals in style, material, and contributors, though it went beyond them in offering a critical service: writers were encouraged to submit manuscripts for detailed criticism. The reading of such manuscripts must have been a thankless task, and one can only assume that Russell undertook it because he was so much under the influence of Pound's ideas and practice. From 1950 he was also engaged in republishing Pound's Fascist and monetary pamphlets, at first in London, and then in Tunbridge Wells, where he set up a hand-press. 'The new press', he announced, 'is to be called The Pound Press, after Mr. Ezra

---

[1] *An Examination of Ezra Pound: A Collection of Essays* (Norfolk, Conn.: New Directions, 1950); published in Britain as *Ezra Pound: A Collection of Essays: To be Presented to Ezra Pound on his 65th Birthday* (London: Peter Nevill, 1950).

Pound, who has done so much to make our publishing programme possible.'[1] Six of Pound's money pamphlets[2] were published from 1950 to 1952, and an edition of *ABC of Economics* in 1953.

Important publications in the early fifties from other firms were Pound's *ABC of Reading* (Norfolk, Conn.: New Directions; London: Faber & Faber, 1951); his translation of *Confucian Analects* (New York: Kasper & Horton, 1951), and of the Confucian classics, the *Ta Hsio* and *Chung Yung*, as *The Great Digest and Unwobbling Pivot* (New York: New Directions, 1951; London: Peter Owen, 1952); a revised edition of *The Spirit of Romance* (London: Peter Owen; Norfolk, Conn.: J. Laughlin, 1953); and a collected edition of *The Translations of Ezra Pound*, with an introduction by Hugh Kenner (London: Faber & Faber; New York: New Directions, 1953). An early example of the enormous number of translations into foreign languages that were made of Pound's works in the fifties was *Cinco Poesías*, a translation by Margaret Bates and others (Miami, Florida: Pandanus Press, 1952). Critical attention was beginning to express itself in book-length works with the appearance of Hugh Kenner's *The Poetry of Ezra Pound* (London: Faber & Faber; Norfolk, Conn.: New Directions, 1951), and H. H. Watts's *Ezra Pound and The Cantos* (New York: Regnery; London: Routledge & Kegan Paul, 1952). By the beginning of 1954 there were enough academics working on Pound to justify the publishing of *The Pound Newsletter*, which helped to gather some of the material for an *Annotated Index to the Cantos of Ezra Pound*, by J. H. Edwards and W. W. Vasse (Berkeley and Los Angeles: University of California Press, 1957).

By the time the *Annotated Index* was published there was a good deal of agitation for Pound's release. In 1958 a motion to free him was filed in the Federal District Court, supported by a report from the Superintendent of St. Elizabeths Hospital stating that Pound was 'permanently and incurably insane' but not 'dangerous', and

---

[1] A statement made in an advertising list, 'Nine News and Bookmart, List No. 6' (February 1952).

[2] *America, Roosevelt and the Causes of the Present War*, trans. J. Drummond; *Gold and Work*, trans. J. Drummond; *An Introduction to the Economic Nature of the United States*, trans. C. Amore; *Social Credit* (2nd ed.); *A Visiting Card*, trans. John Drummond; and *What is Money For? and, Introductory Text Book* (2nd ed.). An American edition of some of these pieces, edited by Noel Stock, appeared a few years ago: *Impact: Essays on Ignorance and the Decline of American Civilization* (Chicago: Regnery, 1960).

by a statement from Robert Frost backed up by comments that Frost had gathered from other writers.[1] The motion was successful. The Government raised no objection to Judge Bolitha J. Laws's dismissal of the 1945 indictment, and his release of Pound into the guardianship of his wife. Pound and his wife went to live with their daughter and son-in-law in Schloss Brunnenburg, near Tirolo in Italy, where Pound has been working on the final section of the Cantos. As one would expect, Pound's name has, since his retreat to the Tyrol, been seen far less often in weekly literary journals. *The Times Literary Supplement*, which mentioned his name in articles or letters in almost every issue of 1957, now mentions it less than once a month; no longer are promising young poets being related to principles and methods that Pound espoused; no longer is his name being introduced, often gratuitously, to every discussion of twentieth-century poetry. A few little magazines still treat him with deference, however, and *X: A Quarterly*, during its brief existence, referred to him frequently.

---

[1] See Anthony Lewis, 'U.S. Asked to End Pound Indictment', *The New York Times*, 15 April 1958; reprinted in *A Casebook on Ezra Pound*, pp. 132–4. Frost's submission is reprinted in *A Casebook*, pp. 135–8.

PART II. THE MAJOR INFLUENCES

---

5. POUND AND YEATS

It has become fashionable to divide the poetry of W. B. Yeats into periods. One of the earliest critics to do so was Edmund Wilson who, in a chapter of *Axel's Castle* (1931), suggested that a second period began for Yeats with the poems of *The Green Helmet*, first published in a small edition in 1910. Wilson describes this period generally as 'Dantesque', and characterizes it as being hard and clear in its union of 'all the vigor of his intellect and all the energy of his passion'.[1] In a lecture some ten years later, T. S. Eliot gave his imprimatur to this kind of theory, though he saw the change as beginning with a few of the poems from the earlier volume *In the Seven Woods* (1904) and as not being fully realized until the poems of *Responsibilities* (1914).[2] Later critics have mostly agreed with Eliot, though a few have attempted to establish further periods within the earlier poetry (which, as Wilson and Eliot pointed out, shows a number of experiments and developments).

The greatest claim that could be made for Pound's influence on Yeats's poetry is that Pound was instrumental in bringing about the change to the second period. The point is that the second period lasted, it is generally agreed, until the poems published in *The Tower* (which marks the beginning of a third period) were written. Now *The Tower* was published in 1928, by which time Pound and Yeats

---

[1] See Edmund Wilson, *Axel's Castle: A Study in the Imaginative Literature of 1870–1930* (New York: Scribner's, 1931), ch. 2, 'W. B. Yeats', especially pp. 34–8.

[2] 'The Poetry of W. B. Yeats': The First Annual Yeats Lecture, delivered to the Friends of the Irish Academy at the Abbey Theatre, June 1940, *The Southern Review*, VII, 3 (Winter 1942), pp. 442–54; reprinted in J. Hall and M. Steinmann, eds., *The Permanence of Yeats: Selected Criticism* (New York: Macmillan, 1950), pp. 331–43.

had been separated for many years and had had little contact with each other, and, although it is true that Yeats developed new ideas and interests very slowly, there is little evidence that the changes apparent in the poems of *The Tower* represent the belated effects of Pound's influence. If a major claim is to be plausibly made for Pound's influence on Yeats's poetry it must be made on the basis of the poems in Yeats's second period, that is to say, on the basis of the poems written when Yeats and Pound knew each other best. The most extensive claim that could be made is that Pound helped to bring about the change to the second period.

Intelligent critics are naturally wary of making such a claim in specific terms, but there have been vague statements that suggest it. John Berryman, in discussing the change in Yeats's style, wrote that he had 'always supposed Pound the motor';[1] and Vivienne Koch suggested that it was 'possibly under the bracing self-criticism which his friendship with Ezra Pound had brought about, that Yeats decided that he must, once and for all, abandon the inversions of his early romantic diction'.[2]

If one accepts Edmund Wilson's theory that the change manifests itself in the poems of *The Green Helmet and Other Poems* it becomes important to establish whether, as a matter of chronology, it was possible for Yeats to have been influenced in the writing of the poems by Pound. (If one accepts Eliot's theory, this question is of little importance, as it is quite obvious that Pound could, as a matter of chronology, have influenced the writing of the poems printed in *Responsibilities*.)

The earliest meeting between Pound and Yeats is one that can be disregarded. It occurred in December 1903, when Yeats was on his first lecture-tour of America. William Carlos Williams records that Pound 'was always far more precocious than I and had gone madly on, even to Yeats—who passed through Philadelphia and read to the Penn students in 1903. I did not hear him.'[3] There is no record

---

[1] 'The Poetry of Ezra Pound', *Partisan Review* (April 1949), p. 379; quoted in Thomas Parkinson, 'Yeats and Pound: The Illusion of Influence', *Comparative Literature*, VI (1954), p. 256.

[2] *W. B. Yeats: The Tragic Phase: A Study of the Last Poems* (London: Routledge & Kegan Paul, 1951), p. 48.

[3] *The Autobiography of William Carlos Williams* (New York: Random House, 1951), p. 52.

of Pound having spoken to Yeats on this occasion. Williams's opinion is that

He knew of Yeats slightly while in America but to my knowledge did not become thoroughly acquainted with Yeats' work until he went to London in 1910. There a strange thing took place. He gave Yeats a hell of a bawling out for some of his inversions and other archaisms, and, incredibly, Yeats turned over all his scripts of the moment to Pound that Pound might correct them. That is not imagination but fact. Yeats learned tremendously from Pound's comments.[1]

At first sight it would appear that Williams had made an obvious error in chronology: Pound first went to London at the end of 1908, not in 1910, as an initial reading of Williams's letter might suggest. But it should be noted that Williams does not say that Pound *first* went to London in 1910; he says that Pound 'did not become thoroughly acquainted with Yeats' work until he went to London in 1910'. Let us follow the sequence of events more closely. Pound arrived in London at the end of 1908. He apparently did not meet Yeats until late in 1909, for in a letter to Lady Gregory written in December of that year Yeats gives the impression that he had not known 'this queer creature Ezra Pound' for very long.[2] At this time, Williams was in Germany, studying medicine at the University of Leipzig. He left Germany in March 1910,[3] and returned to America, travelling via London. It was on this visit to London that Pound took him to see Yeats. They found Yeats reading Ernest Dowson's 'Cynara' to a small group of disciples. As they were leaving the room, having received neither greeting nor farewell, Yeats called Pound back for a few words. Williams's comment in his autobiography reads: 'I don't know whether or not that was Ezra Pound's first acquaintance with Yeats.'[4] It was not, of course, the first meeting between Yeats and Pound, but the fact that Williams thought it might have been is another indication that their acquaintance was not of long standing. A few months after this meeting—that is,

---

[1] Letter from W. C. Williams to Babette Deutsch, 18 January 1943; *The Pound Newsletter*, 8 (October 1955), p. 23; *The Selected Letters of William Carlos Williams*, pp. 210-1. The version given here is a conflation of the two transcripts, neither of which appears to have been very carefully proof-read.

[2] *The Letters of W. B. Yeats*, ed. A. Wade (London: Hart-Davis, 1954), p. 543.

[3] See *The Selected Letters of William Carlos Williams*, p. 21.

[4] *The Autobiography of William Carlos Williams*, p. 114.

during the summer of 1910—Pound returned to America because of an attack of jaundice, and remained there until February the following year. While he was in America, Yeats's volume, *The Green Helmet and Other Poems*, was printed and published.

In May 1911, Pound met Yeats again, this time in Paris. Their acquaintance deepened, and Pound wrote to his father:

Yeats I like very much. I've seen him a good deal, about daily, and he has just gone back to London. As he was here for quiet, one got a good deal more from him than when, as before, he has been occupied with other affairs. He is as I have said once before, a very great man, and he improves on acquaintance.[1]

The tone of this letter should be sufficient to establish that Pound could hardly have influenced Yeats's work previously, at least in the manner suggested by Williams. A consideration of the shortness of the period during which the two men could possibly have discussed literary matters supports the same conclusion. After their introduction towards the end of 1909, Yeats and Pound were together in the British Isles for only about six months before Pound returned to America. For about six weeks of this time—in January and February 1910—Yeats was in Ireland.[2] The poems in *The Green Helmet and Other Poems* that could possibly have been written under the direct and immediate influence of Pound are thus reduced to a very small number. They are 'King and No King', 'A Drinking Song', 'The Fascination of What's Difficult', 'A Woman Homer Sung', 'Peace', 'Against Unworthy Praise', 'These are the Clouds', and 'Brown Penny', the latest of them being written in May 1910.[3] One poem was written during Pound's absence in America; it is 'The Mask', written in August 1910 for *The Player Queen*. Two further poems, written after Pound's return from America, were added to *The Green Helmet and Other Poems* for its 1912 edition: they are 'On Hearing That the Students of Our New University

[1] Letter to Homer L. Pound, May 1911, American Literature Collection of the Yale University Library; printed in Parkinson, loc. cit., p. 257.

[2] See *The Letters of W. B. Yeats*, pp. 546–9.

[3] For the dating of these poems, see G. B. Saul, *Prolegomena to the Study of Yeats's Poems* (Philadelphia: University of Pennsylvania Press, 1957), *passim*; Richard Ellmann, *The Identity of Yeats* (London: Macmillan, 1954), p. 288; and Joseph Hone, *W. B. Yeats: 1865–1939*, 2nd ed. (London: Macmillan, 1962), p. 237. The date of 'Brown Penny' is still uncertain.

Have Joined the Agitation against Immoral Literature', and 'At the Abbey Theatre'.[1]

If Pound had been instrumental in bringing about Yeats's change to a second period, one would expect the critics who describe the beginnings of this period to single out for comment the poems that Pound might, on chronological grounds, have influenced. In fact, however, Edmund Wilson mentions only poems that could not possibly have been influenced by Pound. He quotes from 'The Coming of Wisdom with Time', written in March 1909;[2] and from 'No Second Troy', which, according to Joseph Hone, is at the beginning of a journal 'started after a visit to Maud Gonne in Paris in December 1908'.[3] The poem that T. S. Eliot singles out from *The Green Helmet and Other Poems* as typical of the second period is 'Peace', which was, admittedly, written after Pound had met Yeats. But it was written in Normandy in May 1910 while Yeats was visiting Maud Gonne; Pound was certainly not with him, and it is doubtful whether in the circumstances Yeats had much interest in any poetic theories that Pound might have discussed with him.

Including those mentioned by Wilson and Eliot, the poems in *The Green Helmet and Other Poems* best exemplifying Yeats's second period would seem to me to be 'No Second Troy', 'Reconciliation', 'Against Unworthy Praise', and 'The Fascination of What's Difficult'. They are tightly-argued and passionate poems which nevertheless avoid the 'strong lines' and contorted syntax of the metaphysicals. 'No Second Troy', perhaps the best of them, shows a fine tension between almost irrepressible emotion and the repression that comes from the need to state an argument clearly:

> Why should I blame her that she filled my days
> With misery, or that she would of late
> Have taught to ignorant men most violent ways,
> Or hurled the little streets upon the great,
> Had they but courage equal to desire?
> What could have made her peaceful with a mind
> That nobleness made simple as a fire,
> With beauty like a tightened bow, a kind
> That is not natural in an age like this,

[1] See Ellman, *The Identity of Yeats*, p. 288.   [2] See ibid.

[3] Hone, op. cit., p. 227.

Being high and solitary and most stern?
Why, what could she have done being what she is?
Was there another Troy for her to burn?[1]

The tone of the poem reflects another tension, a tension between blind consuming love on the one hand, and bitterness and reproach on the other: some of the questions that Yeats asks suggest one of these forces, some the other. The tension is summed up (but not resolved) in the finely compressed thought of the final line, a line which—like the final stanzas of many of Vaughan's or Traherne's poems—sets the mind off on an exploration of its many possibilities.

The same consecutiveness of argument is to be found in 'Reconciliation', where it is matched by a lengthening and complicating of the sentences. The first twelve lines of 'Reconciliation' form a single sentence, the complexity of which stands in sharp contrast to the simplicity of Yeats's normal sentences in his first period (which typically consist of a few clauses loosely connected by 'ands' and 'buts', as in, for instance, 'The Two Trees' or 'When You are Old').

The complicating of sentence-structure in the second-period poems is a natural concomitant of the argumentativeness that they embody. A second natural concomitant is the loosening and freeing of the iambic rhythm that was Yeats's normal vehicle in the first period. This loosening and freeing had been going on almost throughout the first period. There is, for instance, a vast difference between the rhythm of 'The Indian Upon God', written at the age of twenty, and the rhythm of the later poems from the first period, such as 'The Secret Rose'. 'The Indian Upon God' begins with a rigid iambic metre that barely allows substituted feet; 'The Secret Rose', written some ten years later, shows a much greater freedom in the substitution of feet (though it still keeps to a set number of syllables per line), and a much greater variety in carrying the syntax over from one line to the next. With some of the poems of *In the Seven Woods* (the title-poem, for instance), Yeats begins to write many lines that are no longer susceptible of scansion according to principles of feet or syllables. At first it is often simply a matter of lengthening the line by ending it with an extra-metrical word, as in

---

[1] *The Variorum Edition of the Poems of W. B. Yeats*, ed. Peter Allt and Russell K. Alspach (New York: Macmillan, 1957), pp. 256–7. In the editions from 1931 onwards, Yeats inserted a comma after 'done' in the second last line.

the line 'The unavailing outcries and the old bitterness' (from 'In
the Seven Woods'), which metrically ends with 'old'. By the time of
The Green Helmet and Other Poems, however, Yeats seems to be
settling upon a rhythm that avoids the unpredictable lengthening of
lines in the poems of *In the Seven Woods*; that keeps fairly closely
to a set eight or ten syllables, with one (but not often more than one)
extra syllable occasionally; and that maintains a basic number of
stresses from line to line within the one poem. It is the basic number
of stresses within the line that gives an individual character to each
of the poems of the second period—that gives, for instance, a quite
different character to 'Pardon, old fathers' and to 'To a Shade' in the
volume *Responsibilities*, 'Pardon, old fathers' having a four-stress
line, and 'To a Shade' a five-stress one.

The final feature of the second-period style that is worthy of note
is the spareness, directness, and simplicity of Yeats's diction. This
quality can be seen, for instance, in the two poems from *The Green
Helmet* already referred to, 'No Second Troy' and 'Reconciliation'.
In them, and in other poems typical of the second period, the archaisms and poeticisms of the first period have been set aside; the
overworking of words like 'dim', 'pale', 'desolate', 'dreams', and
'sorrow', and the enervating interest in the trappings of 'kings,
Helmets, and swords' have given way to current, colloquial, prosaic
expressions.

It can be seen that, if it is right to characterize the second period
by the features mentioned, there is a considerable resemblance between Yeats's practice and Pound's theory as expressed in, for instance, the Imagist Manifesto and 'A Few Don'ts'. Pound was
advising young poets in 1913:

Don't chop your stuff into separate *iambs*. Don't make each line stop dead
at the end, and then begin every next line with a heave. Let the beginning
of the next line catch the rise of the rhythm wave, unless you want a
definite longish pause.[1]

On the question of diction he was saying:

Don't use such an expression as 'dim lands *of peace*'. It dulls the image.
It mixes an abstraction with the concrete. It comes from the writer's not
realizing that the natural object is always the *adequate* symbol.[2]

---

[1] 'A Few Don'ts', *Literary Essays*, p. 6.   [2] Ibid., p. 5.

G

These statements do not, of course, cover all the features of Yeats's second-period style. The basic features of argumentativeness and complexity of syntax may be partially covered by Pound's frequently reiterated statement that 'Poetry must be as well written as prose'. But, in any case, the matter is not of great importance, for Pound himself seems to admit that Yeats's new style was created with little help from him. In part of the essay called 'A Retrospect', a part which he dated December 1911—that is, only a few months after his more intimate acquaintance with Yeats began—Pound stated, presumably with reference to the poems of *The Green Helmet*:

Mr Yeats has once and for all stripped English poetry of its perdamnable rhetoric. He has boiled away all that is not poetic—and a good deal that is. He has become a classic in his own lifetime and *nel mezzo del cammin*. He has made our poetic idiom a thing pliable, a speech without inversions.[1]

The distinction between rhetoric and oratory on the one hand, and poetry on the other was one that Yeats had long been aware of. In *Reveries over Childhood and Youth* he records that in the 1880s he 'would say, quoting Mill, "Oratory is heard, poetry is overheard".'[2] And from the same period he records a dislike for abstraction:

We should write out our own thoughts in as nearly as possible the language we thought them in, as though in a letter to an intimate friend. We should not disguise them in any way; for our lives give them force as the lives of people in plays give force to their words. Personal utterance, which had almost ceased in English literature, could be as fine an escape from rhetoric and abstraction as drama itself. . . . I tried from that on [*sic*] to write out of my emotions exactly as they came to me in life, not changing them to make them more beautiful. 'If I can be sincere and make my language natural, and without becoming discursive, like a novelist, and so indiscreet and prosaic,' I said to myself, 'I shall, if good luck or bad luck make my life interesting, be a great poet; for it will be no longer a matter of literature at all.'[3]

These words were written in 1914, many years after the incidents described, and one might feel that Yeats was reading into the past his later critical attitudes. The statement made in the last quotation is very similar to one made in his diary about two years earlier, with,

[1] *Pavannes and Divisions* (1918); reprinted in *Literary Essays*, pp. 11–12.
[2] W. B. Yeats, *Autobiographies* (London: Macmillan, 1956), p. 97.
[3] Ibid., pp. 102–3.

of course, no overtones of retrospectivity; he was describing his theory of art:

First Principles

Not to find one's art by the analysis of language or amid the circumstances of dreams but to live a passionate life, and to express the emotions that find one thus in simple rhythmical language. The words should be the swift natural words that suggest the circumstances out of which they rose.[1]

The objectives set out in this statement are very similar to those I have suggested he achieved in his second period. But there remains the suspicion that Yeats has pre-dated the principles governing the second period. Ellmann draws attention to an essay of 1898 in which Yeats states principles quite contradictory to those under discussion. In this essay, 'The Autumn of the Body',[2] Yeats says:

I see, indeed, in the arts of every country those faint lights and faint colours and faint outlines and faint energies which many call 'the decadence,' and which I, because I believe that the arts lie dreaming of things to come, prefer to call the autumn of the body. . . . communion of mind with mind in thought and without words, foreknowledge in dreams and in visions, and the coming among us of the dead, and of much else.[3]

The solution to the apparent contradiction is not, I think, that Yeats pre-dated his discovery of the principles exemplified in his second-period poetry. It is rather that in the late 1880s and the 1890s Yeats held concurrently a 'hard' and a 'soft' view of the nature of poetry. Yeats was never a consistent theorizer, and it might not be going too far to suggest that he never realized the contradiction: his philosophy always had within it the elements that he later systematized in the doctrines of the gyres and of the self and the anti-self, elements that allowed him to hold contradictory notions without concerning himself about their truth.

By the time Yeats met Pound it is almost certain that he had rejected the 'soft' view and confirmed his belief in the 'hard'; the

[1] A diary note dated Christmas 1912, quoted in Richard Ellmann, *Yeats: The Man and the Masks* (London: Macmillan, 1949), p. 214.

[2] So named in W. B. Yeats, *Essays and Introductions* (London: Macmillan, 1961); Ellmann, using the original version as a copy-text, substitutes 'flesh' for 'body' in the title and in the text of the essay when he quotes from it in *Yeats: The Man and the Masks*, p. 214.

[3] *Essays and Introductions*, pp. 191–2.

selection of subjects and the treatment of them in *The Green Helmet and Other Poems* indicates that the 'soft' view, the view exemplified by the earlier 'Celtic Twilight' poems, had been almost completely abandoned. The adoption of a consistent view had been a long process, partly because Yeats was for a long time holding concurrently the 'Celtic Twilight' view, and partly because he had difficulty putting his 'hard' theory into practice. This difficulty is referred to in his autobiographical essays. In discussing 'The Lake Isle of Innisfree', which was written at the end of 1888, he recalled in 1922 that 'A couple of years later I would not have written that first line with its conventional archaism—"Arise and go"—nor the inversion in the last stanza.'[1] In discussing still earlier poems he noted that, although they were written in an attempt to set down his emotions exactly as they happened, 'when I re-read those early poems which gave me so much trouble, I find little but romantic convention, unconscious drama. It is so many years before one can believe enough in what one feels even to know what the feeling is.'[2]

By the time of *The Green Helmet and Other Poems* Yeats did, however, know what the feeling was, and had been able to embody it in highly satisfactory verse. It has been shown that the best of the second-period poems in *The Green Helmet and Other Poems* could not have been influenced by Pound. There remain a few poems that it is possible for him to have influenced.[3] These have not so far been discussed, and I do not propose to spend much time on them now. 'A Woman Homer Sung' is a very melodramatic poem, containing such abstractions as 'shook with hate and fear', and such archaisms as

> And trod so sweetly proud
> As 'twere upon a cloud.

'King and No King' is written in a fairly conversational tone, though it has lines of studied formality of which Pound would have disapproved, lines such as

> And I that have not your faith, how shall I know
> That in the blinding light beyond the grave
> We'll find so good a thing as that we have lost?

The poem has, in any case, so many personal references to the

---

[1] *Autobiographies*, pp. 153-4.   [2] Ibid., p. 103.   [3] Listed above, pp. 78-9.

relationship between Yeats and Maud Gonne that it is unlikely Pound was allowed to see it before publication. 'Against Unworthy Praise' is also too personal for Pound to have been of any use in making suggestions during its composition. 'A Drinking Song' is a very conventional, sentimental fragment. 'These are the Clouds' looks as if Pound had little influence on its composition, for its first few lines are full of abstractions and vague, unidentified generalizations:

> These are the clouds about the fallen sun,
> The majesty that shuts his burning eye;
> The weak lay hand on what the strong has done,
> Till that be tumbled that was lifted high . . . .

'Brown Penny' is so full of Yeats's earlier romanticism that there can be no question of possible influence from Pound: Yeats had been using material like

> For he would be thinking of love
> Till the stars had run away,
> And the shadows eaten the moon

long before he had heard of Pound. Of the two poems added to the 1912 edition, one is a fragment of satire, 'On Hearing That the Students . . .', and the other, 'At the Abbey Theatre', is an imitation of Ronsard.

It can, therefore, be confidently asserted that as the best of the poems in *The Green Helmet* could not have been influenced by Pound, and as the others appear not to have been, Yeats's second period began quite independently of Pound. In view of this, the most that could plausibly be asserted for Pound's influence is that he confirmed Yeats in the direction he was taking for the second period, and helped him, by suggestions about individual words and lines, to embody his theories more adequately in his verse. There is, in fact, some evidence to support this suggestion. William Carlos Williams's assertion that 'Yeats turned over all his scripts of the moment to Pound that Pound might correct them' could well be true, provided that Williams's dating of 1910 is rejected in favour of 1912. When Yeats was speaking in 1914 at a banquet arranged in his honour in Chicago by the magazine *Poetry*, he said:

When I returned to London from Ireland, I had a young man go over all my work with me to eliminate the abstract. This was an American poet,

Ezra Pound. Much of his work is experimental; his work will come slowly, he will make many an experiment before he comes into his own. . . .[1]

'When I returned to London' could mean 1910, when Yeats was in London for an Abbey Theatre season and later for a series of lectures; but it is more likely to mean 1912, when Lennox Robinson took over management of the Abbey Theatre and left Yeats with more time to spend outside Dublin. Early in December of that year, Yeats returned to 18 Woburn Buildings, London, intending to spend the winter there.[2] It was a miserable winter for him, as he was restricted to a milk diet by a digestive disorder, he suffered from headaches, and his eyes were too sore for him to read much.[3] In these difficulties, Pound, ever ready to help anyone in distress, was invaluable. He read to Yeats in the evenings, and helped to improve his health by teaching him to fence. It must have been during this winter that Pound went over Yeats's work in an attempt to eliminate the abstract. It is, unfortunately, impossible to know exactly which poems were corrected. William Carlos Williams says that they were 'all [Yeats's] scripts of the moment'; if this were so the corrections might or might not be in Pound's handwriting on any of the extant manuscripts or typescripts. Yeats says that the scripts corrected were 'all my work'; if this were so one would expect changes to have been made in subsequent editions of the earlier work. The first edition of the early work to follow Pound's correction of Yeats's poems was a revision of *Poems* (1895), reprinted from standing type in London in 1913; it introduced almost no new readings. Another revision was made in 1919, once again introducing almost no new readings. The poems from *The Wind among the Reeds* and subsequent works up to 1921 were published in 1922 as *Later Poems*. It was of this volume and of a new volume of plays that Yeats was thinking when he wrote to Olivia Shakespear: 'These books have meant a great deal of work, and I am tired and in a rage at being old.'[4] The 'great deal of work' was apparently caused by the alterations that Yeats made for the volumes, alterations which, in the case

---

[1] Quoted in Harriet Monroe, *A Poet's Life*, p. 338.
[2] See *The Letters of W. B. Yeats*, pp. 569–73.
[3] See Joseph Hone, op. cit., p. 271.
[4] 7 June 1922; *The Letters of W. B. Yeats*, p. 685.

of the poetry, apparently caused some protests from readers.[1] Yet
the alterations were not really extensive. The most altered poem
was 'The Folly of Being Comforted'. It had been printed in 1908,
in the first volume of the collected edition; in 1913, in *A Selection
from the Love Poetry of William Butler Yeats*, published by The
Cuala Press; and in 1921, in the American edition of the *Selected
Poems*. These versions differ from each other only in punctuation.
The 1922 version introduces further punctuation changes, but also
some substantive changes. Where the 1913 version read:

> 'Time can but make it easier to be wise,
> Though now it's hard, till trouble is at an end;
> And so be patient, be wise and patient, friend.'
> But, heart, there is no comfort, not a grain;

the 1922 version read:

> 'Time can but make it easier to be wise
> Though now it seem impossible, and so
> Patience is all that you have need of.'
> No,
> I have not a crumb of comfort, not a grain . . . .[2]

It will be readily seen that even these changes are of little importance. They certainly seem to bear no marks of Pound's tuition, for
Yeats was quite capable of making such changes by himself, and in
any case Pound was not present when the changes were made.

As no poem was altered more than 'The Folly of Being Comforted', and as alterations made in other poems are of the same type
as those in this poem, it can be suggested with some confidence
that Pound had virtually no influence on the revision of the poems
written by Yeats before he met Pound. Yet it is known that Pound
did alter some of Yeats's poems during the period of their close
friendship. The first of these were the poems sent to Pound by
Yeats in response to his request for something to print in *Poetry*.
Five poems by Yeats were printed in the December 1912 number:
'The Realists', 'The Mountain Tomb', 'To a Child Dancing in the
Wind', 'A Memory of Youth', and 'Fallen Majesty'. Some or all of
these were altered by Pound without consulting Yeats before they

---

[1] See Hone, op. cit., p. 346.   [2] See *Variorum Edition*, pp. 199–200.

were sent on to *Poetry*. Yeats was at first annoyed, but then rather impressed by Pound's brashness.[1]

Several readings in the five poems occur only in the version printed in *Poetry*. This is quite usual for those of Yeats's poems that were first published in magazines, but in this case there could be the suggestion that Yeats later got rid of the readings that Pound had inserted. The readings altered in subsequent editions of three of the poems are of little importance: they concern mostly punctuation and single words. These poems are 'The Realists', 'The Mountain Tomb', and 'Fallen Majesty'. Some of the alterations to 'To a Child Dancing in the Wind' are more interesting. One of them changed the line 'And he, the best warrior, dead' to 'Nor the best labourer dead'. 'The best warrior' would presumably have been a reference to John O'Leary, who died in 1907; 'the best labourer' is generally taken, though perhaps wrongly, as a reference to John Synge, who died in 1908.[2] This is an interesting alteration, but hardly one that could plausibly be attributed to Pound's interference in either reading. The other important alteration in the poem is the change from

> What need that you should dread
> The monstrous crying of wind?

to

> What need have you to dread
> The monstrous crying of wind?

It is most unlikely that Pound, with his concern for colloquialism in the language of poetry, would have altered the second of these readings to the first; that is to say, it is most unlikely that Yeats originally put down the second reading only to have it altered to the first by Pound, and then reverted to his original reading for subsequent editions. It is possible that Pound pointed out to Yeats at some time after the publication of the poem in *Poetry* the possibility of using a more colloquial expression, and that Yeats took his

---

[1] Hone reports this incident on p. 235 of his *W. B. Yeats: 1865–1939*, in a section dealing with the events of the years 1907 to 1910. The incident must, however, have occurred over the publication in the December 1912 number of *Poetry*, as this was the first publication of Yeats's poems in any magazine with which Pound was connected after the time of Yeats's first meeting with him in London.

[2] See, for instance, John Unterecker, *A Reader's Guide to William Butler Yeats* (New York: Noonday, 1959), p. 126.

advice for subsequent editions; but this must remain a surmise. In the remaining poem, 'A Memory of Youth', the changes are more substantial still, and once again they can hardly be reversions to an original reading changed by Pound. The sixth line was altered from 'And she seemed happy as a king' to 'A cloud blown from the cut-throat North': the robust colloquialism 'cut-throat' may be due to a suggestion made by Pound after the publication in *Poetry*, but there is no positive evidence for this. In the following line, 'Love's moon was withering away' became 'Suddenly hid love's moon away' in subsequent editions: Pound disliked the colourlessness of the verb 'to be', and so this change might be due to him. The remaining substantial change, the change of the last line from 'Threw up in the air his marvellous moon' to 'Tore from the clouds his marvellous moon' is the sort of improvement that Yeats might well have made without any help from Pound.

It might be wondered why, in the light of these discouraging findings, one would persist with a study of Pound's influence on Yeats. It has been indicated so far that Pound's influence on the poems published up to almost the end of 1912 in either their original or corrected versions is undemonstrable and probably negligible, and that Yeats formed his second-period style without help from Pound. But it should be remembered that the end of 1912 takes us to only the beginning of the closer friendship between the two men, and that the poems discussed so far had all been published before the time when, according to Yeats, 'I had a young man go over all my work with me to eliminate the abstract.' On the assumption that 'all my work' means in this context 'all my work that I had written but not then published' and perhaps also 'all the work that I subsequently wrote', it becomes important to investigate the poems written but not published in December 1912, and the poems written between then and the time when Yeats made the statement at the end of February or the beginning of March 1914. Now it would seem that possibly only two of Yeats's poems had been written but not published by December 1912: 'A Coat', written in 1912, and first published in *Poetry* in May 1914; and the double poem, 'The Witch' and 'The Peacock', written in May 1912, and first published with 'A Coat'.[1] Two poems were certainly

[1] See Ellmann, *The Identity of Yeats*, p. 289.

written during December 1912: 'The New Faces',[1] and 'To a Wealthy Man' (written on 24 December).[2] 'Two Years Later' may have been written in this December, or it may belong to the following one.[3] 'The Grey Rock' was written at the end of December 1912, or in the first few days of January 1913.[4] During the winter of 1913/1914, two poems were written: the Prefatory Poem of *Responsibilities* in December,[5] and the Epilogue early in 1914.

The first thing to be noticed is that very few poems were written by Yeats while Pound was with him. During the winter of 1912/1913, when Pound was looking after Yeats's health in London, and during the winter of 1913/1914, when he was acting as Yeats's secretary in London and later in Sussex, Yeats wrote, at most, six poems. Compared with this five months for six poems, one month (September 1913) when Pound was not with Yeats sufficed for the writing of eight poems: 'September 1913', 'To a Friend Whose Work Has Come to Nothing', 'Paudeen', 'To a Shade', 'When Helen Lived',

---

[1] See A. N. Jeffares, *W. B. Yeats: Man and Poet* (London: Routledge & Kegan Paul, 1949), p. 163.

[2] See Ellmann, *The Identity of Yeats*, p. 288.   [3] Ibid., p. 289.

[4] Joseph Hone, op. cit., p. 269, says that the poem 'appeared in the *Literary Digest* for November 1912', but the first printing of the poem is given in both *The Variorum Edition of the Poems of W. B. Yeats*, p. 270, and G. B. Saul, op. cit., pp. 89–90, as the issues of *Poetry* and *The British Review* for April 1913. Ellmann, in *The Identity of Yeats*, p. 288, gives the date of composition as 1913. Part of the poem was printed in *The Literary Digest* (New York) for 15 November 1913 (pp. 958–9), and it must be this printing that Hone had in mind.

In a letter to Lady Gregory dated 'Jan 8' and postmarked 1913, Yeats referred to the poem in relation to Mabel Beardsley:

> Strange that just after writing those lines on the Rhymers who 'unrepenting faced their ends' I should be at the bedside of the dying sister of Beardsley, who was practically one of us. She had had a week of great pain but on Sunday was I think free from it. She was propped up on pillows . . . . Beside her a Xmas tree with little toys containing sweets, which she gave us.
>
> (*The Letters of W. B. Yeats*, p. 574)

The reference to 'on Sunday' (which is also used in connexion with another incident described in the letter) suggests that the visit to Mabel Beardsley took place on the Sunday previous to the writing of the letter. This Sunday would have been the 5th of January, a date which explains the 'Xmas tree with little toys' satisfactorily. 'Those lines on the Rhymers' must, then, have been written at most a few days before the 5th, because it was 'just after writing' them that the visit to Mabel Beardsley occurred. Ellmann is probably right, then, in giving the date of composition as '1913'.

It is true that in the letter quoted Yeats assumes Lady Gregory to be familiar with the lines referred to, but this does not, of course, imply prior publication; he probably enclosed the poem in manuscript or typescript with this letter, or with a previous one.

[5] See Ellman, *The Identity of Yeats*, p. 288.

'Running to Paradise', 'The Magi', and 'The Dolls'.[1] This was, of course, an exceptional month, but it serves to indicate the fact that when Pound was with Yeats he did not spend his time correcting and revising poems as they were being written. Nor, it would seem, did he spend his time correcting the poems that had been written. I have shown that there were very few unpublished poems available for Pound to revise during the winter of 1912/1913, and that in regard to the poems already published the corrections made some years later were of a minor nature and were only very doubtfully due to Pound's influence. It may now be asked whether the same position existed for the winter of 1913/1914. In the eight months that elapsed from the end of Pound's first winter with Yeats to the beginning of the second, Yeats wrote the eight poems of September 1913, and three others: 'The Three Hermits', 'Beggar to Beggar Cried' (both written on 5 March 1913[2]), and 'The Hour Before Dawn', written on 19 October 1913.[3] Of these eleven poems, five had been published by the time Pound and Yeats came together for the winter of 1913/1914: 'The Three Hermits' had been published in *The Irish Times* for 8 September 1913; and it had also, together with 'To a Friend Whose Work Has Come to Nothing', 'Paudeen', and 'To a Shade', appeared in *Poems Written in Discouragement*, published by The Cuala Press in October. Now these five poems were all republished in one place or another in 1914, after Pound and Yeats had spent the winter together. If Pound's services in eliminating the abstract had been made use of during the winter and if Yeats had taken much notice of the suggested emendations, one would expect the 1914 versions of these poems to be substantially altered from the original printed versions. In fact, however, the only alterations made were in spelling, punctuation, and the spacing between stanzas.

In the absence of any direct evidence of Pound's corrections on Yeats's manuscripts or typescripts, these five poems provide an important test case for judging the extent of his influence on the writing of the poems. Four of them (the exception is 'The Three Hermits') were printed within a month of being written; as Yeats was in Ireland during that month and Pound in England, and as

---

[1] According to Ellmann's dating, ibid., p. 289.
[2] See ibid.   [3] See ibid.

their arrangements to spend the winter had already been made,[1] it is unlikely that Pound saw the poems before publication. Pound's first opportunity to discuss the poems with Yeats would have been during the following winter: yet this discussion, if it occurred at all, produced no significant alterations in the text of the poems.

The evidence that has been brought forward suggests that Pound's emendation of Yeats's poems was of very small extent. It is true that this evidence has been entirely drawn from poems written when Pound and Yeats were separated from each other and not from poems written when they spent the winters together. Yet the undiscussed evidence, the evidence that might be drawn from the manuscripts written during the winters, is, for two reasons, not of great importance. The first of these is that the poems written during the winters were very few in number. The second is that even Pound's handwriting on these manuscripts would not prove conclusive evidence; corrections in his handwriting might, for instance, have been the result of his acting as an amanuensis for Yeats rather than as a critic. In any case, none of those who have looked at the manuscripts have ever mentioned the presence of Pound's handwriting on them. A. N. Jeffares, in 'W. B. Yeats and His Methods of Writing Verse', *The Nineteenth Century and After*, CXXIX (1946), pp. 123–128, discusses corrections made by Yeats to his original drafts, including the draft of 'A Coat' (written in 1912), without mentioning the presence of any other handwriting than Yeats's. Corrections in Yeats's handwriting might, of course, be the result of discussions with Pound who, according to Yeats, 'helps me to get back to the definite and concrete, away from modern distractions, to talk over a poem with him is like getting [Lady Gregory] to put a sentence into dialect. All becomes clear and natural.'[2] But such corrections might be the result of Yeats's own rethinking, and so they provide very inconclusive evidence.

Statements made by Pound in 1914 add support to the suggestion that he had had little to do with Yeats's poetry until then. The poems written after publication of *The Green Helmet and Other Poems* were published or republished in *Responsibilities* (Church-

---

[1] See *The Letters of W. B. Yeats*, p. 584.
[2] Letter to Lady Gregory, probably written during the winter of 1913/14; quoted Hone, op. cit., p. 272.

town, Dundrum: The Cuala Press, 1914). Pound reviewed this volume for *Poetry*,[1] and the tone of the review indicates that his part in the poems was probably negligible. He refers to a 'new note' in Yeats's work—'you could hardly call it a change of style'. This 'new note' seems, for Pound, to have been partly a matter of Yeats's coming to deal 'with things as they are and no longer romantically Celtic',[2] and partly a matter of his presentation of his subjects 'becoming gaunter, seeking greater hardness of outline'. This change, according to Pound, had become apparent in the poems of *The Green Helmet and Other Poems*, the example he quotes being 'No Second Troy'. In the poems of *Responsibilities* the gauntness and hardness had become intensified, he thought, the poems he especially praises being 'The Grey Rock', 'When Helen Lived', 'The Realists', 'To a Child Dancing in the Wind', and 'The Magi'. These poems could not, as has been already shown, have been much influenced by Pound in either their original or corrected versions. One further piece of evidence that this is so is provided in the review by Pound's statements about 'The Grey Rock', which was written when he was meeting Yeats every day:

> *The Grey Rock* is, I admit, obscure, but it outweighs this by a curious nobility, ...

> . . . .

> I have said that *The Grey Rock* was obscure; perhaps I should not have said so, but I think it demands unusually close attention. It is as obscure, at least, as *Sordello*, but I can not close without registering my admiration for it all the same.

These are hardly the statements of a man who was in consultation with the poet during the composition of the poem. Pound goes no further than the expression of this pious bewilderment: he offers no help with the obscurity, so that one suspects that even at this time he was not quite certain of the meaning of the poem.

If it is accepted that Pound had little influence on the writing or correcting of Yeats's poetry up to the beginning of 1914, the problem still remains of why Yeats records that 'I had a young man go

---

[1] *Poetry*, IV, 2 (May 1914), pp. 64–9; reprinted in *Literary Essays*, pp. 378–81.

[2] This is, presumably, part of the reason why Pound praised 'Child Dancing' and 'The Realists' in a letter to Harriet Monroe.

over all my work with me to eliminate the abstract'. If the effects of this 'going over' are virtually indiscernible in the revised version of the poems concerned, why does Yeats mention it? The answer is probably that one is taking too naïve a view of influence to expect Pound to have an effect on the actual construction or content of any particular poem. Yeats may have agreed with Pound that there was something wrong with many of his poems, but either Pound was not able to suggest specific emendations to correct the faults, or else Yeats felt that it was better to try to take account of the principles of Pound's objections in the writing of subsequent poems. If this were so, one would look not for specific verbal influence but rather for a general movement of Yeats's poems in the direction of Pound's principles. But such a movement could hardly be a very great one, for it has been shown that Pound's and Yeats's principles were very similar at this time and that Pound considered Yeats to be putting his intentions fairly successfully into practice.

Although Yeats's second-period style had been quite firmly established by the beginning of 1914, there may, nevertheless, have been a few minor changes made in it later because of Pound's influence. There are a few poems in *The Wild Swans at Coole*, Yeats's next major volume, that at first sight seem to have a connexion with Pound. 'A Thought from Propertius' looks as if it might have some connexion with Pound's *Homage to Sextus Propertius*, but, though Pound may have suggested that Yeats read Propertius, Yeats's poem has a much more reverent and elevated tone than Pound's and in any case was almost certainly written earlier.[1] 'Ego Dominus Tuus' mentions one of Pound's abiding interests, Guido Cavalcanti, in a fleeting reference which may have been due to Pound's influence. 'The Balloon of the Mind' is Yeats's most imagistic poem:

> Hand, do what you're bid:
> Bring the balloon of the mind
> That bellies and drags in the wind
> Into its narrow shed.

This seems to invite comparison in structure with Pound's poem, 'The Bath Tub', written a couple of years before, or with 'April'. Beyond these few points, however, there is nothing to be said about

[1] Ellmann, *The Identity of Yeats*, p. 290, dates 'A Thought from Propertius' as 'by Nov. 1915'. *Homage to Sextus Propertius* was finished in 1917.

any new influence by Pound on Yeats discernible in the poems from *The Wild Swans at Coole*. Pound seems to have thought that the poems in this volume represented a decline, for between its publication and the publication of Yeats's next major volume he wrote to William Carlos Williams that Yeats had 'faded'.[1] This judgement was probably made because of Yeats's increasing interest in magical systems, but even if one leaves out of account the poems representing this interest it is, I think, impossible to see in the poems of *The Wild Swans at Coole* any further influence by Pound.

Apart from poetry, there are two other fields in which Pound may be thought to have influenced Yeats: the drama, and critical theory. I have already touched on the second of these. The first is, however, far more important, and deserves a lengthier treatment. During the first winter that Yeats and Pound spent in Sussex, Pound was working on the Fenollosa manuscripts that had recently come into his charge. About the time that Yeats left England for his American lecture tour, Pound finished the first piece of material from the manuscripts to be ready for publication, the Noh play, *Nishikigi*. In sending it to Harriet Monroe for publication in *Poetry*, Pound said, in a letter dated 31 January 1914: 'You'll find W.B.Y. also very keen on it.'[2] Although this suggests that Pound had already discussed the Noh drama with Yeats, it would seem that the discussion, if it occurred, made little impression on him, so little impression, in fact, that most writers assume that Yeats did not learn of the Noh drama until the following winter.[3] At any rate, Yeats worked on only one play during 1914, the much revised *The Player Queen*, and in writing about it to his father he did not mention Noh drama.[4] Even during the following winter, there is little evidence that Yeats was greatly interested in Noh: he certainly was not making any practical use of such an interest, for the only play he was working on was still *The Player Queen*. During 1915, however, he saw a good deal of Pound—he was, for instance, concerned in Pound's project to get a pension for James Joyce—and he probably joined in discussions about the Noh with Arthur Waley and

---

[1] 11 September 1920; *Letters*, p. 223. [2] *Letters*, p. 69.
[3] F. A. C. C. Wilson, for instance, writes: 'Then in the winter of 1914–15, Ezra Pound introduced him to the Noh . . .'. *W. B. Yeats and Tradition* (London: Gollancz, 1958), p. 41.
[4] See *The Letters of W. B. Yeats*, p. 588.

Edmund Dulac at Pound's lodgings. The discussions must at first have been rather academic, for none of the participants had ever seen a Noh play, and Fenollosa's notes do not provide a coherent description. Towards the end of 1915, however, some of the practical difficulties were solved by Pound's chance meeting with the young Japanese dancer, Michio Ito. He had never acted in the Noh —in fact he had not seen a performance since the age of seven—but he did his best to familiarize himself with the conventional gestures and to demonstrate them to Pound and his group.[1]

By the winter of 1915/1916, Yeats was ready to adopt some of the conventions of the Noh in his own plays, the first product being *At the Hawk's Well*, which he dictated to Pound early in 1916.[2] Apart from the still unfinished *The Player Queen*, this was the first play Yeats had written for six years, and it is doubtful whether, but for Pound's enthusiasm, he would at this time have returned to the writing of plays. Some of the dissatisfaction that he felt with the conventional playwright's task comes out in the introduction he wrote a few months later for *Certain Noble Plays of Japan*. This volume contained four Noh plays translated by Ernest Fenollosa and Pound, together with Yeats's introduction, which speaks less about the plays in the volume than about the inspiration Yeats himself had drawn from Noh. Yeats begins by describing the preparations made for the staging of *At the Hawk's Well*, contrasting them very favourably with the elaborate preparations required for a conventional play. He then claims to 'have invented a form of drama, distinguished, indirect, and symbolic, and having no need of mob or Press to pay its way—an aristocratic form'.[3] His interest in Noh seems, in fact, to have been mainly in its aristocratic elements: in the commercial possibility of playing to a small and discriminating audience in a restrained and delicate style. Such a form made it possible to introduce in a completely symbolic way the esoteric doctrines that he was interested in. Pound emphasized similar

---

[1] It has often been suggested (e.g., by Hone, op. cit., p. 289; Ellmann, *Yeats: The Man and the Masks*, p. 217) that Ito had acted in Noh in Japan. Anthony Thwaite, in 'Yeats and the Noh', *The Twentieth Century*, CLXII (1957), pp. 235–42, shows this to be an error.

[2] Ellmann, *Yeats: The Man and the Masks*, p. 215.

[3] W. B. Yeats, Introduction to *Certain Noble Plays of Japan*: from the manuscripts of E. Fenollosa, chosen and finished by Ezra Pound (Churchtown, Dundrum: E. C. Yeats, The Cuala Press, 1916); and *Essays and Introductions* (1961), p. 221.

elements in the Introduction to his '*Noh*' or *Accomplishment*, published later in the same year:

The art of allusion, or this love of allusion in art, is at the root of the
Noh. These plays, or eclogues, were made only for the few; for the
nobles; for those trained to catch the allusion.[1]

A comparison of Yeats's Introduction with Pound's indicates
that the form of drama that Yeats said he had 'invented' and the
traditional Japanese Noh were almost identical. (*At the Hawk's Well*
has, in fact, been converted into a traditional Noh play and acted
on the professional stage in Japan.[2]) It should not, however, be
assumed that Yeats was over-estimating his contribution in speaking of invention, or that Pound should be credited with introducing
to Yeats a new form of drama. Before he encountered Noh drama
Yeats had, in fact, committed himself, either in theory or in practice,
to most of its elements. As early as 1897 he had clearly stated a
theory of symbolic, non-representational drama in a letter to Fiona
Macleod:

My own theory of poetical or legendary drama is that it should have no
realistic, or elaborate, but only a symbolic and decorative setting. A forest,
for instance, should be represented by a forest pattern and not by a forest
painting. . . . The plays might be almost, in some cases, modern mystery
plays.[3]

About the same time, he wrote an essay along similar lines, emphasizing the importance of an intimate theatre to present plays with a
spiritual theme:

We must make a theatre for ourselves and our friends, and for a few simple
people who understand from sheer simplicity what we understand from
scholarship and thought. We have planned the Irish Literary Theatre
with this hospitable emotion, and that the right people may find out
about us, we hope to act a play or two in the spring of every year; and
that the right people may escape the stupefying memory of the theatre of
commerce which clings even to them, our plays will be for the most part
remote, spiritual, and ideal.[4]

[1] Introduction to '*Noh*' or *Accomplishment: A Study of the Classical Stage of Japan*,
including translations of fifteen plays by Ernest Fenollosa and Ezra Pound (London:
Macmillan, 1916); reprinted in *The Translations of Ezra Pound*, p. 214.

[2] See Thwaite, loc. cit., p. 242.

[3] Printed in E. A. Sharp, *William Sharp (Fiona Macleod): A Memoir* (London: Heinemann, 1910), pp. 280-1.

[4] 'The Theatre' (1899); reprinted in *Essays and Introductions*, p. 166.

There is little doubt, then, that the principles that Pound and Yeats believed to be inherent in the Noh drama had been held by Yeats for many years, and had guided him in the writing of some of his plays. But in his connexion with the Abbey Theatre Yeats had found difficulty in keeping his principles unsullied by the demands of audiences, actors, and managers, and this difficulty seems ultimately to have produced a *malaise* that kept him from writing any new plays between 1910 and 1916. Pound's study of the Noh traditions was important for Yeats, not merely in providing an external thrust of enthusiasm to turn him once more to the writing of plays, but also in confirming the principles that he had only partially been able to put into practice, and in providing suggestions for techniques by which they might be put completely into practice. I have already suggested that not all these techniques were new to him. He had anticipated the supernatural figures of Noh drama with the faeries, demons, and spirits of *The Countess Cathleen, The Land of Heart's Desire, The Green Helmet,* and *The Hour-Glass.* The plays he wrote before his introduction to the Noh are full of symbolic objects and actions, as for instance the helmet and the sword of *The Green Helmet* and the action prescribed in the same play when 'Suddenly three black hands come through the windows and put out the torches.'[1] The helmet has virtually the purpose of the Noh mask, and one can see Yeats almost needing masks for the metamorphoses and revelations at the end of *The Countess Cathleen* and *The Land of Heart's Desire*; in *The Land of Heart's Desire,* for instance, a mask or masks for the Faery Child would have enabled some of the points to be made with greater effect, and if Yeats had had masks available to him he would no doubt have expanded the final balletic scene where 'there are dancing figures, and it may be a white bird, and many voices singing'[2] into something like the dance of the hawk in *At the Hawk's Well. The Land of Heart's Desire* is the only play before his introduction to Noh in which Yeats makes much use of dancing to reinforce a mood and ethos, but in almost all his early plays he uses singing to do this and to act as a chorus-like comment on the inner meaning of the play. He had also anticipated the elevated and noetic language of the Noh, and had given much thought

---

[1] *The Collected Plays of W. B. Yeats,* 2nd ed. (London: Macmillan, 1952), p. 241.
[2] Ibid., p. 72.

to the way in which it should be delivered. The question of delivery is taken up with reference to dramatic poetry as well as lyric in Yeats's essay of 1902, 'Speaking to the Psaltery'.[1] The simplicity of setting demanded by the Noh play was something that he had been groping towards: he had been impressed in 1902 by the stage settings of Gordon Craig, who, he said, 'has discovered how to decorate a play with severe, beautiful, simple, effects of colour, that leave the imagination free to follow all the suggestions of the play';[2] and the Abbey Theatre's production of *The Countess Cathleen* in 1911 used minimal and non-realistic scenery.[3]

It is fairly obvious, then, that Yeats's own experiments had prepared him for an appreciation of the Noh drama. It is strange that he did not make use of the Noh form as soon as Pound told him about it, but the reason may be that Pound had not at that time (during the winter of 1913/1914) clarified in his own mind the essential features of the form or the features that would appeal to Yeats; or it may be that Yeats was still rather dubious about the possibilities of success in practical drama.

When he did combine his own experience with the tradition of the Noh in *At the Hawk's Well*, he produced a very fine play. But part of the success is due not to any dramatic experience but to the improvement that Yeats had been making in his non-dramatic verse. This was the first new play he had written since establishing his second-period style. The combination of the second-period style with the stark symbolism required by the form produced in *At the Hawk's Well* verse which is markedly more condensed than the verse of his previous plays: it lacks the oratorical repetition and the atmospheric elaboration of his earlier dramatic verse; it avoids the long, loosely constructed sentences of his earlier plays, but instead of replacing them with the long, tightly constructed sentences of his second-period non-dramatic verse it replaces them with short, urgent sentences; and, appropriately enough in view of these

---

[1] Reprinted in *Essays and Introductions*, pp. 13–20. The methods described in this essay seem to have influenced Pound when he was later writing his operas.

[2] Letter to the Editor, *Saturday Review*, 5 March 1902; *The Letters of W. B. Yeats*, p. 366.

[3] See *The Collected Plays*, p. 3; for details of the revision of this play see George Brandon Saul, *Prolegomena to the Study of Yeats's Plays* (Philadelphia: University of Pennsylvania Press, 1958), pp. 25–6.

characteristics, the lines are generally shorter and the rhythms more broken. Some of these points can be illustrated by comparison of a passage from *The Shadowy Waters* with a passage from *At the Hawk's Well*. These two plays were written about ten years apart. In *The Shadowy Waters*, Forgael searches for the meaning of the magic ship as the sailors are boarding it; the birds that hover over the mast provide him with an omen:

> There! there! They come! Gull, gannet, or diver,
> But with a man's head, or a fair woman's,
> They hover over the masthead awhile
> To wait their friends, but when their friends have come
> They'll fly upon that secret way of theirs,
> One—and one—a couple—five together.
> And now they all wheel suddenly and fly
> To the other side, and higher in the air,
> They've gone up thither, friend's run up by friend;
> They've gone to their beloved ones in the air,
> In the waste of the high air, that they may wander
> Among the windy meadows of the dawn.
> But why are they still waiting? Why are they
> Circling and circling over the masthead?
> Ah! now they all look down—they'll speak of me
> What the Ever-living put into their minds,
> And of that shadowless unearthly woman
> At the world's end. I hear the message now,
> But it's all mystery. There's one that cries,
> 'From love and hate'. Before the sentence ends
> Another breaks upon it with a cry,
> 'From love and death and out of sleep and waking'.
> And with the cry another cry is mixed,
> 'What can we do, being shadows?' All mystery,
> And I am drunken with a dizzy light.
> But why do they still hover overhead?
> Why are you circling there? Why do you linger?
> Why do you not run to your desire,
> Now that you have happy winged bodies?
> Being too busy in the air, and the high air,
> They cannot hear my voice. But why that circling?[1]

In *At the Hawk's Well*, the hawk is similarly used as an image, though less as an omen of what will happen than as a pure symbol

[1] *The Collected Plays*, pp. 153–4.

of certain mental and spiritual forces. When the hawk's cry is first
heard, Cuchulain discusses its meaning:

> It sounded like the sudden cry of a hawk,
> But there's no wing in sight. As I came hither
> A great grey hawk swept down out of the sky,
> And though I have good hawks, the best in the world
> I had fancied, I have not seen its like. It flew
> As though it would have torn me with its beak,
> Or blinded me, smiting with that great wing.
> I had to draw my sword to drive it off,
> And after that it flew from rock to rock.
> I pelted it with stones, a good half-hour,
> And just before I had turned the big rock there
> And seen this place, it seemed to vanish away.
> Could I but find a means to bring it down
> I'd hood it.[1]

The first passage is full of oratorical repetition, of rather relaxed
and meaningless description, and of expressions of mystery. By
contrast, the second passage moves at a much faster pace, wastes
no words, and uses description in a pointed, meaningful way (for
symbolism or irony). The technique of the first passage is largely
incantatory; and this technique relies on oratorical repetition,
vague description ('In the waste of the high air', 'happy winged
bodies', and so on), and constant assertions of mystery ('that secret
way of theirs', 'that shadowless unearthly woman At the world's
end', 'All mystery, And I am drunken with a dizzy light', and so on).
The technique of the second passage is largely symbolic and imagistic; and this technique relies on bare precision of detail ('no wing
in sight', 'I'd hood it', and so on), and the avoidance of direct assertions of meaning or mood. Even small details like the hawk's attempting to tear Cuchulain with its beak or attempting to blind him
probably have some symbolic significance. Both actions are connected in mythology and tradition with the revelation of knowledge
and with physical or spiritual impotence, that is, they have symbolic
meanings that would be relevant to the theme of the play.

Yeats's technique of using symbolism in the form of clear pictorial images probably owes something to Pound and his ideas of
imagism. Yeats had, of course, managed to avoid the unnecessary

[1] Ibid., p. 214.

word and concentrate on essentials in his non-dramatic verse a few years before he met Pound, but there are one or two idiosyncrasies in the application of this technique in *At the Hawk's Well* that he seems to have picked up from Pound. Pound was fond of using sensory details in a way that almost separated them from the object to which they applied. This 'disembodied' use of detail can be illustrated from a poem in *Lustra*, 'Liu Ch'e':

> The rustling of the silk is discontinued,
> Dust drifts over the court-yard,
> There is no sound of foot-fall, and the leaves
> Scurry into heaps and lie still . . . .[1]

It will be noticed that the details are introduced in such a way that there is sometimes no need for an article before the noun, and that this very usage itself reinforces the generalized, 'disembodied' effect. (Pound was to drop the article very frequently in the narrative parts of his Cantos, but there are much earlier examples of this habit, including 'The Seafarer'.) Yeats seems to have appropriated these habits in a few places in *At the Hawk's Well*. In the speech by Cuchulain that has already been quoted, he uses the expression 'But there's no wing in sight', where he might have referred to the whole bird instead of to only one detail. In a speech by the First Musician there is the statement 'I have heard water plash',[2] which seems to separate the sound from the object causing it. Again, in an early speech by Cuchulain there is the same breathless, article-less narrative as in Pound's 'The Seafarer':

> A rumour has led me,
> A story told over the wine towards dawn,
> I rose from table, found a boat, spread sail,
> And with a lucky wind under the sail
> Crossed waves that have seemed charmed, and found this shore.[3]

These are minor matters, but they have the importance of showing the extent of Pound's influence on Yeats in stylistic matters. *At the Hawk's Well* was written at a time when Yeats was probably far more inclined to listen to Pound than he was when writing the non-dramatic lyrics that have been discussed earlier in this chapter. Yet even so, there is little evidence of Pound's influence on the play.

---

[1] *Personae: Collected Shorter Poems*, p. 118.   [2] *Collected Plays*, p. 217.
[3] Ibid., p. 212.

Yeats was too full of his own theories to give much time to Pound's suggestions except where they affected detail.

There is one exception to this statement, one instance where Yeats followed Pound's advice in a major matter. This was in connexion with *The Player Queen*, which Yeats had been trying to write ever since 1908. Ellmann's version of what happened is as follows:

It was Pound who, hearing that Yeats had spent six or seven years trying to write *The Player Queen* as a tragedy, suggested that it might be made into a comedy, with such effect that Yeats completely transformed the play at once.[1]

This account is supported by Yeats's note to a 1922 edition of the play, and by a statement in *Wheels and Butterflies*.[2] Nobody has, I think, ever suggested that the change from a verse tragedy to a prose farce was a mistake, but in any case the main point is that without Pound's intervention the play would almost certainly not have been finished when it was.

Pound's advice regarding *The King of the Great Clock Tower* some years later was neither so helpful nor so welcome. Yeats was worried in 1933 and 1934 because it was a couple of years since he had written verse. He decided to force himself to write, and then to ask advice about the results. He visited Pound in Rapallo, but Pound confined his advice to a single word, 'Putrid'.[3]

Yeats's visit suggests that he did expect to get some help from Pound. This expectation was based not just on their experiences during the second decade of the century but also on Yeats's experiences with Pound in Rapallo during the few years previous to the visit. Pound had in fact persuaded Yeats to live for a time in Rapallo, and the visit of 1934 was largely undertaken to dispose of a flat in the Via Americhe and to bring back some furniture.[4] Yeats had spent some part of the winters of 1927/1928, 1928/1929, and 1929/1930 in Rapallo, and had made good use of Pound while he was there. During his first visit Pound helped him punctuate some

[1] Ellmann, *Yeats: The Man and the Masks*, p. 215.

[2] *Plays in Prose and Verse* (London: Macmillan, 1922), notes to *The Player Queen*; *Wheels and Butterflies* (London: Macmillan, 1934), introduction to *The Resurrection*.

[3] See Preface to *The King of the Great Clock Tower* (Dublin: The Cuala Press, 1934); reprinted in *The Variorum Edition of the Poems of W. B. Yeats*, p. 856.

[4] See Hone, op. cit., p. 437.

of the poems in *The Winding Stair and other Poems*.[1] While in Rapallo on this occasion Yeats made plans for the following winters, plans in which Pound had a part: in writing to Lady Gregory, Yeats mentioned that he wanted to keep Pound 'as a friendly neighbour, for I foresee that in the winter he must take [George] Russell's place of a Monday evening'.[2] Pound seems to have fitted in with Yeats's expectations, at least during the winter of 1928/1929. This was the only one of the three winters when Yeats was well enough to work. He wrote to Lady Gregory: 'I see Ezra daily. We disagree about everything, but if we have not met for 24 hours he calls full of gloomy and almost dumb oppression.'[3] Some weeks later another letter to Lady Gregory states that

I have written seven poems—16 or 18 lines each—since Feb 6 and never wrote with greater ease. The poems are two 'meditations' for *A Packet for Ezra Pound* which Lolly is printing and the first five of *Twelve Poems for Music*. The getting away from all distractions has enriched my imagination. I wish I had done it years ago.[4]

Yeats's statements about Pound at this time have a patronizing, and at times a calculating, tone. It is quite obvious that Yeats had no intention of taking his advice: indeed, by this time, with his theory of the Phases of the Moon as applied to human personality fully developed, Yeats could even have explained why it was impossible to take his advice, for Pound belonged to one of the primary Phases, 23, whereas Yeats belonged to the ideal antithetical Phase, 17.[5] In any case, careful study of the lyrics written during the winter of 1928/1929 fails to show any evidence of Pound's influence. The one poem from *The Winding Stair and Other Poems* that looks as if it might have been influenced by Pound, 'Spilt Milk', was in fact written on 8 November 1930, when Yeats was in London.[6]

It can be said with some confidence that Pound had almost no influence on Yeats during the winters spent in Rapallo. Yeats's

---

[1] See *The Letters of W. B. Yeats*, p. 738.   [2] Ibid., p. 739.

[3] Letter to Lady Gregory, 21 January 1929; quoted Hone, op. cit., p. 402.

[4] 9 March 1929; *The Letters of W. B. Yeats*, pp. 759–60.

[5] See W. B. Yeats, *A Vision*, revised reissue (New York: Macmillan, 1956), pp. 88–9, 140–5, 163–9; Ellmann, *Yeats: The Man and the Masks*, p. 240; H. W. Häusermann, 'W. B. Yeats's Criticism of Ezra Pound', *English Studies: A Journal of English Letters and Philology* (Amsterdam), XXIX (1948), p. 103.

[6] See Ellmann, *The Identity of Yeats*, p. 291.

attitude to him was even more patronizing than it had been during the winters spent in Sussex, and Yeats was by this time less susceptible to influence: he had become more confident of his own abilities as a result of his esoteric system, and he had consciously adopted the mask of the elderly, assured man of letters. If Pound did have any influence it would have been simply in encouraging him to write during the winter of 1928/1929. This, and the winter of 1915/1916 were the only times that Yeats wrote freely when in Pound's company. During the 1915/1916 winter Pound had actually had some influence on the material written, for he had introduced Yeats to Noh drama, but there was no influence of this kind during the winter of 1928/1929.

Yeats was unlike most of the other objects of Pound's influence in that he was an older and more successful writer than Pound himself. Although he allowed Pound to perform kindnesses for him, the relationship between them seems always to have been that Yeats looked on the kindnesses as his right, and Pound looked on them as his duty. Pound was always strangely subservient to Yeats, and this attitude probably precluded his having much influence.

6. POUND AND ELIOT

On 22 September 1914, T. S. Eliot presented himself at 5 Holland Place Chambers to meet Pound for the first time. The meeting had been suggested by Conrad Aiken, who had been trying unsuccessfully to get Eliot's poems printed and who knew that Pound had connexions with publishers. After the visit, Pound wrote to Harriet Monroe, saying that he thought Eliot had 'some sense'.[1] Some time in the next week Pound read 'The Love Song of J. Alfred Prufrock', and was more than confirmed in his first impression. He wrote to Harriet Monroe:

> I was jolly well right about Eliot. He has sent in the best poem I have yet had or seen from an American. *PRAY GOD IT BE NOT A SINGLE AND UNIQUE SUCCESS*. He has taken it back to get it ready for the press and you shall have it in a few days.
>
> He is the only American I know of who has made what I can call adequate preparation for writing. He has actually trained himself *and* modernized himself *on his own*. The rest of the *promising young* have done one or the other but never both (most of the swine have done neither). It is such a comfort to meet a man and not have to tell him to wash his face, wipe his feet, and remember the date (1914) on the calendar.[2]

Three days later he sent 'Portrait of a Lady' to H. L. Mencken with a commendation.[3] But neither Harriet Monroe nor Mencken shared his enthusiasm. Miss Monroe, as Pound pointed out to her later, at first 'loathed and detested Eliot',[4] and she raised many objections to printing 'Prufrock', at least in the form in which it was submitted.[5] Mencken did not print 'Portrait of a Lady' in *The Smart Set*, and it was almost a year before it gained publication, in Alfred Kreymborg's *Others*.[6]

There is little doubt that Pound was the first person who both recognized Eliot's talent and was able to do something about

---

[1] Harriet Monroe, *A Poet's Life*, p. 394.   [2] *The Letters of Ezra Pound*, p. 80.
[3] 3 October 1914; *Letters*, p. 81.   [4] Letter, 24 April 1917; *Letters*, p. 165.
[5] See *Letters*, pp. 85, 92–3, 101, 107 n.
[6] *Others*, I, 3 (September 1915), pp. 35–40.

promoting his reputation. He did this in the face of opposition from reputable critics, and it was only his remarkable persistence that secured publication for Eliot at all. But it is important to realize that Pound acclaimed Eliot because of the poems he had written before their meeting, poems written when Eliot knew little of Pound's work. Theories to the contrary have been explicitly denied by Pound himself.[1] What Pound did for Eliot was to secure publication for his poetry, and it is noteworthy that Eliot has acknowledged this as his greatest debt to Pound. In an article first published in 1946 he gives credit to Pound for being able to get 'Prufrock' published after Aiken had tried to without success, and for getting his first volume, *Prufrock and Other Observations*, published in 1917.[2]

As Pound admitted, Eliot had already, by the time of their meeting, 'trained himself *and* modernized himself *on his own*'. This remains true, despite the fact that Eliot had read Pound's early poems in 1910. According to Eliot,

I was introduced to *Personae* and *Exultations* in 1910, while still an undergraduate at Harvard. The poems did not then excite me, any more than did the poetry of Yeats: I was too much engrossed in working out the implications of Laforgue. I considered them, however, the only interesting poems by a contemporary that I had found.[3]

The volume that Eliot read was, presumably, Pound's first American edition, *Provença: Poems selected from Personae, Exultations, and Canzoniere of Ezra Pound* (Boston: Small, Maynard, 1910). Now even if the poems in this volume had 'excited' Eliot, he would not have learnt much from them about modernity in poetry; none of them were imagistic, most were highly derivative. Eliot's own verse technique at the time was, in fact, a good deal more modern than Pound's. Even when they met, some four years later—four years in which Eliot wrote very little and Pound continued his intensive

---

[1] See his Letter to the Editor, *The Times Literary Supplement*, 26 July 1957, p. 457.

[2] See 'Ezra Pound', *Poetry*, LXVIII (1946), p. 327; reprinted in *Ezra Pound: A Collection of Essays*, pp. 25–6. Eliot states in this essay that he met Pound in 1915, an error that he repeated in a letter to *TLS*, 9 August 1957, p. 483, and corrected in another letter, *TLS*, 23 August 1957, p. 507. It would seem as if Eliot, knowing that 'Prufrock' was not published in *Poetry* until June 1915, could not, in retrospect, believe that it was as far back as September 1914 that Pound had assured him that the magazine would accept his recommendation to publish it as soon as possible. Presumably Pound did not spoil the impression of great influence that he presented to Eliot by letting him know of the difficulty he had persuading Harriet Monroe to print the poem.

[3] 'On a Recent Piece of Criticism', *Purpose*, X, 2 (June 1938), pp. 91–2.

apprenticeship—Eliot's technique was in some ways more modern than Pound's. In his own terms, Pound at the time was an imagist and a vorticist, but not yet a practiser of ideogrammic techniques. Eliot, in the same terms, was all three.

The best exemplar of an imagist poem is probably Pound's 'In a Station of the Metro', which he discusses as a 'one image poem' in his article 'Vorticism'.[1] It reads:

> The apparition of these faces in the crowd:
> Petals, on a wet, black bough.

The method of such a poem is described by Pound as 'a form of super-position, that is to say it is one idea set on top of another'. Other examples of the form that are quoted by Pound include the two *haiku*:

> The fallen blossom flies back to its branch:
> A butterfly;

and

> The footsteps of the cat upon the snow:
> (are like) plum-blossoms.

This method of setting down two equally detailed images in a metaphorical linkage is used occasionally in Eliot's verse. One example occurs right at the beginning of 'Prufrock', and this may have influenced Pound's favourable response to the poem; it is in the frequently quoted lines:

> When the evening is spread out against the sky
> Like a patient etherised upon a table.[2]

Another example occurs in 'Portrait of a Lady':

> And four wax candles in the darkened room,
> Four rings of light upon the ceiling overhead,
> An atmosphere of Juliet's tomb.

Longer imagist poems apply the same technique two or three times in their simultaneous description of a scene and a mood. Hulme's 'Autumn', the first of the poems Pound printed as 'The Complete Poetical Works of T. E. Hulme', may be taken as typical:

---

[1] *The Fortnightly Review*, XCVI (1914), pp. 461–71.

[2] *Collected Poems: 1909–1935* (London: Faber & Faber, 1936), p. 11. All quotations from Eliot's verse follow the text of this volume, unless otherwise stated.

A touch of cold in the Autumn night—
I walked abroad,
And saw the ruddy moon lean over a hedge
Like a red-faced farmer.
I did not stop to speak, but nodded,
And round about were the wistful stars
With white faces like town children.

Eliot's 'Preludes' obviously use the same technique, but there are examples in other early poems, such as the description of the attitude of both the women who 'come and go Talking of Michelangelo' and of Prufrock by means of the description of the fog:

The yellow fog that rubs its back upon the window-panes,
The yellow smoke that rubs its muzzle on the window-panes
Licked its tongue into the corners of the evening,
Lingered upon the pools that stand in drains,
Let fall upon its back the soot that falls from chimneys,
Slipped by the terrace, made a sudden leap,
And seeing that it was a soft October night,
Curled once about the house, and fell asleep.

Eliot, unlike Hulme, avoids the crudity of separate individual similes, but the sharpness of the description and its two-fold orientation are the same. The attention is, furthermore, focused on the image, so that Pound's dictum is followed: 'The point of Imagisme is that it does not use images *as ornaments*. The image is itself the speech. The image is the word beyond formulated language.'[1]

The clarity, precision, and concreteness that Pound and his fellow-Imagists strove after caused them frequently to describe sense-impressions or details with little reference to the object or person of which they were a part. In discussing Yeats I mentioned the 'disembodied' quality of the images to be found in Pound's 'Liu Ch'e', or 'The Encounter'. Eliot's early poetry, quite independently, has the same quality. In 'Prufrock' he says

And I have known the arms already, known them all—
Arms that are braceleted and white and bare
[But in the lamplight, downed with light brown hair!]
Is it perfume from a dress
That makes me so digress?
Arms that lie along a table, or wrap about a shawl.

His 'Preludes' contain many sense-impressions so 'disembodied'

[1] 'Vorticism', loc. cit., p. 466.

that they can be mentioned in the plural: 'smell of steaks'; 'faint stale smells of beer'; 'the sawdust-trampled street With all its muddy feet'; 'all the hands That are raising dingy shades'; 'the yellow soles of feet'; and 'short square fingers stuffing pipes'.

The techniques that have been mentioned so far do not make up the whole of imagist and vorticist practices, but they do form the most distinctive and individual of those practices. The techniques that have not been mentioned are the more elementary and less individual ones that could be assimilated during the apprenticeship of any poet, imagist or not. We may assume, with Pound, that Eliot had mastered these matters, that he had in Pound's terms, 'trained himself . . . *on his own*'. It is not unreasonable, then, to conclude that Pound could offer Eliot nothing through his advocacy of imagism or vorticism. Eliot had assimilated the best of the practices suggested by these doctrines, and was, in fact, in advance of Pound in 'modernity'. He had even put into practice the sort of technique that Pound was later, under the influence of Fenollosa, to call the 'ideogrammic' method. The exposition of this method offered by Pound in *A B C of Reading* presents it as a more complex form of Imagism. The 'Image' was an attempt to present 'an intellectual and emotional complex in an instant of time' through a precise and vivid picture. The ideogram was an attempt to present 'a general idea' (presumably something of wider significance than 'an intellectual and emotional complex') through a series of pictures, each of them having the idea that is being presented. Poems written according to imagist doctrine present two images, one superimposed on the other: in short poems the two images are presented very simply, sometimes in just a single detail; in longer ones the two images may be taken up alternately in order to add further details. In a poem written according to the 'ideogrammic' method one would expect more than two images; one would expect as many images as were necessary to single out unmistakably the idea that the poet wanted to present as being common to them all.

Such a procedure of superimposition inevitably calls to mind 'montage', a method which has been much developed this century in theory and in practice by Russian film-makers.[1] Or again, it calls

[1] See, for instance, Sergei M. Eisenstein, *The Film Sense*, tr. Jay Leyda (New York: Harcourt, Brace, 1942).

to mind Conrad Aiken's theory of placing 'poetic tones' in juxta-
position in order to produce a complex result, because '*a*, it is clear,
if it is preceded by *c* and followed by *e*, is not quite the same as *a*
standing alone . . . a peculiar light has been cast across it, which
throws certain parts of it into stronger relief than others'.[1] The
Russian theory of 'montage', and Aiken's theory of 'poetic tones'
were both being worked out at the same time as Pound's theory of
the ideogram, that is, during the first and second decades of this
century.

It may be objected that neither of these theories is quite the same
as the theory of the ideogram. This is true, of course, but I would
suggest that the results such theories would produce in poetry are
indistinguishable from the results produced by the theory of the
ideogram. The point is that, just as one does not have to be an Imagist in theory to produce poems that can rightly be claimed as imagistic, so one does not have to know or to believe in Pound's theory
of the ideogram to produce poems that can rightly be claimed as
'ideogrammic'. In short, the techniques Pound was advocating were
not as original as the theories he used to explain and justify them;
and the techniques could quite easily be employed by those holding
alternative theories or no theories at all.

In practice, the film-makers' theory of 'montage', Aiken's theory
of 'poetic tones', and Pound's theory of the ideogram produce
results similar to those of Eliot's early poems, which were written
without the help of any of these theories, though admittedly under
the influence of Laforgue's poetry. Pound's use of the ideogram
can be seen very clearly in *Hugh Selwyn Mauberley*: instead of
arguing about the position of the poet in contemporary society,
Pound presents a number of short scenes of that society, and of its
sources of inspiration in the past; all of these scenes are designed to
display materialism and the use of substitutes for culture, and the
effects these are likely to have on the poet: this is the idea that is
being conveyed ideogrammically, that is, by a number of scenes
having one feature in common. The same technique is applied not
just at the level of the eighteen separate parts of *Mauberley* but also
at various levels within each of the parts. When Pound says, for

[1] See Aiken's article, 'Counterpoint and Implication', in his *Collected Poems* (New
York: Oxford University Press, 1953), pp. 873–7.

instance, that 'His true Penelope was Flaubert' he is superimposing the biography of his poetic *persona* and of Flaubert on the story of Odysseus in order to make a point that is common to all of them: it is an exemplification of the 'ideogrammic' method. But Eliot had been using this method in the poems written before he met Pound. Eliot was, in fact, throughout his career, always more abrupt than Pound in superimposing one scene on another. In his early attempts at using the ideogrammic method, such as the one that has just been referred to, Pound often indicated where his scenes were analogous: 'E.P.', for instance, corresponds to Odysseus; Flaubert to Penelope. Eliot, however, even in his early poems, had no qualms about setting two scenes down side by side without much overt indication of where they corresponded. 'Prufrock' begins with the cinematic technique of showing in alternation Prufrock on his way to the tea-party; the women already there, 'Talking of Michelangelo'; the fog; and people and institutions along the way that Prufrock is taking. These are all in some way related to the 'overwhelming question', and Prufrock's attitude to it. Even these scenes are not the only ones superimposed to make the ideogram: when Eliot represents Prufrock considering whether his life might be symbolized by the vague, unmeditative existence of 'lonely men in shirt-sleeves', he goes on to superimpose another, quite disparate, image reinforcing this symbol: he says:

> I should have been a pair of ragged claws
> Scuttling across the floors of silent seas.

Or again, in another verse-paragraph, he superimposes the tea-party; a reference to a love-poem by Marvell; references to the raising of Lazarus and to the parable of Dives and Lazarus; and a hypothetic bedroom scene:

> And would it have been worth it, after all,
> After the cups, the marmalade, the tea,
> Among the porcelain, among some talk of you and me,
> Would it have been worth while,
> To have bitten off the matter with a smile,
> To have squeezed the universe into a ball
> To roll it toward some overwhelming question,
> To say: 'I am Lazarus, come from the dead,
> Come back to tell you all, I shall tell you all'—

If one, settling a pillow by her head,
   Should say: 'That is not what I meant at all.
   That is not it, at all.'[1]

With these techniques of imagism and the ideogrammic method at his disposal before their meeting, Eliot could learn little from Pound. But Pound's enthusiastic reception of his poetry seems to have turned him back to writing. Eliot says that 'I had kept my early poems . . . in my desk from 1911 to 1915'; it appears, then, that he wrote virtually no poetry in the years 1912, 1913, and 1914.[2] In 1915, however, that is, after coming to know Pound and being assured that his work would be published, Eliot wrote 'Morning at the Window', 'The *Boston Evening Transcript*', 'Aunt Helen', 'Cousin Nancy', and 'Mr. Apollinax', all of which were published in *Poetry*.

The satire of these poems is rather less solemn and more jocular than the satire of Eliot's early poems. The difference can be seen in the descriptions of human activities. In the early poems, the descriptions are realistic and serious, and the irony arises from the whole portrait rather than from the details. But in the poems written after Eliot met Pound, the details themselves carry the irony, and are wryly exaggerated rather than seriously exact. 'Mr. Apollinax' describes its subject thus:

[1] The tea-party of the first few lines, and the hypothetical bedroom scene of the last few lines are quite obvious. On the connexion between this poem, the Biblical story of the raising of Lazarus, and Dostoevsky's *Crime and Punishment*, see John C. Pope, 'Prufrock and Raskolnikov Again: A Letter from Eliot', *American Literature*, XVIII (January 1947), pp. 319–21. The reference to the parable of Dives and Lazarus is suggested by the appropriateness of the lines spoken by Lazarus in the poem to the Biblical account of Dives' speech: 'I pray thee therefore father, that thou wouldest send [Lazarus] to my father's house . . . if one went unto them from the dead, they will repent.' (S. Luke, xv. 27, 30.) The reference to Marvell's poem, 'To His Coy Mistress', comes in with the lines

   To have squeezed the universe into a ball
   To roll it toward some overwhelming question,

which are obviously related to Marvell's lines

   Let us roll all our Strength, and all
   Our sweetness, up into one Ball:
   And tear our Pleasures with rough strife,
   Thorough the Iron gates of Life.

[2] In a letter to the editor of *The Times Literary Supplement*, 8 July 1960, p. 433, Eliot says that he thinks he made some additions to 'Prufrock' in 1912, but is 'grateful to Mr. Aiken for having perceived at once that the additions were of inferior quality' and for suppressing them. Aiken, however, denies any knowledge of this suppression: see *TLS*, 3 June 1960, p. 353.

I

When Mr. Apollinax visited the United States
His laughter tinkled among the teacups.
I thought of Fragilion, that shy figure among the birch-trees,
And of Priapus in the shrubbery
Gaping at the lady in the swing.
In the palace of Mrs. Phlaccus, at Professor Channing-Cheetah's
He laughed like an irresponsible foetus.
His laughter was submarine and profound
Like the old man of the sea's . . . .

This more direct, more pointedly verbal, and perhaps less delicate
form of irony is the prevailing tone of Pound's verses of the same
time and a little earlier—it is to be seen, for instance, in 'The Tem-
peraments'. The same tone occurs in Eliot's verses so promptly
after his meeting with Pound, that the natural assumption is that
Eliot was influenced by Pound.[1]

But beyond this, there is little trace of influence. Borrowings or
adaptations, which would provide good evidence of influence if they
existed, were specifically discouraged by Pound. Eliot was prevailed
on by Pound to alter a single word in 'Morning at the Window' because it was the same as one in Pound's 'Les Millwin'; Marianne
Moore was prevailed on to avoid the word 'pneumatic' in one of her
poems because Eliot had just previously used it in 'Whispers of Immortality'.[2] Eliot seems to have accepted Pound's point of view not
just in this specific case but also in general. In a review of Pound's
Collected Poems that he wrote for *The Dial* in 1928, he said: 'I have,
in recent years, cursed Mr Pound often enough; for I am never
sure that I can call my verse my own; just when I am most pleased
with myself, I find that I have only caught up some echo from a
verse of Pound's.'[3] It is not surprising, then, that one looks in vain
for close verbal parallels between the work of the two poets. Eliot
was obviously aware of the danger of borrowing from Pound, and
was constantly trying to avoid it.

Pound often made a distinction between poets whom one could
imitate and poets from whom one could learn. In a letter to Harriet
Monroe written in 1913 he classed Verlaine and Baudelaire in the

---

[1] A similar point to the one made in this paragraph is made by Grover Smith in
T. S. Eliot's Poetry and Plays: A Study in Sources and Meaning (Chicago: The University of Chicago Press, 1956), pp. 31–2.

[2] See letter to Marianne Moore, 16 December 1918; *Letters*, p. 203.

[3] 'Isolated Superiority', *The Dial*, LXXXIV, 1 (January 1928), p. 5.

first category, and Gautier and Gourmont in the second.[1] Three years later, in recommending the study of Gautier to Iris Barry, he wrote:

Théophile Gautier is, I suppose, the next man who can write. Perfectly plain statements like his 'Carmen est maigre' should teach one a number of things. His early poems are many of them no further advanced than the Nineties. Or to put it more fairly the English Nineties got about as far as Gautier had got in 1830, and before he wrote 'L'Hippopotame.'[2]

At about the same time as this letter was written, Pound was talking to Eliot about Gautier. They agreed that a study of *Emaux et camées*, Gautier's maturest poetry, would be a useful antidote to the insidious influence of decadent imagism:

That is to say, at a particular date, in a particular room, two authors, neither engaged in picking the other's pocket, decided that the dilutation of *vers libre*, Amygism, Lee Masterism, general floppiness had gone too far and that some counter-current must be set going. Parallel situation centuries ago in China. Remedy prescribed 'Emaux et Camées' (or the Bay State Hymn Book). Rhyme and regular strophes.
Results: Poems in Mr. Eliot's *second* volume, not contained in his first 'Prufrock' (Egoist, 1917), also 'H. S. Mauberley'.[3]

This statement, which purports to be one of agreement between two equals, really seems like a statement of Pound's instruction of Eliot. Pound's description of the parlous condition of verse which provided the reason for the movement is very much like his description of the condition which prompted Imagism, with the names of one or two new *bêtes noires* thrown in. Now the remedy prescribed in Imagism seemed to Pound to be summed up in the aphorism 'Poetry must be as well written as prose', which he took over from Ford Madox Hueffer.[4] The aphorism covers at least the second and third points of the original Imagist Manifesto, the injunctions to avoid superfluity and a metronomic rhythm. But this kind of remedy has its danger, specifically named by Pound as *vers libre* and 'Lee Masterism'. It would seem as if Pound, with Eliot's agreement, now proposed what was virtually the opposite kind of remedy, 'Rhyme and regular strophes', that is, the very features of verse that

[1] See *Letters*, p. 60.   [2] 27 July 1916; ibid., p. 139.
[3] Ezra Pound, 'Harold Monro', *The Criterion*, XI, No. 45 (July 1932), p. 590.
[4] See Ford Madox Ford, *Thus to Revisit: Some Reminiscences* (London: Chapman & Hall, 1921), p. 201; Pound, *Letters*, p. 91.

distinguish it from prose. For Pound, this would have been nothing
new, for his interest in the troubadours had led him to practise these
features. But for Eliot, whose primary influences until this time had
been Laforgue and Jacobean drama, it was a new, and perhaps an
unwise, departure. In the Introduction that he wrote for Pound's
Selected Poems in 1928, Eliot recognized the influences on Pound
as having been of two kinds: those of Browning and the poets of the
nineties, which taught him the importance of *'verse as speech'*; and
those of his 'more antiquarian studies', which taught him the importance of *'verse as song'*.[1] In Eliot's terms, then, Pound was at this
time insisting that they both ought to concentrate on 'verse as song'.

Pound's imitation of Gautier's metre was, in fact, rather free.
He preserved the quatrain and its rhyme scheme, but ignored
Gautier's *'vers de huit pieds'*, preferring to use a line of varying
length and to place the stresses in it with great freedom. Eliot, on
the other hand, followed Gautier with less freedom. The poems he
wrote in Gautier-like quatrains, 'Burbank with a Baedeker',
'Sweeney Erect', 'A Cooking Egg', 'The Hippotamus', 'Whispers
of Immortality', 'Mr. Eliot's Sunday Morning Service', and
'Sweeney Among the Nightingales', are all written with a basic
eight-syllabled line, from which a variation of even one syllable is
rare. It is true that, with the exception of 'The Hippopotamus',
they omit Gautier's rhyme at the end of the first and third lines, but
Pound rarely preserved the double rhyme either. Apart from
rhythm, there are a few other connexions between Eliot's poems and
Gautier's: 'The Hippopotamus' is obviously related to Gautier's
'L'Hippopotame' (from *Póésies diverses*, not *Emaux et camées*); and
the lines about Grishkin in 'Whispers of Immortality',

> Grishkin is nice: her Russian eye
> Is underlined for emphasis,

are obviously related to the opening lines of 'Carmen':

> *Carmen est maigre,—un trait de bistre*
> *Cerne son œil de gitana.*[2]

---

[1] T. S. Eliot, Introduction to *Selected Poems* by Ezra Pound (London: Faber & Gwyer,
1928), p. ix.

[2] See Grover Smith, op. cit., p. 40, for the date, *'ca* 1918', of 'Whispers of Immortality'. Grover Smith also draws attention to the resemblance between Gautier's lines
and Eliot's.

It is particularly interesting that these two resemblances to Gautier are resemblances to the two poems that Pound had mentioned to Iris Barry in 1916. They appear to have been great favourites of Pound's, for in addition to recommending them to his friends he also used the opening lines of one of them, 'Carmen', in his own poem, 'To a Friend Writing on Cabaret Dancers'.

The important difference between Pound's and Eliot's use of Gautier is in the length of line. Eliot adopted a much more rigid form, which was simply not suited to what he had to say. His ideo-grammic technique, his satire and irony, and the jocularity that he had learnt from Pound had previously been exercised in free forms. But he now wanted to use these methods in 'rhyme and regular strophes', a task which was virtually impossible. One result was a resort to line-filling and flabby rhyming, as in the following stanzas:

> Observing that hysteria
>   Might easily be misunderstood;
> Mrs. Turner intimates
>   It does the house no sort of good.
>   ('Sweeney Erect')

> I shall not want Honour in Heaven
>   For I shall meet Sir Philip Sidney
> And have talk with Coriolanus
>   And other heroes of that kidney.
>   ('A Cooking Egg')

> Under the penitential gates
> Sustained by staring Seraphim
> Where the souls of the devout
> Burn invisible and dim.
>   ('Mr. Eliot's Sunday Morning Service')

> The silent man in mocha brown
> Sprawls at the window-sill and gapes;
> The waiter brings in oranges
> Bananas figs and hothouse grapes.
>   ('Sweeney Among the Nightingales')

In all of these examples, there is a debility in the last line. Eliot's reduction of the rhymes within the stanza places great emphasis on the remaining two rhyming lines, the second and the fourth, so that, because of this and because of the short lines, the stanza approximates to a closed couplet. Where this innate form is exploited for the purpose of bathos, the result is quite acceptable, as in the opening stanza of 'Burbank with a Baedeker', in which the notion of 'Descending' in the first two lines degenerates into the 'fell' at the end of the last two:

> Burbank crossed a little bridge
> Descending at a small hotel;
> Princess Volupine arrived,
> They were together, and he fell.

But such an effect of bathos is only one of the many effects that Eliot is striving after. His ideogrammic technique probably suffers most from the rigid form: it degenerates into the obscurity of allusion that has often been complained of in these poems. Yet the obscurity caused by compression is often combined with line-filling: what Eliot wants to say is inevitably too long to be expressed in the form, but when it is compressed it is too short. Consider, for instance, the second stanza of 'Burbank with a Baedeker':

> Defunctive music under sea
> Passed seaward with the passing bell
> Slowly: the God Hercules
> Had left him, that had loved him well.

'Defunctive music' is a quotation from 'The Phoenix and Turtle'. On one level it refers to the death of love between Burbank and Princess Volupine, a death which is referred to rather repetitively in 'Passed' and 'passing bell'. This death of love is apparently due to a sexual failure by Burbank: the virile god, Hercules, deserts him, leaving him in what the Elizabethans might have called a 'dying' condition. On another level, 'Defunctive music' suggests that the love of Burbank and Volupine fails because it cannot triumph over their lack of similarity as the love of the phoenix and the turtle-dove did: their love is a modern debasement of the love celebrated by Shakespeare. On a third level, the reference to Shakespeare in 'Defunctive music', and in 'the God Hercules Had left him, that had loved him well' suggests the interests of the relatively cultured Burbank, who is capable of 'meditating on Time's ruins, and the seven laws'. The reference to Hercules is a curiously inverted form of two lines in *Antony and Cleopatra*:

> 'Tis the god Hercules, whom Antony lov'd,
> Now leaves him.[1]

For Eliot to suggest that the God Hercules had 'loved [Burbank] well' is to invert Shakespeare's idea in a peculiarly obscure (and perhaps meaningless) way. The reference to Antony's love of Hercules occurs just before the battle, so that any sexual connotation of love is suppressed; the reference to Hercules' love of Burbank occurs in a passage about physical love, so that the sexual connotation (which seems to be quite unwanted) is emphasized. These difficulties spring, I suggest, partly from the condensation dictated by the quatrain form, and partly from the need to fill out the form. Eliot has to rely on a bare quotation of 'Defunctive music' to bring in the relevance of 'The Phoenix and Turtle', but having reduced this reference to a minimum he is forced to repeat the idea of 'Defunctive' in 'Passed' and 'passing bell'. Again, having introduced 'the God Hercules', the form seems to have forced him to invert the Shakespearian reference in a meaningless way, and to make use of the unnecessary word 'well' (which is not in Shakespeare) to produce a rhyme: in this case, what ought to have been the most significant word in the whole stanza has been used simply to satisfy the form.

Pound, who was also using Gautier as a basis, and being equally allusive, had two manifest advantages. First, he was prepared to shorten or lengthen the line to suit what he had to say; a single stanza from 'Yeux Glauques' will illustrate this:

> The thin, clear gaze, the same
> Still darts out faun-like from the half-ruin'd face,
> Questing and passive. . . .
> 'Ah, poor Jenny's case' . . .

Secondly, he apparently realized that in such an essentially condensed form it was better to avoid allusions through quotation and to concentrate on allusions through what might be termed proper-noun metaphor, a method which could, if necessary, reduce the reference to a single word. By this means, Eliot's problems of a condensation in reference, and expansion through line-fillers were avoided. Using this technique, then, Pound was able to write lines like 'His true Penelope was Flaubert', 'Christ follows Dionysus',

---

[1] IV. iii., ll. 16–17.

'Caliban casts out Ariel', 'The English Rubaiyat was stillborn', 'Headlam for uplift; Image impartially imbued', and so on.[1]

Pound, in other words, adapted the form to his material, and produced results that justify his study of Gautier. He explored the possibilities of a neglected form, and showed how it could be used for the purposes of a modern poet. Eliot, on the other hand, in attempting to use the same form, failed in two ways: he failed to modify the form in order to make it suitable for the ideogrammic method that he wanted to use in miniature; and he failed to shape the allusions that he wanted to use to the form in which they were to be expressed. For him, the imitative study of Gautier produced no very valuable results, though it may have been a useful apprenticeship. Pound was probably in a position to have pointed out where Eliot was making his mistakes. For some reason, he did not do so. His influence on Eliot was, therefore, rather unfortunate.

But neither Pound nor Eliot seems to have thought so. After Eliot had finished the first draft of *The Waste Land* while convalescing in Lausanne,[2] his first thought was to call in on Pound and leave the draft with him for his comments.[3] It 'left his hands, reduced to about half its size, in the form in which it appears in print'.[4] Pound's most valuable advice was that 'The *POEM* ends with the "Shantih, shantih, shantih" ', an opinion which he stressed by saying: 'The thing now runs from "April . . ." to "shantih" without a break. That is 19 pages, and let us say the longest poem in the English langwidge. Don't try to bust all records by prolonging it three pages further.'[5] But apart from advising Eliot what to omit and what to leave in, Pound queried some details, especially in 'A Game of Chess' and 'The Fire Sermon'. In almost every case, Eliot offered an alternative reading, which Pound accepted.[6] Eliot has summed up the help he received in this way: 'Pound . . . tried first to understand what one was attempting to do, and then tried to help one do it in one's own way.'[7]

A few months after helping Eliot with the poem, Pound wrote to Dr. Schelling: 'Eliot's *Waste Land* is I think the justification of the

---

[1] These lines are all from *Hugh Selwyn Mauberley*: see *Personae*, pp. 197–202.
[2] See *Time*, LV, 10 (6 March 1950), p. 16 (Pacific Overseas ed.).
[3] See Eliot, 'London Letter', *The Dial*, LXXII (May 1922), p. 510.
[4] Eliot, 'Ezra Pound' (1946); reprinted in *Ezra Pound: A Collection of Essays*, p. 28.
[5] *Letters*, p. 234.   [6] See ibid., pp. 236–7.   [7] 'Ezra Pound', loc. cit., p. 33.

"movement," of our modern experiment, since 1900.'[1] This is, I suppose, incontestable, yet it should be remembered that *The Waste Land* for the most part puts into operation, on a larger scale and with greater mastery, the techniques that Eliot possessed before he met Pound. There is, however, a greater daring in the representation of colloquial speech; and a new departure for Eliot in the use of foreign quotations within the poem instead of merely in the epigraph. The representation of colloquial speech was more daring and more extensive than anything Pound had attempted by this time, but the use of foreign quotations had probably been picked up from Pound, who had, for instance, used Greek and Provençal in *Hugh Selwyn Mauberley*.

Eliot was certainly grateful for Pound's help in tidying-up the poem. One of his letters making inquiries about emendations is superscribed 'Cher maître',[2] and his dedication of the poem is, of course, 'For Ezra Pound: *il miglior fabbro*'.

Eliot may also have been grateful to Pound for the publication of *The Waste Land*, which seems to have been arranged, at least in part, by him. Pound had only recently changed his New York publisher. *Lustra* (1917) and *Pavannes and Divisions* (1918) had been published by Alfred A. Knopf, whom Pound had probably been instrumental in persuading to publish Eliot's *Ezra Pound: His Metric and Poetry* (1917), *Poems* (1920), and *The Sacred Wood* (1921). Before *The Sacred Wood* appeared in February 1921, however, Pound had already had a volume published by his new publisher, Boni and Liveright; it was *Instigations* (1920). This volume was followed by another from the same house, *Poems 1918–21*, published in 1921. Eliot's first American publication after *The Sacred Wood* was *The Waste Land*, and it also was published by Boni and Liveright. The suggestion is, then, that Pound persuaded Eliot to change his publisher. But there is also evidence for the further suggestion that Pound handled some of the negotiations with Boni and Liveright. He was asked for a comment on the publication when the Gotham Book Mart's catalogue *We Moderns* was being prepared, and he wrote:

The bearing of this poem was not over-estimated, nevertheless the immediate reception of it even by second rate reviewers was due to the purely

[1] *Letters*, p. 248.   [2] Ibid., p. 236.

fortuitous publication of the notes, and not to the text itself. Liveright wanted a longer volume and the notes were the only available unpublished matter.[1]

This seems to suggest that Pound had negotiated the publication, and this suggestion is the most obvious interpretation of the 'squib' that Pound included in a letter to Eliot. The important lines of these verses, which Eliot thought of printing as a preface to *The Waste Land*, run thus:

> These are the poems of Eliot
> By the Uranian Muse begot;
> A Man their Mother was,
> A Muse their Sire.
>
> How did the printed Infancies result
> From Nuptials thus doubly difficult?
>
> If you must needs enquire
> Know diligent Reader
> That on each Occasion
> Ezra performed the caesarean Operation.[2]

This seems to mean that Pound had arranged for the publication of each of Eliot's volumes of poetry. There is no doubt that he had 'performed the caesarean Operation' for *Prufrock and Other Observations*; it seems likely that he had done the same thing for Eliot's second collection, and was in the process of doing it again for *The Waste Land*.

Eliot's other debts to Pound in the field of poetry may be dealt with fairly briefly. Verbal echoes, such as the reminiscence of the opening of Pound's 'The Return' in 'Little Gidding' III and V, are very few in number, because Eliot was constantly seeking to avoid them. There are in his work, however, a few imitations of Pound's method, tone, and subject. These imitations are of a minor nature, and are not nearly so numerous as some critics would lead one to believe.

The chief imitation of method occurs, I think, in Eliot's attempt in some of the speeches of *Murder in the Cathedral* to emulate

---

[1] Gotham Book Mart, *We Moderns* (New York, 1940), p. 24; quoted in Donald Gallup, *T. S. Eliot: A Bibliography* (London: Faber & Faber, 1952), p. 7.

[2] Letter to T. S. Eliot, 24 December 1921; *Letters*, p. 234.

Pound's revival of Anglo-Saxon metres.[1] In 'The Seafarer' Pound
used a basically four-stress line, frequently divided by a caesura,
with two or three alliterating sounds in many lines. While keeping
fairly close to the sense of the Anglo-Saxon, Pound was not nearly
so strict in his division into half-lines or in his pattern of alliteration
as the Anglo-Saxon poets were, but it is evident that these matters,
together with the much more strictly observed four stresses in the
line, form a basis for his verse. In *Murder in the Cathedral*, Eliot
makes considerable use of a four-stress line, and there are times
when its breaking into half-lines and its pattern of alliteration suggest an imitation of Pound. Occasional examples of single lines fall-
ing into this metre—lines such as 'Seven years and the summer is
over', or 'Does the watchman walk by the wall?'[2]—could be dis-
counted as being fortuitous. But where there are passages in which
several lines fairly close together fall into the metre, the probability
of influence is very strong. When, furthermore these passages are all
spoken by one group of characters in the play, the Tempters, the
adoption of the metre appears almost certainly deliberate. The
second speech of the First Tempter provides the first example:

> Spring has come in winter. Snow in the branches
> Shall float as sweet as blossoms. Ice along the ditches
> Mirror the sunlight. Love in the orchard
> Send the sap shooting. Mirth matches melancholy.[3]

It is true that most of the half-lines have three stresses, but then so
do some of Pound's, and so, of course, do many Anglo-Saxon ones.
The second speech of the Second Tempter also contains the Poundian metre:

> Power obtained grows to glory,
> Life lasting, a permanent possession.
> A templed tomb, monument of marble.
> Rule over men reckon no madness.[4]

This Tempter's speeches are particularly rich in the metre, perhaps
because they purport to represent an attitude of patriotism shared
by all the English people except the barons, an attitude for which

---

[1] This point is mentioned by Louis MacNeice, in *Modern Poetry: A Personal Essay*
(London: Oxford University Press, 1938), p. 129.

[2] *Murder in the Cathedral*, 3rd ed. (London: Faber & Faber, 1937), pp. 12, 42.

[3] Ibid., p. 24.   [4] Ibid., p. 27.

the traditional metre, untouched by Norman influence, might be considered appropriate. Two further examples may be quoted:

> Shall he who held the solid substance
> Wander waking with deceitful shadows?
> Power is present. Holiness hereafter.[1]

.   .   .   .   .

> Yes! Or bravery will be broken,
> Cabined in Canterbury, realmless ruler,
> Self-bound servant of a powerless Pope,
> The old stag, circled with hounds.[2]

Eliot's version of the metre often uses a separate alliterating sound in each of the halves forming one line. Both the Anglo-Saxon poets and Pound avoid this, but it is an obvious development of the basic metre. In the last two quotations there is, furthermore, the elliptical syntax that Pound uses very often in 'The Seafarer': Eliot's 'Holiness hereafter' and 'realmless ruler' are parallel to Pound's 'Days little durable' and 'Bitter breast-cares'. The remaining Tempters make less use of the Poundian metre: it occurs only in an isolated line or two, such as the Fourth Tempter's

> Wantonness is weakness. As for the King,
> His hardened hatred shall have no end.[3]

A different type of imitation of Pound can be seen in Eliot's 'Journey of the Magi', which approximates in tone to Pound's 'Exile's Letter'.[4] These two poems share the confidential tone of an old man talking to a friend; in both there is a good deal said of the operation of memory across a span of years, and there is a contrasting of the hardships of a journey with the comfort of palaces; there is also a certain amount of imagery in common, the most noticeable example being the valleys. The confidential tone, which is expressed with almost exactly the same level of colloquialism in the two poems, may be exemplified by a quotation from each:

> I went up to the court for examination,
> Tried Layu's luck, offered the Choyo song,
> And got no promotion.
>
> ('Exile's Letter')

---

[1] *Murder in the Cathedral*, p. 27.   [2] Ibid., p. 29.   [3] Ibid., p. 35.
[4] This point is mentioned by Grover Smith, op. cit., p. 123. For 'Exile's Letter' see *Personae*, p. 144–6; for 'Journey of the Magi' see *Collected Poems: 1909–1935*, pp. 107–8.

But there was no information, and so we continued
And arrived at evening, not a moment too soon
Finding the place; it was (you may say) satisfactory.

('Journey of the Magi')

Pound's speaker reviews the operation of memory in this way:

And all this comes to an end.
And is not again to be met with.

Eliot's does the same in these words:

All this was a long time ago, I remember,
And I would do it again . . . .

Pound's speaker compares the roughness of the journey with the luxury of a palace:

And what with broken wheels and so on, I won't say it wasn't hard going,
Over roads twisted like sheep's guts.
And I was still going, late in the year,
     in the cutting wind from the North,
And thinking how little you cared for the cost,
     and you caring enough to pay it.
And what a reception:
Red jade cups, food well set on a blue jewelled table, ...

Eliot's does the same:

'. . . Just the worst time of the year
For a journey, and such a long journey:
The ways deep and the weather sharp,
The very dead of winter.'
And the camels galled, sore-footed, refractory,
Lying down in the melting snow.
There were times we regretted
The summer palaces on slopes, the terraces,
And the silken girls bringing sherbet.

And finally there is the use of valleys as a place of refreshment.
Pound writes of his traveller coming

Into a valley of the thousand bright flowers,
That was the first valley;
And into ten thousand valleys full of voices and pine-winds.

Eliot's traveller reports that

Then at dawn we came down to a temperate valley,
Wet, below the snow line, smelling of vegetation;
With a running stream and a water-mill beating the darkness,
And three trees on the low sky . . . .

The main point to be made, however, is that in all these quotations the tone of the two poems is very similar. Both poems are the reminiscences of an old man speaking quietly to a friend and letting his mind wander over his experiences. The wandering or rambling quality is perhaps not very apparent from the examples quoted, but it can be easily established by noting the large proportion of lines in the two poems that begin with 'And'; about a quarter in Eliot's poem, and almost a half in Pound's.

The final kind of imitation of Pound that I want to mention is imitation in subject. To be convincing, demonstration of such imitation needs to deal with particularized rather than generalized subjects. Yet the best example with Pound and Eliot happens to be in a subject that is common to most Romantic poets, namely the work of the poet himself. Eliot's imitation is a rather remote one, yet I think it is true to say that he would not have written as he did without knowing Pound's work. The most effective comparison can be made between, on the one hand, the first part of *Hugh Selwyn Mauberley* and the third part of 'Mauberley 1920', and, on the other, 'East Coker', II and V.[1] Pound and Eliot both suggest that poetry is a difficult art, requiring concentration: Pound says that 'He strove to resuscitate the dead art Of poetry'; Eliot that he faced 'the intolerable wrestle With words and meanings'. In both of them, too, there is a feeling of dismay at their lack of success: Pound speaks of being left with

> Nothing, in brief, but maudlin confession,
> Irresponse to human aggression;

Eliot speaks of the same wallowing in emotion,

> In the general mess of imprecision of feeling,
> Undisciplined squads of emotion.

Both yearn for a classic discipline in their work, Pound speaking of

> Emendation, conservation of the 'better tradition',
> Refinement of medium, elimination of superfluities,
> August attraction or concentration;

Eliot speaking of getting 'the better of words', and, by implication,

---

[1] The relevant passages in 'East Coker' will be found in *Four Quartets* (London: Faber & Faber, 1944), pp. 17, 21–2.

of 'precision' and 'discipline'. Yet both have a feeling that what they have to say is in advance of their technique of saying it: Pound speaks of resuscitating a 'dead art', of maintaining ' "the sublime" In the old sense', of being born in a country that was culturally 'out of date'; Eliot speaks of writing 'A periphrastic study in a worn-out poetical fashion' and of mastering words only 'For the thing one no longer has to say, or the way in which One is no longer disposed to say it'.[1]

All of these similarities are similarities of ideas rather than of words. They could, therefore, be plausibly attributed simply to Eliot and Pound's sharing of certain attitudes to the art of poetry, rather than to an influence of Pound's poem on Eliot's. Yet even if this point of view were adopted, there would remain the possibility that Pound was partly responsible for Eliot's sharing his critical attitude. The need to examine this possibility leads me to a consideration of Pound's influence on Eliot's critical ideas.

This discussion will be even more tentative than the discussion of Pound's influence on Eliot's poetry, because so little is known of Eliot's ideas before he met Pound. Apart from two brief reviews in *The Harvard Advocate*, there is almost nothing to indicate his early ideas about literature. There is, therefore, virtually no possibility of comparing the ideas he held before meeting Pound with those he held after meeting him. Yet there can be little doubt that an influence was exerted by Pound on Eliot's critical theory and practice. Eliot himself said in 1927 that 'Pound's critical influence is immense, and beneficial. . . . My own critical debt to him is as great as my debt in versification.'[2] Had Eliot said '. . . as great as my debt in poetry' one might have suspected that he was referring simply to Pound's ability to secure publication for his criticism as well as for his poetry, but the use of the word 'versification' precludes such an interpretation. Eliot genuinely meant that he believed Pound had

---

[1] Pound probably had in mind a statement made by Yeats in a speech that Pound reported. Eliot may well have seen the report, the relevant passage of which reads:

> If I take up today some of the things that interested me in the past I can no longer use them. They bore me. Every year some part of my poetical machinery suddenly becomes of no use.
>
> Reported in Ezra Pound, 'Homage to Wilfred Blunt',
> *Poetry*, III, 6 (March 1914), p. 223.

[2] 'Isolated Superiority', rev. of *Collected Poems* by Ezra Pound, *The Dial*, LXXXIV, 1 (January 1928), p. 7.

helped to formulate his critical ideas. Some ten years later, he implied the same thing, when he referred to 'Mr. Pound, who, as
literary critic alone, has been probably the greatest literary influence
of this century up to the present time'.[1]

It is true to say, I think, that Pound was instrumental in introducing Eliot to some of the ideas that were to become quite important in his critical theory and practice. These ideas can be
grouped under two main headings: the first is the poetic method,
the techniques and attitudes that the poet requires in order to create
worthwhile poetry; the second is the poetic tradition, a view of the
relative merits of the chief poets writing in European languages. A
third, but quite minor, heading could be made for listing the critics
to whom Pound directed Eliot's attention.

In the matter of poetic method, everyone who came in contact
with Pound was impressed by the seriousness of his attitude to the
poet's task. This attitude received its lengthiest exposition in the
article, 'The Serious Artist', which Pound contributed to *The
Egoist* in 1913,[2] but there were many other manifestations over a
period of many years. Eliot acknowledged his debt in the words:

> I think that Pound was original in insisting that poetry was an art, an
> art which demands the most arduous application and study; and in see-
> ing that in our time it had to be a highly conscious art.

.   .   .   .

> Pound's great contribution to the work of other poets (if they choose
> to accept what he offers) is his insistence upon the immensity of the
> amount of *conscious* labour to be performed by the poet; and his invalu-
> able suggestions for the kind of training the poet should give himself—
> study of form, metric and vocabulary in the poetry of divers literatures,
> and study of good prose.[3]

This notion of the poet's task, a notion far removed from the popular Romantic one of 'unpremeditated art', came to be accepted in
theory and in practice by Eliot. In his essay of 1919, 'Tradition and
the Individual Talent', at a point where he is mainly concerned to
demonstrate the unconscious fusion of disparate elements in the
mind of the poet (the converse of the 'dissociation of sensibility'

---

[1] 'T.S.E.', 'Commentary', *The Criterion*, XVI, No. 65 (July 1937), p. 668.
[2] I, 9 (15 October 1913), pp. 161–163; reprinted in *Literary Essays*, pp. 41–57.
[3] 'Ezra Pound' (1946); reprinted in *Ezra Pound: A Collection of Essays*, p. 35.

that he was to speak about later), he nevertheless inserts a sentence
or two reminding his readers of the conscious elements in the writing
of poetry:

Of course this is not quite the whole story. There is a great deal, in the
writing of poetry, which must be conscious and deliberate. In fact, the
bad poet is usually unconscious where he ought to be conscious, and conscious where he ought to be unconscious.[1]

If Eliot simply asserted that the poet's task was a difficult one, and
that the finished poem must pass through various stages of criticism
and revision, one could dismiss the thought of any influence from
Pound; such a notion would be too common and obvious to require
attribution to a source. But Pound and Eliot go beyond this notion.
According to them, the poet's task—or at any rate the modern poet's
task—is not merely to exercise taste and discretion in deciding on the
final form of his poem, but also to train himself to be able to do this.
This was a subject that Pound never tired of treating. Eliot's essays,
on the other hand, have always dealt more with the product than
with the process of creation, and they have rarely dealt with modern
poetry; it is difficult, therefore, to find in them an overt statement
on this subject. Just as Eliot was scrupulous in excising from his
poetry the verbal echoes of Pound that he detected, so in his criticism he seems to have scrupulously avoided using Pound's notions,
at least without attribution. (The same scrupulousness can be seen
in Pound's invariable attribution of 'No *vers* is *libre* for the man
who wants to do a good job' to Eliot, and of 'Poetry must be as well
written as prose' to F. M. Ford.[2]) Yet there are in his criticism
occasional references to Pound's theory of the poetic method. In the
essay, 'William Blake', Eliot casually mentions that 'It is important
that the artist should be highly educated in his own art . . .';[3] and
over twenty years later, in writing of the apprenticeship of a poet,
he referred to the necessity both of studying and assimilating
English poetry and of formally studying the classics:

The only way to learn to manipulate any kind of English verse seemed
to be by assimilation and imitation, by becoming so engrossed in the

[1] *Selected Essays*, 3rd ed. (London: Faber & Faber, 1951), p. 21.
[2] For another example of the use of 'No *vers* is *libre* . . .' in Pound's work, see *Literary
Essays*, p. 12; for 'Poetry must be as well written as prose', see *Letters*, p. 91.
[3] *Selected Essays*, p. 319.

K

work of a particular poet that one could produce a recognizable derivative. . . . I do not recommend any other way of beginning the study of
Greek and Latin verse than with the aid of those rules of scansion which
were established by grammarians after most of the poetry had been
written.[1]

In this statement he comes very close to the ideas that he considered
to be 'original' in Pound.

This influence of Pound on Eliot's ideas about the poetic method
may seem rather unimportant. The same can not, however, be said
about a second point of influence in these ideas, namely influence
concerning the theory of the poet's impersonality. Eliot's form of
this theory was more coherent and less paradoxical than either
Yeats's or Pound's. Both Yeats and Pound believed that the poet
should strive after an expression of his true personality: Yeats
speaks of 'personal utterance', and of trying 'to write out of my
emotions exactly as they came to me in life';[2] Pound of the ' "search
for oneself" ', and of ' "sincere self-expression" '.[3] This objective
was to be reached through a process of using one mask after another:
in a diary entry Yeats asks himself about the narrator in one of his
stories: 'Is it simply the doctrine of the Mask? The choosing of
some one mask? . . . Is it becoming Mask after Mask';[4] Pound
speaks of himself in his early poems as 'casting off, as it were, complete masks of the self in each poem'.[5] Ultimately, such a process
would lead, according to Yeats, to a

> Poem maybe as cold
> And passionate as the dawn.[6]

According to Pound, it would lead to poetry that was 'impersonal',
or imagistic. To say that a search for 'sincere self-expression' ought
to end in 'impersonality' would seem, at least at first sight, to be
paradoxical. It is only fair to Pound, therefore, to quote a passage in
which he explains the procedure:

In the 'search for oneself,' in the search for 'sincere self-expression,'
one gropes, one finds some seeming verity. One says 'I am' this, that, or
the other, and with the words scarcely uttered one ceases to be that thing.

---

[1] *On Poetry and Poets* (London: Faber & Faber, 1957), p. 27.
[2] *Autobiographies*, pp. 102, 103.   [3] 'Vorticism', loc. cit., p. 463.
[4] Extract from 1908 diary, quoted in Ellman, *Yeats: The Man and the Masks*, p. 190.
[5] Loc. cit.   [6] 'The Fisherman', *Variorum Edition*, p. 439.

I began this search for the real in a book called *Personae*, casting off, as it were, complete masks of the self in each poem. I continued in a long series of translations, which were but more elaborate masks.

Secondly, I made poems like 'The Return,' which is an objective reality and has a complicated sort of significance, like Mr. Epstein's 'Sun God,' or Mr. Brzeska's 'Boy with a Coney.' Thirdly, I have written 'Heather,' which represents a state of consciousness, or 'implies,' or 'implicates' it.

. . . .

These two latter sorts of poems are impersonal, and that fact brings us back to what I said about absolute metaphor. They are Imagisme . . . .[1]

What Pound meant by saying that imagistic poems were 'impersonal' was, I presume, that they dealt with an emotion or idea without dealing with the poet's relation to the expression of that emotion or idea: the question of whether the poet had experienced the emotion or idea was not being raised; it was assumed that he had, but the process by which he came to choose a particular image to express the emotion or idea was not part of the poem. The plausibility of this interpretation of 'impersonal' lies in the fact that most imagist poems satisfy it. The first principle of Imagism, 'Direct treatment of the "thing," whether subjective or objective', seems, for Pound at least, to have implied impersonality.

Eliot's relation to these theories is at its most obvious and mechanical in his use of Pound's term 'persona' to refer to the poet's mask. Pound had used the term in the title of a volume of poems as early as 1909, and in critical essays at least as early as 1914. When, later than this, Eliot is found using the term with reference to Pound's poetry, the obvious conclusion is that he had derived it from Pound. In a review of Pound's *Quia Pauper Amavi* printed in 1919, Eliot refers to 'persona';[2] and in the introduction to Pound's *Selected Poems* (published by Faber & Gwyer in 1928) he says that *Homage to Sextus Propertius* 'is not a translation, it is a paraphrase, or still more truly (for the instructed) a *persona*'.[3] The usage of the word in this last context makes it almost certain that Eliot was deriving the term from Pound: he is applying it to Pound's poetry

---

[1] Pound, loc. cit., pp. 463–4.
[2] 'T.S.E.', 'The Method of Mr. Pound', *The Athenaeum*, 24 October 1919, p. 1065.
[3] Page xxiii.

in the way Pound himself did, a way quite different from that in which Jung (who is the only other likely source of Eliot's usage) applies it to an aspect of human personality. Later still, Eliot applied the term to Arnold's poetry (as Pound had done to Browning's): this was in *The Use of Poetry and the Use of Criticism*, and it may well be that this particular instance of the usage of the term has caused it to become such a common critical counter since then.[1] Eliot wrote: 'The poem about Heine is good poetry for the same reason that it is good criticism: because Heine is one of the *personae*, the masks, behind which Arnold is able to go through his performance.'[2] Immediately after this sentence, Eliot goes on to use one of Yeats's theories, the theory of the purpose of the anti-mask: he thus indicates once again the close relationship between his critical ideas on this point and the ideas of Pound and Yeats.

But this usage of a single term is merely the most obvious point of relationship. A second, and almost equally obvious point, is the notion of impersonality. In the same year as that in which I have noticed Eliot's first use of 'persona', he also wrote of the poet's need to achieve impersonality. This was in the article, 'Tradition and the Individual Talent', first published in *The Egoist* in 1919, in which he wrote that

The business of the poet is not to find new emotions, but to use the ordinary ones and, in working them up into poetry, to express feelings which are not in actual emotions at all. And emotions which he has never experienced will serve his turn as well as those familiar to him. . . . Poetry is not a turning loose of emotion, but an escape from emotion; it is not the expression of personality, but an escape from personality.[3]

The conclusion reached about impersonality is, of course, vastly different from that reached by Pound and Yeats, who believed in 'self-expression'. Yet both Pound and Yeats speak so confusedly that Eliot may even have thought that they would approve of his conclusion. If one did not accept the interpretation of Pound's

[1] Rupert Brooke used it in an early review of Pound; it was later used by Conrad Aiken, R. P. Blackmur, Louis MacNeice, and Cleanth Brooks in contexts where Pound's influence is almost certain; and in the fifties and sixties it became a vogue word used, for instance, by such diverse writers as John Speirs, Laurence Lerner, Randolph Quirk, Fredson Bowers, J. B. Priestley, and Derek Stanford.

[2] 'Matthew Arnold', *The Use of Poetry and the Use of Criticism* (London: Faber & Faber, 1933), p. 112.

[3] *Selected Essays*, p. 21.

theory of impersonality that I have offered, or some similar theory, one might think that Pound meant by impersonality what Eliot meant, 'an escape from personality'. What I am suggesting is that, whether or not Eliot made this mistake, his notion of impersonality probably took as its starting point Pound's ideas about the essential impersonality of imagism.

The major, and least questionable, influence of Pound on Eliot's theories of the poetic method seems, however, to concern Eliot's doctrine of the objective correlative. This, like the doctrine of impersonality, springs from the first principle of Imagism, 'Direct treatment of the "thing".' Richard Aldington has a very interesting elaboration of what he calls this 'fundamental doctrine':

1. Direct treatment of the subject. This I consider very important. We convey an emotion by presenting the object and circumstance of that emotion without comment. For example, we do not say 'O how I admire that exquisite, that beautiful, that—25 more adjectives woman, you are cosmic, let us spoon for ever,' but we present that woman, we make an 'Image' of her, we make the scene convey the emotion. Thus, Mr. Pound does not say 'His Muse was wanton, though his life was chaste,' but he says that he and his songs went out into the 4 a.m. of the world composing albas.[1]

This statement, written when Aldington was still a loyal 'Imagiste' in the Pound tradition, makes it very clear that 'Direct treatment of the "thing" ' means direct description of an object or set of circumstances in which an emotion or thought was experienced, without the emotion or thought itself being described. (It also provides, incidentally, further justification for the interpretation of Pound's theory of impersonality that I have offered above.) In his article 'Vorticism' Pound gives a practical example of this procedure when he explains the genesis of his poem

> The apparition of these faces in the crowd:
> Petals, on a wet, black bough.

The words of the poem are, he indicates, an 'equation'[2] for an experience that he had in a 'metro' station. In the same article he offers the same sort of explanation for poems like 'Heather': this

---

[1] 'Modern Poetry and the Imagists', *The Egoist*, I, 11 (1 June 1914), p. 202.
[2] Loc. cit., p. 465. Pound had said much the same thing in general terms in *The Spirit of Romance*, p. 14.

poem, he says, 'represents a state of consciousness, or "implies," or 'implicates" it'. Some three years later, Eliot commented on the objectivity and lack of emotion in some examples of this imagist technique.

One of the ways by which contemporary verse has tried to escape the rhetorical, the abstract, the moralizing, to recover (for that is its purpose) the accents of direct speech, is to concentrate its attention upon trivial or accidental or commonplace objects. This tendency is common to a very great variety of poets: what is less noticed is the divergence of form which it takes. To be concrete, if perhaps facile in generalization, I may divide the tendency into its English and its American currents. With the American the effect is more usually an arrest at the object in view; the American poet is fearful of betraying any reaction beyond that revealed in the choice and arrangement; the effect is of an ingenious if sometimes perverse visual imagination in complete detachment from any other faculty.[1]

In this statement Eliot is simply repeating the ideas of Pound and Aldington, though admittedly with more detachment from the ideas. Two years later he had dropped the slight tone of denigration, and was stating the same ideas with a curious twist, given to them presumably by his theory of impersonality. He assumes that the poet's task is to describe an object or set of circumstances which represent an emotion or an idea, but he implicitly denies any auto-biographical connexion between the object and the emotion. This is his famous doctrine of the 'objective correlative', stated in the review entitled 'Hamlet and His Problems'; in this review he says that

The only way of expressing emotion in the form of art is by finding an 'objective correlative'; in other words, a set of objects, a situation, a chain of events which shall be the formula of that *particular* emotion; such that when the external facts, which must terminate in sensory ex-perience, are given, the emotion is immediately evoked.[2]

In 'Tradition and the Individual Talent', an essay which was prob-ably written within a month of 'Hamlet and His Problems', Eliot had stated that the emotions a poet expresses need not be his own; in the 'objective correlative' doctrine he simply applied this belief

[1] 'T.S.E.', 'Reflections on Contemporary Poetry', *The Egoist*, IV, 8 (September 1917), p. 118.
[2] *Selected Essays*, p. 145.

to Pound's interpretation of the first principle of Imagism. Pound had assumed that the poet experienced an emotion in a particular set of circumstances, and then wrote a poem made up of a description of the circumstances together with another image or images to provide an 'equation' for the emotion. In the very simple poem that he instances, 'The apparition of these faces in the crowd' is the original set of circumstances; and 'Petals, on a wet, black bough' is the image providing the 'equation' for the unstated emotion that went with the 'apparition'. As, according to Eliot's theory of impersonality, the poet need not have experienced the original set of circumstances or the emotion that accompanied them, there is no need to describe the circumstances; all that is needed to satisfy his theory is 'a set of objects, a situation, a chain of events' to provide the 'objective correlative', the 'formula', or, using Pound's word, the 'equation' of the emotion that the poet desires to express.

A final point of contact between Pound's and Eliot's ideas on the poetic method concerns the distinction they both make between imitation and influence. In 'A Few Don'ts' Pound indicated that the writer should be influenced by as many great writers as possible, but that he should avoid imitating them by repeating their vocabulary. In a letter to Harriet Monroe written in 1913, he deplored the imitation of Baudelaire and Verlaine, and held up Gautier and Gourmont as useful influences.[1] Eliot made the same distinction in a review of Pound's *Collected Poems*. He went further than Pound, however, by attempting to define the nature of 'influence', and by introducing a third term, 'discipleship'. Pound, he wrote,

has been a great deal imitated, but that matters still less; and with his imitators neither I nor any one else can be concerned. But apart from imitation and plagiarism, there are these two things which are not the same: influence and discipleship. Sometimes they are united in the same persons; but I have suggested that Pound has great influence but no disciples. And I think the reason is this: that influence can be exerted through form, whereas one makes disciples only among those who sympathize with the content.[2]

It is, perhaps, a fairly obvious distinction to make, but because Pound made it before Eliot, because he obviously reiterated it, and

[1] See *Letters*, p. 60.
[2] 'Isolated Superiority', *The Dial*, LXXXIV, 1 (January 1928), p. 4.

because Eliot first made it in writing of Pound, there is the suggestion of influence.

Apart from influence on Eliot's theories of the poetic method, Pound's main influence was on Eliot's theories of the poetic tradition. Pound and Eliot disagreed on the valuation of many poets—such as Dryden, Pope, and Swinburne—but on the merits and demerits of Dante, Shakespeare, and Milton they were in agreement. It could be true, of course, that they gained their relative estimates of these poets independently during their undergraduate days, but as their estimate of Milton is so different from the one current in American universities at the beginning of the century and as it is expressed with certain points of similarity, this seems unlikely.

Yet although their general attitude to Dante, Shakespeare, and Milton is similar, Pound and Eliot rarely make the same specific points. On Milton, for instance, they agree that he is much inferior to Dante and Shakespeare, they agree that he was a bad influence on English poetry, they agree that he has certain admirable qualities, but they agree on little else, at least in their printed criticism. This is, presumably, because Eliot would have considered it a waste of time to repeat what Pound had written. Where there is agreement, Eliot is scrupulous in giving Pound the credit for priority. In his first essay on Milton, he acknowledges Pound as having called his attention to Milton's 'misdeeds'.[1] In his second essay, he suggests the reason why he and Pound thought Milton's influence so repugnant. Basically, the suggestion is that Milton represents the farthest remove from the 'verse as speech' that he and Pound were striving for. After comparing the modern movement's desire for contemporary speech in poetry to the desires of Dryden and Wordsworth, he goes on to point out that

Milton does, as I have said, represent poetry at the extreme limit from prose; and it was one of our tenets that verse should have the virtues of prose, that diction should become assimilated to cultivated contemporary speech, before aspiring to the elevation of poetry. Another tenet was that the subject-matter and the imagery of poetry should be extended to topics and objects related to the life of a modern man or woman; that we were to seek the non-poetic, to seek even material refractory to trans-

[1] *On Poetry and Poets*, p. 138.

mutation into poetry, and words and phrases which had not been used in poetry before. And the study of Milton could be of no help here: it was only a hindrance.[1]

Here, then, is the reason for the antipathy of Pound and Eliot to Milton: Milton's poetry ran counter to the theory of Imagism. Now Eliot learnt of the theory of Imagism from Pound, and it seems likely that it was Pound who pointed out to him the opposition between this theory and the poetry of Milton. In any case, Eliot himself ascribes his dislike of Milton to his holding of the imagistic theory, so that even if Pound did not point out the opposition between this theory and the poetry of Milton he was at least indirectly responsible for Eliot's dislike.

The belief on which this opposition is based, the belief that 'Poetry must be as well written as prose' or that one ought to strive after 'verse as speech', is one of the peripheral tenets of Imagism. Eliot also uses, however, one of the central tenets in his criticism of Dante, Shakespeare, and Milton. This is the tenet about 'Direct treatment of the "thing" ', which, as we have seen earlier, was interpreted to mean concentration on the image as an 'equation' or 'objective correlative' for an emotion. He applies it to Dante in his essay of 1929 when he discusses the reasons for the immediacy of the impact that he makes even on readers not skilled in the language. This occurs, says Eliot, because Dante offers 'the objective "poetic emotion" ';[2] in his poetry 'the word is lucid, or rather translucent';[3] and his allegorical method results in 'clear visual images'.[4]

There can be little doubt that Eliot's ideas about the relative importance of Dante, Shakespeare, and Milton (as expressed, for instance, in the same essay) were to some extent formed under Pound's influence. These ideas rested on two of the tenets of Imagism, which Pound had introduced to Eliot. Eliot was, however, a good deal more original in his approach to the question of Milton than other critics influenced by Pound, such as Middleton Murry and F. R. Leavis.[5]

---

[1] Ibid., p. 160.

[2] *Dante* (London: Faber & Faber, 1929); reprinted in *Selected Essays*, p. 238.

[3] Ibid., p. 239.   [4] Ibid., p. 242.

[5] See John Middleton Murry, rev. of *Milton's Prosody* by Robert Bridges, *The Athenaeum*, 26 March 1921; and his *The Problem of Style* (London: Oxford University Press, 1922), pp. 109–21, 141–3; and F. R. Leavis, 'Milton's Verse', in his *Revaluation:*

One other notion about the poetic tradition seems to have come to Eliot from Pound. This is the well-known, somewhat metaphysical, theory that 'The existing monuments form an ideal order among themselves, which is modified by the introduction of the new (the really new) work of art among them.'[1] This theory was expressed in an essay of 1919. In 1933, Pound suggested that the theory was as much his as Eliot's. In the preface to *Active Anthology* he said that 'Mr Eliot and I are in agreement, or "belong to the same school of critics", in so far as we both believe that existing works form a complete order which is changed by the introduction of the "really new" work.'[2] Because Pound was always scrupulous about acknowledging literary debts, I feel sure that he had not borrowed the idea from Eliot. At the least, it would seem that Pound and Eliot arrived at the same idea together. But it seems likely to me that Pound arrived at it first, because it is implied by another idea that Pound certainly had before Eliot. This is the theory that it is possible to criticize an existing work by creating a new one. This theory was not stated explicitly until 1934, when Pound, in *Make It New*, described 'the most intense form of criticism' existing as being 'Criticism in new composition'.[3] But long before 1934 he had been striving to achieve this kind of criticism, in his Provençal, his Chinese, and his Japanese poems, and above all in *Homage to Sextus Propertius*. Before 'Tradition and the Individual Talent' was written, Pound had claimed this kind of criticism for the *Homage* when he wrote in a letter that one of its critics had 'never *understood* anything but syntax and never seen the irony of Propertius'.[4] A few years later, he wrote in another letter:

I do think, however, that the homage has scholastic value. MacKail (accepted as 'right' opinion on the Latin poets) hasn't, apparently, *any* inkling of the *way* in which Propertius is using Latin. Doesn't see that S.P. is tying blue ribbon in the tails of Virgil and Horace, or that sometime after his first 'book' S.P. ceased to be the dupe of magniloquence and began to touch words somewhat as Laforgue did.[5]

Tradition and Development in English Poetry (London: Chatto & Windus, 1936), pp. 42–67.

[1] 'Tradition and the Individual Talent'; reprinted in *Selected Essays*, p. 15.
[2] *Active Anthology*, p. 9.   [3] Reprinted in *Literary Essays*, p. 75.
[4] Letter to A. R. Orage, [? April 1919]; *Letters*, p. 211.   [5] *Letters*, pp. 245–6.

Pound, then, before Eliot published his statement, was beginning
to assert that at least one of his own works, because it offered a new
approach, altered the position of Propertius in the literary tradition.
This assertion was, I suggest, the source of Eliot's theory.

The idea of a literary tradition incorporating (and discriminating
amongst) all periods and all languages strongly suffuses the practical
criticism of both Pound and Eliot. It is an idea that may well have
come to them both from their academic training, for they were
undergraduates at a time when the comparative study of literatures
was fashionable in American universities, and both of them gained
facility in several languages. It is significant, however, that both
explicitly expressed adherence to the doctrine of universal critical
standards, and did so in similar terms. In *The Spirit of Romance*,
Pound asserted that 'What we need is a literary scholarship, which
will weigh Theocritus and Yeats with one balance . . . .'[1] Five
years later, in his essay on Lionel Johnson, he referred to his 'Having
held out for a uniform standard of appreciation, having insisted that
one should weigh Theocritus and one's neighbour in one balance...'.[2]
After another five years, Eliot, in an essay full of 'We needs', was
saying: 'We need a digestion which can assimilate both Homer and
Flaubert.'[3]

The practical result of adherence to this doctrine was that Pound
and Eliot could never discuss a writer without referring to several
other writers, generally from different periods, in an attempt to
place their subject in a tradition. In his essay on Rémy de Gourmont, for instance, Pound refers to Henry James, Thomas Hardy,
Swinburne, Yeats, Samuel Butler, Emerson, Tennyson, Beerbohm,
and Strindberg in the first three pages. Some of these references are
of genuine help; others seem to betray irrelevance or ostentation.
Eliot is, however, probably even more addicted to this sort of display than Pound. Edmund Wilson has parodied the technique in his
chapter on Eliot in *Axel's Castle*:

'We find this quality occasionally in Wordsworth,' he will write, 'but it is
a quality which Wordsworth shares with Shenstone rather than with

[1] Page 8.   [2] *Literary Essays*, p. 362.
[3] 'Euripides and Professor Murray', *The Sacred Wood*, p. 77. The similarity between
the statements of Pound and Eliot is referred to by Stanley Edgar Hyman in *The Armed
Vision: A Study in the Methods of Modern Literary Criticism* (New York: Alfred A.
Knopf, 1948), p. 97.

Collins and Gray. And for the right sort of enjoyment of Shenstone, we must read his prose as well as his verse. The 'Essays on Men and Manners' are in the tradition of the great French aphorists of the seventeenth century, and should be read with the full sense of their relation to Vauvanargues, La Rochefoucauld and (with his wider range) La Bruyère. . . .'[1]

As Wilson goes on to point out, 'we should have to read the whole of literature in order to appreciate a single book, and Eliot fails to supply us with a reason why we should go to the trouble of doing so.'

Pound suggested, no doubt, that Eliot read many books, including books of criticism; this was something that he suggested to all his friends. But there is one critic that he recommended who had as profound an effect (and a far less unfortunate one) on Eliot's criticism as Gautier's *Emaux et camées* had on his poetry. This was Rémy de Gourmont, by whom, according to Eliot, he was 'much stimulated and much helped'[2] at the time when he was writing the essays gathered in *The Sacred Wood*. Now although there can be little doubt that this is true, Eliot never acknowledged that his interest in Gourmont had been excited by Pound. In an earlier chapter I have shown that Pound was very enthusiastic about Gourmont during the life of *The Egoist*, and probably induced Richard Aldington to read his work. It seems likely that the same thing happened with Eliot. It is certainly true that Pound recommended Gourmont to Iris Barry in 1916; and to William Carlos Williams in 1917.[3] It would be very surprising if Pound's enormous enthusiasm had not been communicated to Eliot. It is significant that at the time when Eliot was first coming to know Gourmont's work, that is, when he was writing the essays of *The Sacred Wood*, Pound was working on a long essay on Gourmont, which was published in *Instigations* (1920), and on a translation of Gourmont's *Poudre aux moineaux*, published as *Dust for Sparrows* in the same year.[4] It is significant, too, that on the only occasion when Eliot quotes from Gourmont he uses a

---

[1] *Axel's Castle: A Study in the Imaginative Literature of 1870–1930* (New York: Scribner's, 1931), p. 124.

[2] Preface to the 1928 Edition, *The Sacred Wood: Essays on Poetry and Criticism*, 7th ed. (London: Methuen, 1950), p. viii.

[3] See *Letters*, pp. 143, 180.

[4] 'Rémy de Gourmont', *Instigations* (New York: Boni & Liveright, 1920), pp. 168–95. *Dust for Sparrows* was published in *The Dial* in instalments from September 1920 to May 1921.

passage that Pound had earlier used in his essay. Eliot's quotation from Gourmont occurs in the essay 'Philip Massinger', in a part which had not appeared in print before the publication of *The Sacred Wood* on 4 November 1920.

Eliot wrote:

In the fine pages which Remy de Gourmont devotes to Flaubert in his *Problème du Style*, the great critic declares:

La vie est un dépouillement. Le but de l'activité propre de l'homme est de nettoyer sa personnalité, de la laver de toutes les souillures qu'y déposa l'education, de la dégager de toutes les empreintes qu'y laissèrent nos admirations adolescentes;

and again

Flaubert incorporait toute sa sensibilité a ses œuvres. . . . Hors de ses livres, où il se transvasait goutte à goutte, jusqu'à la lie, Flaubert est fort peu intéressant. . . .[1]

Earlier in the same year,[2] in *Instigations*, Pound had quoted the first of these passages,[3] and had quoted another passage similar in substance to the second:

Etre impersonnel c'est être personnel selon un mode particulier: Voyez Flaubert. On dirait en jargon: l'objectif est une des formes du subjectif.[4]

The cumulative evidence does point, then, to Eliot's having gained his enthusiasm for Gourmont from Pound.

In this matter, as in most of the matters raised in this chapter, it may be thought that I have been too ready to assume that similarity implies influence. It is true that this assumption has often been made, but where it is established that Pound ante-dated Eliot with a technique or an idea it does not seem to be an unreasonable assumption, at least for the period up to the early 1920s. There is a difference between the amount of evidence needed to make a theory of influence by Pound on Yeats plausible, and the amount needed for a theory of influence by Pound on Eliot. Yeats was an older man than Pound, and he treated Pound as a subordinate. Eliot was a slightly younger man, owing his reputation largely to Pound, and treating him with deference. The relationship between Pound and

---

[1] *The Sacred Wood*, p. 139. [2] See *Letters*, p. 220.
[3] Reprinted in *Literary Essays*, p. 354. [4] Reprinted ibid., p. 353.

Eliot was, therefore, far more conducive to influence. In this chapter, it has been assumed that Eliot is right in admitting influence by Pound, and the problem has simply been one of establishing the extent of that influence. In general, this is less than Eliot's statements would lead one to expect. There are, I suggest, two reasons for this. The first is that Eliot deliberately avoided putting into print work that showed traces of Pound's influence: this was partly because he was an intelligent man, and partly because Pound disapproved of the practice. The result has been that there is little tangible evidence of Pound's influence: this influence has stimulated Eliot's thought in various ways, but where it has produced anything resembling the original stimulus that thing has been suppressed or altered beyond recognition. The second reason is that Eliot was so grateful for Pound's help in gaining publication that he over-estimated the extent of Pound's influence. It is significant that his later statements about Pound's influence are more moderate than his earlier ones: in 1946, for instance, he said (quite rightly, I believe) that his 'greatest personal debt' concerned the arrangements for the publication of *Prufrock*.

PART III. LESSER INFLUENCES

7. FIVE IMPORTANT POETS

YEATS and Eliot are the two great poets with whom Pound came
into close personal contact in conditions favourable for influence.
There were other considerable poets (though certainly not so great
as Yeats and Eliot) whose work he influenced—poets like William
Carlos Williams and Archibald MacLeish—but this influence was
chiefly exerted at a distance; in some cases it was exerted without
Pound's being aware of it, in others it was exerted partly through
correspondence. There were, also, other poets whom Pound influenced through close personal contact—people like John Cournos,
John Rodker, and Basil Bunting—but their work is of minor importance.

Apart from Yeats and Eliot, then, the important poets whose
work Pound influenced were influenced from a distance, largely
through his poetic practice. This kind of influence, where the evidence is more literary than biographical, may in some ways be more
interesting than the direct and specific hortatory kind of influence
that predominates with Yeats and Eliot, but it is much harder to
establish. When Pound exerts influence in a personal way one can
be sure that his strong personality attenuates the effect of other influences; when his influence is exerted at a distance one can not
be sure of any such effect. When Pound meets a poet and that poet's
work shows signs of influence, one can be sure that the influence has
come directly; when Pound is separated from a poet whose work
shows signs of influence, one can rarely be sure that the influence is
not coming at second-hand from one of Pound's followers.

The likelihood of indirect or secondary influence is borne out by the fact that Pound's influence was felt much more by important American poets than by important British ones. Apart from Eliot, Pound's influence was felt most by William Carlos Williams, Marianne Moore, Hart Crane, E. E. Cummings, and Archibald MacLeish, all, of course, Americans.

Of these, the one whose work has been touched at the greatest number of points by Pound, and the one who has shown the greatest ability to avoid mere imitation, is William Carlos Williams. Williams was obviously a man of strong personality, who was never prepared to let Pound dominate him. In his autobiography he recalls that even in their undergraduate days Pound 'used to assault me (as he still does) for my lack of education and reading. He would say that I should become more acquainted with the differential calculus—like himself, of course'; but Williams's reply would be that 'a course in comparative anatomy wouldn't at all harm him, if it came to that'.[1] The 'Prologue' to Williams's *Kora in Hell* (1920) was a vehement attack on the values that Pound was upholding, and in it he referred to Pound as 'the best enemy United States verse has'.[2] From Williams's point of view the relationship between the two men was that of equals; from Pound's point of view it was usually that of teacher to pupil. Yet Williams always admitted that Pound was in a much better position than himself to recommend books to be read, and that he had learnt more from Pound than Pound had from him. He wrote to Robert McAlmon that Pound was

a one-sided bastard if there ever was one, who has borrowed from everybody, including myself in the old days, but he's done a good job, surpassingly good. And I've borrowed from him much more than I've given. Everyone has who has followed him. Yeats especially.[3]

In the early years of the acquaintance, the learning naturally tended to be a one-way process. Although Pound was a couple of years younger than Williams, he was more precocious, and had begun to write verse before coming up to the University of Pennsylvania. Williams, on the other hand, deliberately chose verse as a medium of artistic creation only after coming up to the University.[4]

---

[1] *The Autobiography of William Carlos Williams*, p. 53.
[2] See *The Letters of Ezra Pound*, pp. 220–1.
[3] *The Selected Letters of William Carlos Williams*, p. 220.
[4] See the beginning of Chapter 1.

Pound, moreover, was committed to a literary career; Williams was committed to poetry only as a spare-time activity. The result was that, according to Williams, Pound 'deeply influenced my formative years'.[1]

If this statement is true, it obviously does not apply to the years when they were both University students. At the beginning of this period, possibly before he had met Pound, Williams wrote a poem in what was to become his characteristic style, a poem that could be called imagistic.[2] This, and similar poems might have provided Pound with material to work on, but if he did work on it he had no immediate effect. When Williams had his first volume of poems printed—privately—in 1909, and sent a copy to Pound, Pound was shocked. His letter of criticism was so damning that he felt obliged to write a note at the beginning: 'I hope to God you have no feelings. If you have, burn this *before* reading'; and to end it with

Vale et me ama!
P.S. And remember a man's real work is what *he is going to do*, not what is behind him. Avanti e coraggio!'[3]

The tenor of his criticism was that Williams's work was not worth printing, not because there were no lines of poetry in it but because what he said had been said better a long time before.

Yet even by this time Williams thought that he was competent to argue with Pound about poetry. In the year before his own volume appeared he had strongly criticized Pound's *A Lume Spento*. Pound's letter in reply indicates how little the two men had in common; he begins with 'Good Lord! of course you don't have to like the stuff I write';[4] and after several pages of self-justification displays a lack of knowledge of and a mild curiosity about Williams's ideas on poetry:

I wish, no fooling, that you would define your ultimate attainments of poesy. Of course we won't agree. That would be *too* uninteresting. I don't know that I can make much of a list.
1. To paint the thing as I see it.
2. Beauty.

[1] *Selected Letters*, p. 324.
[2] 'A black, black cloud'; see the beginning of Chapter 1.
[3] *The Letters of Ezra Pound*, p. 42.   [4] Ibid., p. 36.

L

3. Freedom from didacticism.
4. It is only good manners if you repeat a few other men to at least do it better or more briefly. Utter originality is of course out of the question.[1]

There can be little doubt, then, that Williams's 'formative years' had not occurred by 1909. If it is true that Pound 'deeply influenced' them, they must have occurred in the succeeding few years. Williams saw a good deal of Pound in 1910: when he was in London on the way back from Germany, he was taken by Pound to see Yeats; and then in the second half of the year Pound was in America recovering from an attack of jaundice. Pound almost certainly took the many opportunities provided by their companionship to elaborate on the criticism of his letter and try to bring Williams up to date on the poetic tradition. The bad Keats, the bad Whitman, the inversions, the inaccurate rhymes, and the inappropriate forms must all have been pointed out.[2] The result was, I suggest, that Williams was forced back on to his original, unpretentious, untutored style, the style of his spontaneous poem, 'A black, black cloud'. This suggestion depends for its plausibility on taking Williams's statement about the composition of this poem at its face value. As almost nothing from Williams's university days has been preserved, the truth of the statement must remain conjectural.

At any rate, whether Williams was reverting to an earlier style or not, his poetry changed between 1909 and 1913 towards the style of Pound. Pound's jewelled world of Rossetti and early Yeats appears in Williams's 'Homage', which begins

> Elvira, by love's grace
> There goeth before you
> A clear radiance
> Which maketh all vain souls
> Candles when noon is.[3]

---

[1] *The Letters of Ezra Pound*, pp. 39–40.

[2] In his *Autobiography*, p. 107, Williams says that he came to realize these faults in his first volume, but implies that he did so without Pound's help. His statement that 'Ezra was silent, if indeed he ever saw the thing, which I hope he never did', is, however, obviously disproved by the evidence of Pound's letter. There can be little doubt that both Williams and Pound are referring to the same volume, *Poems*, a pamphlet privately printed by Reid Howell, in Rutherford, New Jersey, in 1909.

[3] *The Collected Earlier Poems of William Carlos Williams* (Norfolk, Conn.: New Directions, 1951), p. 18.

Yet the poem is by no means a slavish imitation. It is not like any particular poem of Pound's, but has merely a generic resemblance in tone and imagery. The absence of rhyme, and the short lines (both very difficult features to handle in a lyric, but ones that Williams seems to have mastered even at this stage of his career) owe nothing to Pound. A different kind of style is apparent in such poems as 'Postlude', 'Mezzo-Forte', and 'First Praise', which have a matter-of-fact, conversational tone that might equally well have come from Pound, or Browning, or from Williams himself; I am inclined to think that their straightforwardness comes directly from Williams's own character and ideas about poetry.

Several of these poems had been printed in *Poetry* before they appeared together in *The Tempers* (London: Elkin Mathews, 1913). Pound does not seem to have been responsible for the publication in *Poetry*. He still did not have a very high opinion of Williams's verse, though he told Harriet Monroe that he was 'glad you're going to print "Bill", i.e. Wm. Carlos Williams'.[1] After seeing the poems in print, however, he was willing enough to make arrangements with his own London publisher for the volume known as *The Tempers*.

What Pound had done for Williams by this time was to force him to study the English poetic tradition. His poetry provides evidence that he had taken Pound's advice, first given in the letter of 1909, but no doubt repeated many times: 'If you'll read Yeats and Browning and Francis Thompson and Swinburne and Rossetti you'll learn something about the progress of Eng. poetry in the last century.'[2] These are the influences that Williams had absorbed by the time of *The Tempers*. They came to him partly perhaps through Pound's example, but mainly through Williams's individual appreciation of them. He does not imitate them; he writes in a highly personal, direct style, but a style that shows an awareness in a few appropriate places of what had been done by 'Yeats and Browning and Francis Thompson and Swinburne and Rossetti'. Some of the things that he learnt from these poets had not been noticed by Pound: he had, for instance, learnt something very important from Yeats's rhythm, something that he pointed out to Harriet Monroe when she objected to the roughness of versification in 'Proof of Immortality':

[1] *The Letters of Ezra Pound*, p. 50. [2] Ibid., p. 42.

Surely if Yeats teaches anything that can be learnt—that is, anything that it would not be copying to take to one's self—he teaches what can be done with the three-syllable foot by dropping the last syllable in the foot every time but once or twice in the entire poem. Witness 'The Mountain Tomb' in your own *Poetry*.[1]

It is interesting that 'The Mountain Tomb', the poem that Williams uses as an authority for his own practice, appears to have been disliked by Pound.[2]

In the following year or so, Williams drew close to formal Imagism, and was included in *Des Imagistes*. For a time he seems to have been dazzled by the superficial tricks of Pound's Imagism, and perpetrated some of his worst poems, such as the Pound-out-of-Whitman 'Rendezvous', printed in *The Egoist* in 1914:

> My song! It is time!
> Wider! Bolder! Spread the arms!
> Have done with finger pointing.
> Open windows, even for the cold
> To come whistling in, blowing the curtains:
> We have looked out through glass
> Long enough, my song . . . .[3]

Most of Pound's poems about 'my song' are wryly self-depreciatory, but Williams's appears to be unironic. Addresses to 'my song' and other trappings of Pound's Imagism were, however, soon discarded by Williams. What he retained was a concentration on the visual image clearly defined, a concentration that he was temperamentally suited to, and that later formed the basis of his 'Objectivist' movement. Williams always had a very perceptive eye for the appearances of things—notably trees—and this made it easy and natural for him to achieve 'Direct treatment of the "thing"'. It was a quality in him that Pound realized almost from the beginning: 'The thing

---

[1] Letter to Harriet Monroe, 5 March 1913; *The Selected Letters of William Carlos Williams*, p. 24.

[2] In her autobiography, *A Poet's Life*, Harriet Monroe quotes from one of Pound's letters in which he writes: ' "Fallen Majesty" is just where he was two years ago.' (p. 264). The cause of Pound's dislike appears, however, to have been the content rather than the style. The poem is a lament for Maud Gonne's lost beauty and leadership—it is backward-looking and pessimistic. It shares these qualities with 'The Mountain Tomb' and 'A Memory of Youth' which Pound condemns by implication in the same letter. The two poems he praises, 'Child Dancing' and 'The Realists', are set in the present, and are, by comparison, optimistic and affirmative.

[3] *The Egoist*, I, 16 (15 August 1914), p. 307.

that saves your work is opacity, and don't you forget it',[1] he wrote
in 1917; and after the publication of *Kora in Hell*:

You have the advantage of arriving in the milieu with a fresh flood of
Europe in your veins, Spanish, French, English, Danish. You had not
the thin milk of New York and New England from the pap; and you can
therefore keep the environment outside you, and decently objective.[2]

But this 'opacity' or 'objectivity' was not confined for long to the
Imagist limits. Williams wrote few truly Imagist poems; many of
his poems begin in an Imagist way, but then depart from the Imagist
programme as Williams discusses the relationship between himself
and the 'thing', a relationship that often amounts to identity. One
of the poems called 'Pastoral' from *Al Que Quiere!* (1917) shows
this very clearly. It begins with a sentence of almost pure Imagism:

> The little sparrows
> hop ingenuously
> about the pavement
> quarreling
> with sharp voices
> over those things
> that interest them.

The last two lines make an assumption that a strict Imagist would
probably not allow, but the next sentence is completely non-Imagistic. It transfers attention completely away from the 'thing':

> But we who are wiser
> shut ourselves in
> on either hand
> and no one knows
> whether we think good
> or evil.[3]

Other poems state uncompromisingly at the beginning the theme
that Williams intends to deal with, before they branch out into one
or more images: some examples are 'January Morning', 'To Waken
an Old Lady', most of the parts of *Spring and All*, and 'Young Syca-
more'.

These poems are representative of the general way in which
Williams assimilated Imagism to his natural liking for direct, un-
compromising statement about himself. But throughout his poetic

---

[1] *Letters*, p. 181.   [2] Ibid., p. 223.   [3] *Collected Earlier Poems*, p. 124.

career he occasionally produced a poem or a passage of strict
Imagism. Many of the best of these come from the period when, it is
generally assumed, he had left Imagism far behind him. What he
called 'that green bottle piece', from *Collected Poems* (1934), he
admitted many years later to be 'a pure imagistic poem—if such a
thing exists'.[1] The poem referred to is 'Between Walls':

> the back wings
> of the
>
> hospital where
> nothing
>
> will grow lie
> cinders
>
> in which shine
> the broken
>
> pieces of a green
> bottle[2]

Another poem from the same collection, 'Nantucket',[3] is equally
imagistic. Again, many passages from *Paterson* are imagistic. The
reason for the frequency of such passages may be that the whole
poem is a symbolic treatment of man through the features of the
city, Paterson, and as this symbolic connexion is partly brought out
through prose interludes, Williams felt that he could indulge in objective description without having to make the relationship between
it and the theme explicit. Whatever the reason, he indulged his gift
for objective description in passages like this, from Book I:

> The river, curling, full—as a bush shakes
> and a white crane will fly
> and settle later! White, in
> the shallows among the blue-flowered
> pickerel-weed, in summer, summer! if it should
> ever come, in the shallow water!

---

[1] Letter to Babette Deutsch, 25 May 1948; *Selected Letters*, p. 264.
[2] *Collected Earlier Poems*, p. 343.   [3] Ibid., p. 348.

On the embankment a short
compact cone (juniper)
that trembles frantically
in the indifferent gale: male—stands
rooted there.[1]

Williams's assimilation and adaptation of Imagism seems to me
to be one of the most successful uses of the technique. Where Amy
Lowell and Hart Crane tried to assimilate the technique to the
jewelled words of which they were so fond—the jewelled words that
Imagism was a reaction against—Williams assimilated the technique
to the urgency, directness, and personal involvement that seem to
have been essential parts of his personality. He applied Imagism
not just to static images but to moving ones: to the swaying of trees,
the flight of birds, and the fall of water. As a result, his imagistic
poems lack the debilitated stillness that occurs in those of Eliot
and MacLeish.

It is perhaps his 'objectivity' or 'opacity', his feeling for the poem
as an object, a work of art, that causes him to indulge in poems that
depend for part of their effect on being seen. The impact of lines
with only one or two words in them was something that Williams
learnt early in his career, something that he and E. E. Cummings at
times carried to extremes. This method draws attention to the look
of the words on the page, and it leads naturally to such 'pictorial'
effects as Williams's representation of an illuminated sign for 'SODA'
in 'The Attic which is Desire'. Pound's letters often have similar
bizarre pictorial effects, but he did not begin to use them in poetry
until after Williams.[2]

Like Edwin Muir and Hugh MacDiarmid, Williams seems to
have learnt from Pound something of how to tell a story succinctly
in verse. This is partly a matter of selecting vivid details, partly a
matter of having an ear for speech, and partly a matter of handling
rhythm. Browning can, of course, do this very well, and so can
Eliot. But both Browning and Eliot are generally concerned to
characterize the narrator of their story; it is on him, in fact, that
interest centres. Pound and Williams, however, write narrative
poems that are not dramatic monologues: they are dramatic, and

[1] *Paterson* (London: Peter Owen, 1953), p. 30.
[2] See, for instance, the club sign in Canto XXII, and the pyramid in Canto XXXIV.

they have some psychological interest, but the attention is focused on the story being told and on its characters, not on the character of the narrator. These poems are like the dramatic monologues of Browning and Eliot, though, in their use of appropriate contemporary language and rhythms. A fairly early example of the type is Pound's 'The Bellaires', which is a satire of lawyers achieved through the story of the Bellaire family. The narrating 'I', who comments that 'for all this I have considerable regret', is left almost completely uncharacterized. Other examples of the type—more competently handled examples for the most part—occur frequently in the Cantos. Williams handled the impersonal contemporary narrative well even in his early volumes. 'Tract'[1] tells the story of a typical respectable town funeral, though the poet's own exasperation and impatience with the trappings of respectability keep breaking through—and the poem is none the worse for it. 'Dedication for a Plot of Ground',[2] written a little later, is a story told with a complete absence of personal intrusion up to the last two lines; it applies the same technique as Pound applied with more suavity and less urgency in 'The Bellaires'. Williams's 'The Last Words of My English Grandmother' tells a story with equal competence, but it also includes extremely realistic speech:

> Wrinkled and nearly blind
> she lay and snored
> rousing with anger in her tones
> to cry for food,
>
> Gimme something to eat—
> They're starving me—
> I'm all right I won't go
> to the hospital. No, no, no
>
> Give me something to eat
>
> .   .   .   .
>
> Oh, oh, oh! she cried
> as the ambulance men lifted
> her to the stretcher—
> Is this what you call

---

[1] *Collected Earlier Poems*, pp. 129–31.   [2] Ibid., pp. 171–2.

making me comfortable?
By now her mind was clear—
Oh you think you're smart
you young people,

she said, but I'll tell you
you don't know anything.[1]

While this is an extremely individual form of expression, it is obvious that the same kind of thing had been done earlier by Pound, in, for instance, 'Mœurs Contemporaines'. Both Pound and Williams are indebted to Browning, but it seems likely that Williams admired Pound's achievement in this field, and was slightly influenced. This kind of ability with narrative persisted through Williams's career and is to be found, for instance, in the late poems 'The Clouds' (1948) and *Paterson*. Part II of *Paterson* is in fact partly constructed on the narrative of the poet's walk through the city park.

The main type of construction in *Paterson* is, however, one that might be called ideogrammic. This construction had been employed on a much smaller scale in the poems of *Spring and All*—the first poem, for instance, juxtaposes 'the contagious hospital' with the 'lifeless', 'dazed', 'naked' appearance of the first shoots of spring: it is the dull uniformity of appearance possessed by the inmates of the one and the individual shoots of the other that is being conveyed. On another level, the separate poems of this volume go together to make up a representation of modern society by a series of images and scenes. It is the same technique as Eliot was concurrently using in *The Waste Land*, despite Williams's abhorrence of that poem. The main difference in the use of the technique is that whereas Eliot passes sharply from one scene to another without explaining the connexion, Williams links his scenes together in a semi-narrative or semi-expository method. Williams's linking was done partly through the long sentences within the poems, which shifted the scene by small steps so that a considerable transition was achieved between the beginning and the end of the sentence, and partly by prose commentaries between the poems. By the time of *Paterson*, this rather tentative use of the ideogrammic method had given way to the sharper juxtapositions characteristic of Eliot and Pound:

[1] *Collected Earlier Poems*, pp. 443–4.

scene follows scene without overt explanation of the connexion between them. In Book II of *Paterson*, for instance, this technique is used to hint at relationships between fiscal policy in the United States and the Evangelical Protestant religion of Germany.

Pound's Cantos may have supplied some suggestions for Williams's use of the technique, but so may Eliot's poems, of which there are many reminiscences in *Paterson*. Pound is obviously the source of much of the material on usury in Books II and IV of *Paterson*, but Eliot has provided some of the diction and cadence. The influence of *Four Quartets* is apparent in

> For the beginning is assuredly
> the end—since we know nothing, pure
> and simple, beyond
> our own complexities.[1]

This influence is mingled with that of *Ash-Wednesday* in the deprecation of the (perhaps unavoidable) fact

> that the poet,
> in disgrace, should borrow from erudition (to
> unslave the mind): railing at the vocabulary
> (borrowing from those he hates, to his own
> disfranchisement)
> —discounting his failures
> seeks to induce his bones to rise into a scene,
> his dry bones, above the scene, (they will not)
> illuminating it within itself, out of itself
> to form the colors, in the terms of some
> back street, so that the history may escape
> the panders.[2]

At the time when this was written, Eliot was probably, for Williams, still one of 'those he hates'.

The influence of Pound's Cantos, especially of Cantos XXXI to XXXIV and LXII to LXXI (the Jefferson-Adams Cantos) can be seen in the selection of material in Books II and IV of *Paterson*. Williams, following Pound's lead, has made considerable use in his verse of historical material from the early years of the American Union. It was Pound's belief that

The true history of the economy of the United States, as I see it, is to be

---

[1] Book I, Preface; ed., cit., p. 11.   [2] Book II; ibid., p. 99.

found in the correspondence between Adams and Jefferson, in the writings of Van Buren, and in quotations from the intimate letters of the Fathers of the Republic. The elements remain the same: debts, altering the value of monetary units, and the attempts, and triumphs of usury, due to monopolies, or to a 'Corner.'[1]

This is the attitude incorporated in the Jefferson-Adams Cantos, and it is the attitude that Pound must have tried to share with Williams after the Second World War, that is, at the time when Williams was planning and writing *Paterson*, Book II. Shortly before this Book was published, Williams indicated in an article that he had been reading some of the sources that Pound referred him to. He wrote:

While I have been here in the country on my vacation I have been reading a very interesting book, The Age of Jackson, by Arthur M. Schlesinger, Jr., a dissertation on the period when Andrew Jackson was the United States president; it includes prominently also the administration of Martin Van Buren who immediately followed Jackson's incumbency of the presidency.

Upon reading of the events which occurred during those years, at the first quarter of the nineteenth century, it is plain that they were of world importance in determining not only the destiny of democracy in this country but in redefining the basic meaning of political democracy the world over. . . .

Ezra Pound discovered this material fairly early and has written of the period originally and ably. But how? He hasn't the vaguest idea of the meaning, the political significance of the period and of its potentialities. He has taken the classic attitude. He has written, here and there appreciatively of a few of the men, 'measuring' them, pontificating about their qualities. And in this he thinks he has been a great leader of thought in the matter. He has used much of this in his later cantos.[2]

From this quotation it is obvious that although he might take Pound's advice about what to read, Williams reserved the right to come to his own conclusions about it. One example of his conclusions differing from Pound's is in his attitude to Alexander Hamilton, the first U.S. Secretary of the Treasury. In several of the prose passages of *Paterson*, Book II, Part II, Williams represents Hamilton

---

[1] 'An Introduction to the Economic Nature of the United States' (1944), tr. from the Italian by Carmine Amore; printed in *Impact: Essays on Ignorance and the Decline of American Civilization*, ed. Noel Stock (Chicago: Henry Regnery Company, 1960), p. 19.

[2] Preface to *Poetry: The Australian International Quarterly of Verse*, No. 25 (10 December 1947) p. 9.

in a far more favourable light than Pound does in Cantos XXXVII, LXVI, LXX, and LXXI. On the question of 'usury', however, his views were very similar to Pound's. One of the prose passages from *Paterson*, Book II, includes the statements:

> The Federal Reserve System is a private enterprise . . . a private monopoly . . . with power . . . given to it by a spineless Congress . . . to issue and regulate all our money.
> They create money from nothing and lend it to private business (the same money over and over again at a high rate of interest), and also to the Government whenever it needs money in war and peace; for which we, the people, representing the Government (in this instance at any rate) must pay interest to the banks in the form of high taxes.[1]

Williams almost certainly arrived at this Gesellite or Douglasite doctrine through the advocacy of Pound, who had applied the same criticism of 'creating money out of nothing' (one of his favourite phrases) to the English monetary system:

> The Bank of England, a felonious combination or, more precisely, a gang of usurers taking sixty per cent interest, was founded in 1694. Paterson, the founder of the bank, clearly stated the advantages of his scheme: 'the bank hath benefit of the interest on all moneys which it creates out of nothing'.[2]

Most of the material suggested by Pound that is incorporated into Book II is reserved for the prose sections. Williams was not yet ready to follow Pound by attempting to versify it. But such an attempt was made in a vehement attack on usury towards the end of Book IV. Partly quoting from what appear to be letters from Pound and partly trying to find poetic equivalents for Pound's economic theories, Williams allowed himself to be influenced to the extent of imitation. It is almost unbelievable that a man who had stood up to the pressure of Pound's attempts to influence him for so long, and who, even a few years later, was to complain 'Ain't it enuf that you so deeply influenced my formative years without your wanting to influence also my later ones?'[3] should have imitated Pound in using material that had furnished the dullest section of the Cantos. As he

---

[1] *Paterson*, ed. cit., p. 90.

[2] 'The Enemy is Ignorance' (1944), tr. from the Italian by John Drummond; *Impact*, p. 101.

[3] Letter to Ezra Pound, 12 April 1954; *Selected Letters*, p. 324.

had done many times before, he read what Pound suggested and, for once, agreed with Pound's opinion about it. This was an unfortunate accident, but why he should have thought that he could make poetry out of the material is a mystery.

Marianne Moore, of the same generation as Pound and Williams, learnt from Pound in some of the same ways. She often uses a technique that can be described as imagist; her use of the ideogrammic method has similar narrative, descriptive, or expository links (as distinct from the sharply cut method of Eliot); she uses quotations in her verse; and she attempts to embrace all kinds of experience as the materials of poetry. Like Williams, too, she has learnt from Eliot, chiefly in her repetitions of a word, and in the rather languid, debilitated air that pervades some of her work. She lacks the verve, enterprise, and independence of Williams, and she lacks his sense of involvement in her material, but in her own smaller field she is equally competent.

Marianne Moore's work was sufficiently 'modern' to be accepted by *Poetry* and *The Egoist* in 1915 when it was submitted by H.D., who had been at Bryn Mawr with her; but she was personally so retiring that three years later Pound, who had at the time noticed her first appearance in *Poetry*,[1] could still ask 'DOES your stuff "appear" in America?' and 'what about your age . . .?'[2] Later, as he came to know her and her work better, Pound thought of her as a worthy candidate for 'Bel Esprit',[3] and as the obvious successor to Harriet Monroe as editor of *Poetry*.[4] She was so close to Pound in general theory in 1932 that she joined such devoted disciples as Louis Zukofsky and Basil Bunting in a manifesto,[5] and, with them, was invited to appear in Pound's *Active Anthology* (1933). In the late forties and early fifties Pound helped her, in much the same way as he had helped Rouse in the thirties, with her translation of La Fontaine's *Fables*, a selection from which was published in 1955.

Her natural predilection for precise, objective description found convenient theoretical justification in Imagism, which she has practised assiduously throughout her poetic career. In an early poem,

[1] Letter to Harriet Monroe, 17 May 1915; *Letters*, p. 104.
[2] Letter to Marianne Moore, 16 December 1918; ibid., pp. 204–5.
[3] See ibid., pp. 239, 250.   [4] See ibid., pp. 315–16, 319.   [5] See ibid., p. 322.

'Poetry',[1] she states the importance of objectively observed pheno-
mena as the materials of poetry; poetry must be made up, she says,
of what is 'genuine', of 'raw material . . . in all its rawness'. And
she distinguishes between a symbolic and an imagistic use of this
material in the same way as Pound does in his article 'Vorticism':
the data of poetry, she says,

> Hands that can grasp, eyes
>   that can dilate, hair that can rise
>   if it must, these things are important not
> because a high-sounding interpretation can be put upon
>   them but because they are
>   useful.

Marianne Moore's major contribution to Imagism was to show
that the theory could be applied over longer and more complicated
poems than the other Imagists attempted. She was prepared to
apply the theory at several levels in the one poem: to have a basic
image that could have been put down in two lines, and to develop it
by illustration and example, the illustrations and examples frequently consisting of new, and almost separable 'one-image' poems.
When other Imagists attempted long poems they were content to
write only parts of them according to strict imagistic principles, and
to allow other parts to be taken up with personal attitudes, or narrative, or dramatic monologue. Marianne Moore, however, preserves
in her long imagistic poems the objectivity and detachment demanded by strict adherence to the principles. It is this quality that
has been partly responsible for criticism of her poetry as 'bloodless',
'anonymous', or 'frigid'; even Pound noticed that 'Marianne is
scarce an exuberance, rather protagonist for the rights of vitrifica-
tion and petrifaxis'.[2] There is another reason for her poems' giving
this impression: it is her use of abstract or generalizing or 'prosaic'
words. Now the use of such words seems to be proscribed in the
primitive form of Imagism; in 'A Few Don'ts', Pound criticized the
mixing of 'an abstraction with the concrete'; advised his followers
to 'go in fear of abstractions'; and asserted that 'the natural object
is always the adequate symbol'.[3] But in practice Pound had always
realized the value of mixing 'an abstraction with the concrete',

---

[1] Marianne Moore, *Collected Poems* (London: Faber & Faber, 1951), pp. 40–1.
[2] Letter to T. S. Eliot, January 1937; *Letters*, p. 377.   [3] *Literary Essays*, p. 5.

especially for the purpose of irony: his *Mauberley*, for instance, abounds in expression like 'He strove to resuscitate the dead art Of poetry'; 'He fished by obstinate isles'; 'No adjunct to the Muses' diadem', and so on. Eliot had learnt the same technique from Laforgue before he met Pound, and he, and later Auden, made considerable use of it.

One of Moore's early poems that best shows these individual adaptations of Imagism is 'A Grave', which Pound discussed in a letter of 1918.[1] The basic image could have formed a 'one-image' poem if it had been set down as

> The sea has nothing to give
> but a well excavated grave.

This basic image is elaborated in such statements as 'the sea is a collector'; 'their [i.e., drowned men's] bones have not lasted'; and 'men lower nets, unconscious of the fact that they are desecrating a grave'. But in this elaboration, new 'one-image' poems occur. Moore, for instance, compares the activity and rapacity of the sea with the passivity and detachment of the fir trees in a line that could have been set out as

> The firs stand in a procession,
> each with an emerald turkey-foot at the top.

Or she describes the fishermen, who

> row quickly away—the blades of the oars
> moving together like the feet of water-spiders.

This image-within-image construction could have been quite successful by itself, provided that the basic image of the sea as a grave was given sufficient prominence. But Moore, in this and in most of her other Imagist poems, seems to have been reluctant to believe that 'the natural object is always the adequate symbol'. She almost always wanted to control her images, to keep their rich sensuousness within bounds, by the use of abstract, prosaic terms. This negation of sensuousness is often expressed in syntactically or logically negative statements: in 'A Grave', for instance, she states that '*repression*, however, is not the most obvious characteristic of the sea'; the fishermen are said to be '*unconscious* of the fact that they

---

[1] *Letters*, pp. 202–3. The poem appears in Moore's *Collected Poems*, pp. 56–7.

are desecrating a grave'; and the movement of things dropped in the ocean is movement '*neither* with volition *nor* consciousness'.

Now it may be objected that the abstract or prosaic words in these quotations are due not to a general method adopted by Moore, but merely to the particular subject of this poem; it may be said that a graveyard is intrinsically negative—that it represents the negation of life—and that abstract, anti-sensuous terms are almost unavoidable in speaking of it. But I think it can be shown that Moore applies the technique of using abstract or prosaic terms to any subject, no matter how positive or sensuous. She seems always to want to be judicial about her subjects, to fit them into logical categories, to explain their relationship within a metaphysical system. In 'The Fish', for instance, after several stanzas each devoted to an objective image of one or more sea creatures, she writes of the sea-bed in abstract terms:

> All
> external
>   marks of abuse are present on this
>   defiant edifice—
>   all the physical features of
>
> ac-
> cident—lack
>   of cornice, dynamite grooves, burns and
>   hatchet strokes, these things stand
>   out on it; the chasm-side is
>
> dead.
> Repeated
>   evidence has proved that it can live
>   on what can not revive
>   its youth. The sea grows old in it.[1]

In this poem, the pure imagery and the abstraction are separated, but this is unusual; normally the two are intermingled. In 'The Monkeys', the zebras are spoken of as being 'supreme in their abnormality'; the elephants as having 'strictly practical appendages'; the parrakeet as being 'trivial and humdrum on examination'.[2] The elephant in 'Melancthon' has a skin which is

[1] *Collected Poems*, p. 38.   [2] Ibid., p. 44.

cut

into checkers by rut
  upon rut of unpreventable experience;

his back is 'full of the history of power'; he perceives 'feats of strength to be inexplicable after all'; but underneath the surface there is a 'beautiful element of unreason'.[1] In these examples the syntactical or logical negation is not so frequent as in 'A Grave', but it does occur in the 'lack' and 'can not revive' of 'The Fish'; and in the 'unpreventable', 'inexplicable', and 'unreason' of 'Melancthon'.

When imagism is extended by the use of the image-within-image method of Marianne Moore it approaches the ideogrammic method, in which the images are taken from separate fields of experience and set down side by side in order to draw attention to some theme that is common to all of them. Moore does use the ideogrammic method, but, like Williams, she uses it in a much less abrupt form than Eliot. She preserves the formal syntactical indicators of the simile or metaphor while building up her separate images; the separate images are rarely set down as separate blocks of meaning, but are fused with each other by comparison and contrast in the one poem.

Moore was probably never committed to the ideogram as a formal method in the same way as Pound. It is not surprising, then, that her work shows examples of images being used not just as similes or as ideograms, but in various ways between these limits. At the stage closest to the simile, she uses what might be described as a metaphysical Homeric simile; it is a simile where the two parts of the comparison have the far-fetched disparateness of the metaphysical conceit, but where the part used for comparison is stretched out to Homeric proportions as if it were the subject in itself. When, for instance, she wants to describe the majestic independence of the frigate-bird, she compares it to Handel, and in mentioning Handel she spends a few lines describing those aspects of his life that are relevant:

    As impassioned Handel—
meant for a lawyer and a masculine German domestic
  career—clandestinely studied the harpsichord
  and never was known to have fallen in love,

[1] Ibid., pp. 45–8.

M

the unconfiding frigate-bird hides
in the height and in the majestic
display of his art.[1]

At one stage closer to the strict ideogrammic method, she can build up several related images in order to draw attention to the features they have in common. In 'Style',[2] for instance, she uses four main images to explain her subject: the leader of a Spanish dancing company, Vincente Escudero; one of the dancers in this company, Rosario Escudero; the woman who danced the title-role in *Soledad*; and the world tennis champion, Pierre Etchebaster. Each of the four has a particular and individual art, but they all have style. This poem uses something like the ideogrammic method at two levels: in the four main images that are brought together in order to explain what style is; and within the description of some of the four images, where several new images are brought together in order to explain the particular art under discussion.

A closer approximation to the ideogrammic method occurs in the much earlier poem, 'Critics and Connoisseurs'.[3] Once again, there are four images (as there are in Pound's description of the Chinese ideogram for red). The first two, the description of the child making an animal stand up, and the description of the child making a pup eat its meat, are very brief and lack detail. They are followed by two more personal images, described at some length, one of the swan at Oxford, the other of the burdened ant. All four are intended to throw some light on what Moore calls 'fastidiousness', or what might be described as painstaking effort. Each image is separated from the others; there is no overt comparison between them, except in the last few lines where there is a review of the material of the poem. Yet even although the four images are set down as separate blocks, Moore is not using the ideogrammic method in quite the way Pound intended, for, like Williams, she has stated her theme at the beginning of the poem: 'There is a great amount of poetry in unconscious fastidiousness.' Throughout the poem, too, she frequently relates the image under discussion to the theme.

Like Williams, and like Hart Crane, Marianne Moore believed

---

[1] 'The Frigate Pelican', *Collected Poems*, p. 32.
[2] *Like a Bulwark* (London: Faber & Faber, 1957), p. 21–2.
[3] *Collected Poems*, pp. 42–4.

that all kinds of experience could be brought together in poetry. This belief produces in her poetry the effect of the metaphysical conceit, as 'The most heterogeneous ideas are yoked by violence together'. In one of her poems, 'Poetry',[1] she carries this belief to the same extreme as Pound, when, after speaking of some of the more common materials of poetry, she refers to Tolstoy's theory that 'poetry is everything with the exception of business documents and school books'; of this theory she says:

> nor is it valid
> to discriminate against 'business documents and

> school-books'; all these phenomena are important.

Now Pound, in his Cantos particularly, included extracts from business documents, if not from school-books. Moore does the same, but whereas Pound (and his disciple, Archibald MacLeish) quotes at great length from such sources, Marianne Moore generally quotes only striking phrases. Pound makes such quotations part of the subject of his poetry, and frequently requires the source as part of an ideogram. In Marianne Moore's poetry, the quotations are not part of the subject but merely useful descriptive phrases, and the source is generally irrelevant. In many cases, if she had not put the phrase into inverted commas and quoted the source in her notes, no one would have recognized it as a quotation. The same is true, of course, of many of the quotations used by T. S. Eliot: they are brief, striking phrases, and they were not, on first publication, recognized as quotations. In Eliot's poetry, however, knowledge of the source often adds a further level of meaning to the poem: the context in which the quotation occurs gives an individual and significant meaning to the words quoted. Thus the affair described at the beginning of Part II of *The Waste Land* is given an added significance by the implied comparison to the love of Antony and Cleopatra conveyed in the opening lines, 'The Chair she sat in, like a burnished throne, Glowed on the marble'. But in Marianne Moore's poetry, the sources rarely have any relevance; the invariable reference to them in the notes is merely due to the scrupulousness gained from Pound about unacknowledged quotation. Pound seems to have persuaded both Eliot and Marianne Moore that the new poetry

[1] Ibid., pp. 40–1.

he was promoting must not fall into the Georgian technique of reminiscence or unconscious pastiche; the new poets had to 'make it new'.

Hart Crane was a far less intelligent, and a somewhat less independent, imitator of Pound than either Williams or Moore. This imitation was achieved despite the fact that he did not know Pound personally—at any rate, he did not meet him, if he met him at all, until he had finished most of his important work. Of the poets so far dealt with in this book, Crane knew Pound least. This fact introduces uncertainties into the study of Pound's influence on him, a study which is further complicated by the mingling of Eliot's influence with Pound's.

Crane acknowledged that Pound had interested him over a period of about five years. This period occurred early in Crane's writing career. It began when Crane, at the age of seventeen, settled in New York, ostensibly to prepare for entry to a college. It was not long before he came to know members of the smaller, more *avant-garde* literary circles. He knew, for instance, Padraic Colum, who had earlier recommended Joyce to meet Pound; he knew Alfred Kreymborg, to whose magazine, *Others*, Pound sometimes sent work; he knew Margaret Anderson and Jane Heap, the editors of *The Little Review*, just at the time (1917) when Pound was beginning his foreign editorship of the magazine; and he knew of, and probably met, Harriet Monroe, the editor of *Poetry*.

Pound began a correspondence with Crane after seeing Crane's poem, 'In Shadow', in *The Little Review*. He was not encouraging: 'Beauty is a good enough egg, but so far as I can see, you haven't the ghost of a setting hen or an incubator.'[1] This was written early in 1918, and it seems to mark the beginning of Crane's consolidation of his vaguely imagistic propensities into a definite discipleship of Pound and Eliot. It was, however, a gradual process. Almost two years after Pound's first letter, Crane could write to Gorham Munson that 'More and more I am turning toward Pound and Eliot and the minor Elizabethans for values.'[2] The overt discipleship to

[1] Quoted by Philip Horton, *Hart Crane: The Life of an American Poet* (Compass Books ed.; New York: The Viking Press, 1957), p. 57.

[2] Letter to Gorham Munson, 27 December 1919; *The Letters of Hart Crane*, ed. Brom Weber (New York: Hermitage House, 1952), p. 28.

Pound was not so lasting as that to Eliot; shortly after it was established, Crane seems to have had doubts. Some eighteen months after the letter to Gorham Munson, he wrote to another friend that 'The people I am closest to in English are Yeats, Eliot, Pound, and the dear great Elizabethans like Marlowe, Webster, Donne and Drayton, whom I never weary of.'[1] The order of the modern poets named in this letter is significant; it is obvious from other evidence that for some months before it was written Crane had been growing increasingly irritated with Pound, and increasingly appreciative of Eliot. He had given up writing an article on Pound in 1921 because 'the subject itself is so complex and (I fancy) the audience interested so small';[2] later in the same year he complained that 'About the only thing to be gathered from Pound's article on Brancusi is that Pound wishes to avoid being obvious at the cost of no matter what else';[3] and early in 1923 he wrote that 'You already know, I think, that my work for the past two years (those meagre drops!) has been more influenced by Eliot than any other modern'.[4]

Over a period of five years, then, Crane became interested in Pound, slowly became a disciple, and then almost immediately forsook him in favour of Eliot. Conscious and overt discipleship is not, of course, necessarily concurrent with influence, and in the case of Crane it is true, I think, that Pound's influence did not produce worthwhile results until after the period of discipleship. But it is unwise to be dogmatic, because of the inextricable intermingling of Pound's influence with Eliot's. One can be certain, however, that if Pound did impress Crane significantly it was during the period from 1917 to 1923. It is true that if Crane ever met Pound he did not do so until his seven-month visit to Europe in 1928/1929, but by this time Crane's best work had been written, and in any case he was in no fit condition during this visit to profit from Pound's advice.

One of the interests that Pound was instrumental in recommending to Crane—an interest that persisted beyond the period of discipleship—was the study of Laforgue, Gourmont, and other French symbolists. In the early twenties, *The Double Dealer* printed

---

[1] Letter to Charmion Wiegand, 6 May 1922; ibid., p. 86.
[2] Letter to Gorham Munson, 22 July 1921; ibid., p. 63.
[3] Letter to Gorham Munson, 21 November 1921; ibid., p. 70.
[4] Letter to Gorham Munson, 5 January 1923; ibid., p. 114.

some of Crane's translations from Laforgue and Gourmont, though he never became a fluent reader of French. Eliot was partly responsible for this interest, and probably almost wholly responsible for Crane's interest in the Elizabethan playwrights, and in Dante.

Crane's earliest extant poems from his New York period exhibit all the faults that the Imagists sought to get rid of. Like most of the Imagists—including Pound himself—his avowed principles seem to have outstripped his practice, but even his principles were rather slow in forming, for he was young, and not particularly intelligent, and it took him some time to grasp the essentials of the movement to which he paid lip service. One of the poems of 1917 that he refused to reprint is quite Swinburnian:

> Up the chasm walls of my bleeding heart
> Humanity pecks, claws, sobs and climbs;
> Up the inside, and over every part
> Of the hive of the world that is my heart. . . .[1]

Another of the poems of the same year, one that he did reprint, shows some imagist tendencies and, more surprisingly, suggests at first sight some influence from Pound's and Eliot's interest in Gautier. It is 'In Shadow':

> Out in the late amber afternoon,
> Confused among chrysanthemums,
> Her parasol, a pale balloon,
> Like a waiting moon, in shadow swims.
>
> Her furtive lace and misty hair
> Over the garden dial distill
> The sunlight,—then withdrawing, wear
> Again the shadows at her will.
>
> Gently yet suddenly, the sheen
> Of stars inwraps her parasol.
> She hears my step behind the green
> Twilight, stiller than shadows, fall.
>
> 'Come, it is too late,—too late
> To risk alone the light's decline:
> Nor has the evening long to wait,'—
> But her own words are night's and mine.[2]

---

[1] 'The Hive', *The Collected Poems of Hart Crane*, ed. with introd. by Waldo Frank (New York: Liveright, 1946), p. 163.

[2] Ibid., p. 76.

These stanzas, which have the same form as those of *Emaux et camées*, were printed in the December issue of *The Little Review*. Now this magazine had, in its July issue, presented Eliot's first poem in imitation of Gautier, 'The Hippopotamus', and because it is well known that Crane had the highest regard for the standard of this magazine and had submitted—unsuccessfully—many poems for publication,[1] one might suspect some influence. But the only real resemblance between the two poems is in the length of line and in the rhyme scheme; Crane's rhythm is much rougher than the 'regular strophes' of Eliot's poem, and he lacks entirely the ironic structure that supports Eliot's verse structure. The partial resemblance may, then, be mere coincidence.

'In Shadow' does, however, show some influence from the imagists, particularly from such impure imagists as Amy Lowell and Conrad Aiken. They, like Crane, were never able to dispense with a liking for Pre-Raphaelite diction and a languid tone; their poems are full of words denoting colour (often muted colour, or colour in shadow), and of an enervated, still atmosphere. Amy Lowell, for instance, had written a poem called 'In a Garden', which has the same sort of details as Crane's 'In Shadow'; it contains the lines:

> Damp smell the ferns in tunnels of stone
> Where trickle and plash the fountains,
> Marble fountains, yellowed with much water.[2]

Both this poem and Crane's have the inversions that were despised by the Imagists ('Damp smell . . .'; '. . . in shadow swims'), but they do concentrate with a certain amount of objectivity on a particular object. Crane is more modern than Amy Lowell in diction, though 'In Shadow' preserves such poeticisms as 'misty hair', 'distill The sunlight', 'the sheen Of stars inwraps', and 'the light's decline'. Even in later poems, similar expressions are always likely to occur, though they were gradually replaced by learned or prosaic words in the style of Eliot or Marianne Moore (or, later, Auden). 'Voyages', III, for instance, shows him trying to inject a few modern, prosaic words into his jewelled diction:

> Infinite consanguinity it bears—
> This tendered theme of you that light

---

[1] See, for instance, Philip Horton, loc. cit.
[2] *The New Freewoman*, I, 6 (1 September 1913), p. 114.

> Retrieves from sea plains where the sky
> Resigns a breast that every wave enthrones;
> While ribboned water lanes I wind
> Are laved and scattered with no stroke
> Wide from your side, whereto this hour
> The sea lifts, also, reliquary hands.[1]

Though he has frequently been called an imagist because of his early poems, it is almost impossible to find a poem that is wholly imagistic. His eagerness to ruminate made it impossible for him to concentrate for any length of time on the opaque image: it is significant that he has been called a mystic, as well as an imagist, though the requirements of the two approaches would appear to be antithetical. What frequently happens in his poetry is that an image provides the starting-point for a non-imagistic piece of rumination. 'North Labrador', for instance, shows this in the first few lines:

> A land of leaning ice
> Hugged by plaster-grey arches of sky,
> Flings itself silently
> Into eternity.[2]

No true imagist could have permitted the last two lines; they are, in fact, the introduction to one of Crane's typical pieces of crude symbolist musing.

It is probably unfair to judge Crane by his minor poems, because his longest poem, *The Bridge*, is a good deal better than anything else he ever wrote. Its structure seems to have been heavily influenced by the ideogrammic structure of *The Waste Land*, which was published two years before Crane began to design *The Bridge*. He was obviously impressed by *The Waste Land*, though he himself preferred to apply Eliot's 'erudition and technique' to a poem or a set of poems that offered an optimistic spiritual truth, rather than the 'pessimism' of *The Waste Land*.[3] The result was *The Bridge*, constructed, as I have suggested, on the ideogrammic principle. Crane described the structure to Otto H. Kahn in these words:

There are so many interlocking elements and symbols at work throughout *The Bridge* that it is next to impossible to describe it without resorting to the actual metaphors of the poem. Roughly, however, it is based on the

---

[1] *Collected Poems*, p. 104.   [2] Ibid., p. 78.
[3] See letter to Gorham Munson, *The Letters of Hart Crane*, pp. 114–15.

conquest of space and knowledge. The theme of 'Cathay' (its riches, etc.) ultimately is transmuted into a symbol of consciousness, knowledge, spiritual unity.[1]

The completed poem consists of large blocks of quite distinct material from which a common theme is intended to emerge; it is, that is to say, ideogrammic. Even within the larger divisions, the same technique of 'montage' is applied, though there is a tendency to revert to a previous block of material for the purpose of summing up or of balance.

The diction of the poem is similar to that of the shorter poems. The frequent sections of prayer and invocation give Crane ample scope for exercising his fondness for jewelled, poetic words—the last line of the poem is 'Whispers antiphonal in azure swing'—and the descriptions of modern mechanical inventions provide opportunities for a rather brash use of modern vocabulary—the supplicatory poem introducing the work speaks of 'elevators', 'cinemas', a 'subway', and 'A rip-tooth of the sky's acetylene'.[2] Attention is never concentrated for long on a particular object, so that there are no outstanding examples of imagism in the poem.

Apart from the structure, there are, however, two clear examples of Pound's influence. The first, and less important, occurs in 'The River' from Part II. Here Crane uses proper names in much the same metaphorical way as Pound does in, for instance, *Mauberley*. The names used by Crane are, however, not such names as 'Penelope', 'Flaubert', 'Christ', 'Caliban', and so on. They are trade names, used partly to establish a mood, partly to establish a rhythmic idiom, and partly as metaphors. 'The River' begins:

> Stick your patent name on a signboard
> brother—all over—going west—young man
> Tintex—Japalac—Certain-teed Overalls ads
> and lands sakes! under the new playbill ripped
> in the guaranteed corner—see Bert Williams what?
> Minstrels when you steal a chicken just
> save me the wing for if it isn't
> Erie it ain't for miles around a
> Mazda—and the telegraphic night coming on Thomas
> a Ediford—and whistling down the tracks
> a headlight rushing with the sound . . . .[3]

---

[1] Ibid., p. 241.   [2] *Collected Poems*, pp. 3–4.   [3] Ibid., p. 13.

The meaning of the trade names in the third line is probably incon-
sequential. At this stage of the poem Crane was more concerned
with the rhythm and obvious commercialism of the names chosen
than with any particular significance in the products referred to.
But with the mention of 'Minstrels', Crane seems to be suggesting
that culture in modern America is a debased affair of travelling
troupes; and with 'Mazda' he seems to be suggesting that the desire
for spiritual light has been sublimated into satisfaction with modern
inventions, just as the values of 'Thomas a Ediford' have supplanted
the values of Thomas à Kempis or Thomas à Becket. This is an
interesting development from Pound's 'His true Penelope was
Flaubert'. Crane has used the same method, but in a less directly
stated, more inferential way: he has, as it were, left out the mention
of 'Penelope', and used the 'Flaubert' in a symbolic way with implications of 'Penelope'.

The second example of Pound's influence occurs in some of the
sea-faring sections of *The Bridge*. The first of them occurs in Part
III, 'Cutty Sark', where Crane writes of

> Bright skysails ticketing the Line, wink round the Horn
> to Frisco, Melbourne . . .
> Pennants, parabolas—
> clipper dreams indelible and ranging,
> baronial white on lucky blue!
>
> Perennial-*Cutty*-trophied-*Sark*!
>
> *Thermopylae, Black Prince, Flying Cloud* through Sunda
> —scarfed of foam, their bellies veered green esplanades,
> locked in wind-humors, ran their eastings down;
>
> *at Java Head freshened the nip*
> *(sweet opium and tea!)*
>
> Buntlines tusseling (91 days, 20 hours and anchored!)
> *Rainbow, Leander*
> (last trip a tragedy)—where can you be
> *Nimbus?* and you rivals two—
>
> a long tack keeping—
>
> *Taeping?*
> *Ariel?*[1]

[1] *Collected Poems*, p. 30.

The condensed syntax of this passage is similar to that of Pound's passages on sea-faring. Both poets seem to have felt that a loose syntax, with phrases and clauses barely hanging together, accompanied by an omission of inessential words such as subjects and articles, and by frequent inversions, was somehow appropriate to such passages. A less exuberant passage than the one quoted from 'Cutty Sark' would come even closer to Pound's style; there is one in, for instance, Part VIII of *The Bridge*, 'Atlantis', where Crane writes that

> We left the haven hanging in the night—
> Sheened harbor lanterns backward fled the keel.
> Pacific here at time's end, bearing corn,—
> Eyes stammer through the pangs of dust and steel.[1]

Crane lacked the enormous metrical virtuosity of Pound, but he did experiment extensively, though more in the direction of onomatopoeia than in Pound's direction of historic forms.

Another poet influenced by Pound who experimented in a similar way to Crane was E. E. Cummings, who went much further in the typographical representation of sound. Cummings's first encounter with Pound's work occurred some time after the publication in 1912 of Pound's *Ripostes*. S. Foster Damon, a friend of Cummings's at Harvard, showed him the volume, and he was very much impressed (as Yeats had been) by 'The Return', the improvisation of 'an unknown Greek masterpiece' as Yeats called it.[2] Some years later, when he was in Paris in the early 1920s, Cummings met Pound, and in the 1930s, when Cummings was still unacceptable to most publishers, Pound 'ballyhooed' him in a review of *Eimi* printed in *The New English Weekly*.[3] The review had no practical results, as no English publisher came forward with an offer, and Cummings's next volume of verse was rejected by several American publishers: it was eventually published privately, with the title *No Thanks*.[4]

---

[1] Ibid., p. 57.

[2] See Charles Norman, *The Magic-Maker: E. E. Cummings* (New York: Macmillan, 1958), p. 43. The quotation from Yeats occurs in the Introduction to *The Oxford Book of Modern Verse* (Oxford: Clarendon Press, 1936), p. xxvi.

[3] See Norman, op. cit., pp. 299–303, 320–4.   [4] See ibid., pp. 304–5.

Cummings was too good a poet to be a slavish imitator of Pound, but his major innovation in twentieth-century poetry, the careful placement of words on the printed page, owes something to Pound. Cummings believes that 'A poem, a painting, lives in itself',[1] a statement that he made when discussing Pound's theory of intensity in art. This belief is obviously very close to the theory of the Objectivists, with at least one of whom, William Carlos Williams, Cummings was in close contact about his experiments. Williams has stated the essential point of Objectivism to be the theory that 'the poem, like every other form of art, is an object'.[2] This theory caused him, just as an almost identical theory caused Cummings, to be concerned about the appearance of the object on the page. I have suggested in an earlier chapter that Objectivism was merely an emphasizing of some of the ideas that had long been held by Pound; I would suggest now that Cummings's belief that 'A poem, a painting, lives in itself' is equally likely to have come from his acquaintance with Pound's ideas. Pound had applied this sort of theory to his poetic practice by being very careful about the appearance of the words: one of his objections to 'free verse' was that there was no justification in sense or rhythm for many of the line units adopted; and his imitation of many forms indicates his care with such matters as line units and indentation. Like Pound, Cummings had enormous trouble with his printers over the setting up of his poems, and like Pound, he demanded many revised proofs.[3]

It would seem that Cummings himself acknowledges Pound's primacy in this concern for the poem as a printed object. When Charles Norman had written a passage praising Cummings as an innovator in this matter, he showed it to Cummings, who disagreed. Norman had written that

Cummings was the first to introduce and develop those structural elements on the printed page which act as doors and passageways to ultimate effects. A simple test is to take any of his poems and note how his lines and divisions of lines help to establish meaning and accent as well as movement. In this respect he is an innovator.[4]

Cummings replied that 'from my standpoint, not EEC but EP is the authentic "innovator"; the true trailblazer of an epoch'.[5]

[1] See Norman, p. 10. [2] *The Autobiography of William Carlos Williams*, p. 264.
[3] See Norman, op. cit., pp. 377–82. [4] Ibid., p. 160. [5] Ibid.

The 'ultimate effects' of which Norman writes include the sound of the poems, which Cummings frequently attempts to represent by typography. Like Crane, he often attempts to suggest the sound of music; a few of the poems from & (1925) recall very strongly Crane's evocations of jazz, and perhaps Eliot's 'O O O O that Shakespeherian Rag'—one of them, for instance, has the lines

> a waiter intones:bloo-moo-n
> sirkusricky
> platzburg
> hoppytoad   yesmam.[1]

In the same volume there is one of Cummings's earliest attempts to represent a dialect. It occurs in a poem the subject of which bears a resemblance to Eliot's 'Preludes', and though the dialect represented is a New York one, it is not dissimilar in its details to the Cockney dialect used by Eliot in 'A Game of Chess':

> raise the shade
> will youse dearie?
> rain
> wouldn't that
>
> get yer goat but
> we don't care do
> we dearie we should
> worry about the rain
>
> huh
> dearie?
> yknow
> i'm
>
> sorry for awl the
> poor girls that
> gets up god
> knows when . . . .[2]

Like Pound, Cummings uses several dialects of English in his poems, his most commonly used one (corresponding to Pound's American Western dialect) being from the Bronx. One of the early examples of Bronx occurs in a poem from VV [ViVa] (1931), where he writes:

---

[1] 'Portraits', IV, *Poems: 1923–1954* (New York: Harcourt, Brace, 1954), p. 87.
[2] 'Portraits', V, ibid., p. 88.

oil tel duh woil doi sez
douyuh unnurs tanmih eesez pullih nizmus tash,oi
dough un giv uh shid oi sez. Tom
oidoughwuntuh doot,butoiguttuh
braikyooz,datswut eesez tuhmih.[1]

A less drunken version of the same dialect occurs later in the same
volume, where Cummings writes about

buncha hardboil guys from duh A.C. fulla
hooch kiddin eachudder bout duh clap an
talkin big how dey could kill
sixereight cops—'I sidesteps im an draws
back huly jeezus'—an—'my
specialty is takin fellers' goils away
frum dem'—. . . .[2]

In the same volume there is a representation of Southern English in
'Lord John Unalive', a poem about an English aristocrat whose
fortune is ascribed to 'the socalled fact that maost faolks rally
demannd canned saounds'.[3] Pound is, of course, always likely to
fall into dialect, either in his letters or in his Cantos. In Canto XIX
he represents himself as saying

Waal haow is it you're over here, right off the Champz Elyza?
And how can yew be here? . . . .[4]

Or in the previous Canto he represents the speech of an English
salesman from the provinces.

Another habit that Cummings owes partly to Pound is his
penchant for indecency, especially for coprology. Pound had some
trouble with his printers and publishers about this matter (there
were lines blacked out in *Blast*, for instance), but even so he seems
to have managed to get a fair amount into print, his most extended
essays being in Cantos XIV and XV. Cummings's troubles began
with *The Enormous Room*, which had to have a four-letter exclama-
tion blacked out before publication.[5] One reason why no publisher
would bring out his *No Thanks* was its coprology; one of the poems
has never yet been printed.[6] Yet Cummings, like Pound, has still

---

[1] 'Portraits' V, p. 224.   [2] Ibid., p. 239.   [3] Ibid.   .   [4] Faber editions, p. 88.
[5] See Norman, op. cit., p. 113.   [6] See ibid., pp. 304–5.

managed to get a good deal printed: his peculiar typographical requirements sometimes conceal the objectionable words.[1]

In his later poems, Cummings developed the technique of offering unpopular opinions in a demagogic way, a technique much used by Pound and Williams. At first the certainty of tone was generally disguised by the use of a dialect or by humour, as in the poem 'economic secu'.[2] But *50 Poems* (1940) and Χαιρε (1950) have a more serious tone, illustrated by the opinion offered in the poem 'a kike is the most dangerous'.[3] The reference to the 'jew' in this quotation is also reminiscent of many of Pound's references, and even of some of Eliot's.

Archibald MacLeish is a far less independent follower of Pound than E. E. Cummings; like Hart Crane, who is also a less independent follower than Cummings, he had little personal knowledge of Pound; and like Crane he was as much influenced by Eliot as by Pound.

MacLeish's first two volumes of poetry, *Tower of Ivory* (1917) and *The Happy Marriage* (1924), were written, quite competently, in an eighteen-ninetyish manner. His acquaintance with Pound's work began when he arrived in Paris in 1923 with the intention of supporting himself by writing. There he met most of the writers mentioned in his poem, 'Sentiments for a Dedication':

> Those of one man's time
> They shall be dead together:
> Dos that saw the tyrants in the lime,
> Ernest that saw the first snow in the fox's feather,
>
> Stephen that saw his wife,
> Cummings his quick fillies,
> Eliot the caul between the ribs of life,
> Pound—Pound cracking the eggs of a cock with the beautiful sword
>   of Achilles.[4]

It is interesting to note that Pound is the only one in this list whose

---

[1] One of his most ingenious disguises is the use of transliteration into Greek characters, as in 'Portraits', IV; *Poems: 1923-1954*, p. 87.

[2] Ibid., p. 341.   [3] Ibid., p. 454.

[4] *Collected Poems: 1917-1952* (Cambridge, Mass.: Houghton Mifflin, 1952), p. 84. 'Dos' is, of course, John Dos Passos; 'Ernest' is Ernest Hemingway; and 'Stephen' is Stephen Vincent Benét.

name causes the poet to pause; then, having repeated the name, he takes longer to characterize him than he had taken with any of the other writers.

The first results of MacLeish's contact with Pound and Eliot were some short poems in the style of T. E. Hulme's Imagist poems, and some pastiches of Eliot. The Imagism can be illustrated by a comparison of Hulme's 'Autumn' with MacLeish's 'March'. Mac-Leish's poem reads:

> Let us think of these
> Winter-stiffened trees
>
> (Posthumously sucking pap
> From the pores of a dead planet
>
> Like the bristles on a butchered pig)
> Every stalk and standing twig
>
> Swollen with delightful sap[1]

This poem has the objectivity and starkness associated with Imagism; the introduction of 'Let us think' would perhaps be avoided by strict Imagists (it is an unnecessary and subjective line), but Hulme introduces 'I' in his poem; in any case, 'think' was a much-used word in MacLeish's poetic vocabulary at the time. The pastiche of Eliot is at its most concentrated in 'L'An trentiesme de mon eage',[2] which, very surprisingly, MacLeish has often republished. The title of the poem, from Arnaut Daniel, had been used by Pound in the first part of *Mauberley*, and had therefore, according to Pound's principles, been forbidden to any other serious modern writer. The Gautier-like stanza form might have come from Pound or from Eliot: the first two stanzas and the last one do not break into two equal parts as Eliot's generally do, but all stanzas lack the lengthening of the line that is typical of Pound. There is a general reminiscence of Eliot in the 'disembodied' sense-impressions, which are given a sub-human quality by being pluralized: MacLeish's 'words', 'faces', 'hands', 'voices', and 'footsteps' correspond to the 'smell of steaks', 'the faint stale smells', 'the hands That are raising dingy shades', 'the yellow soles of feet', and so on of Eliot's 'Preludes'. Then there are specific reminiscences, notably of Eliot's

---

[1] MacLeish, *Collected Poems*, p. 21.   [2] Ibid., p. 15.

favourite imagery of stairs and doors as found in *Prufrock*, 'Portrait of a Lady' (III), *The Waste Land*, and *Gerontion*; the parallel is especially obvious in MacLeish's stanza:

> By voices, by the creak and fall
> Of footsteps on the upper floor,
> By silence waiting in the hall
> Between the doorbell and the door.

In the last line quoted there may also be a reminiscence of a passage in Eliot's *The Hollow Men*, written just before MacLeish's poem:

> Between the idea
> And the reality
> Between the motion
> And the act . . . .[1]

Both the imagism and the pastiche of Eliot recur in MacLeish's poetry throughout his career. The recurrence of imagism is perhaps explained by MacLeish's continuing to believe that.

> A poem should be equal to:
> Not true.
>
> .   .   .   .
>
> A poem should not mean
> But be.[2]

This famous statement comes very close to Pound's notion (set out in his article, 'Vorticism') that the image (and therefore the poem) is an 'equation'; and to the notions of Pound, Williams, Cummings, and others, that the poem is an 'object'. In any case, MacLeish, despite his depreciatory question in 'Invocation to the Social Muse', 'Who recalls the address now of the Imagists?',[3] frequently reverted to the imagist technique. Even in some poems of the nineteen-fifties he uses the technique—in, for instance, 'A Man's Work':

> An apple-tree, a cedar and an oak
> Grow by the stone house in the rocky field
> Where I write poems when my hand's in luck,
> The cedar I put in: the rest are wild—

---

[1] The part of *The Hollow Men* from which this quotation is taken, Part V, was not printed until the poem appeared as a whole in *Poems 1909–1925*, published on 6 January 1926. But MacLeish's poem is later than this: it was first published under the title 'In my thirtieth year' in *The Saturday Review of Literature*, II (3 July 1926), p. 897.

[2] 'Ars Poetica'; *Collected Poems*, p. 41.   [3] *Collected Poems*, p. 94.

N

> Wind dropped them. Apples strew the autumn ground
> With black, sweet-smelling pips. The oak strews air,
> Summers with shadow, winters with harsh sound.
> The cedar's silent with its fruit to bear;[1]

or in the 'one-image' poem:

AUTUMN
Sun smudge on the smoky water[2]

Most of his plays, too, show signs of imagist technique. Like *Murder in the Cathedral*, and like some parts of Eliot's other plays, MacLeish's plays concentrate on the presentation of an emotion or an impression rather than on the presentation of an action. Even *Panic*, which contains a good deal of melodramatic action in the stage directions, has an imagistic stillness in most scenes. It is interesting that Pound considered Imagism and Vorticism to be applicable to plays; he said that

The Japanese, who evolved the hokku, evolved also the Noh plays. In the best 'Noh' the whole play may consist of one image. I mean it is gathered about one image. Its unity consists in one image, enforced by movement and music.[3]

Pastiche of Eliot occurs in several comparatively late poems. The wheel imagery at the beginning of 'Pole Star' seems to owe something to the same imagery used in *Murder in the Cathdral*. In his play, Eliot had used the lines:

> For good or ill, let the wheel turn.
> The wheel has been still, these seven years, and no good.
> For ill or good, let the wheel turn;

and

> that the wheel may turn and still
> Be forever still.[4]

The play was first published in an edition for general circulation in June 1935. In the issue of *The New Republic* for 1 January 1936, MacLeish had a poem, then entitled 'Pole Star for this Year', which began:

> Where the wheel of light is turned,

[1] *Collected Poems*, p. 156.   [2] Ibid., p. 153.   [3] 'Vorticism', loc. cit., p. 471 n.
[4] *Murder in the Cathedral*, pp. 18, 21.

> Where the axle of the night is
> Turned, is motionless, where holds
> And has held ancient sureness always . . . .[1]

In the nineteen-forties he had a poem reminiscent of the section of *The Hollow Men* already quoted; it is 'Tricked by Eternity the Heart', which contains the lines:

> Between the cause and the effect,
> Time, like the custom of the street,
> Teaches our eyes till they expect
> What is no longer theirs to meet . . . .[2]

From the same period, 'The Spanish Lie' is highly reminiscent of *The Hollow Men* and of *Ash-Wednesday*. Finally, in the early nine-teen-fifties there is a poem with the title, 'Hypocrite Auteur' and the epigraph, '*mon semblable, mon frère*';[3] this has, at any rate, the virtue of obvious and acknowledged irony.

MacLeish's chief debt to Pound is in his narrative technique. When Pound tells a story he generally does so through an explicit or implicit 'persona'; he tells it from what the critics of the novel would call a 'point of view'. By this means he manages to convey an atmo-sphere (which often seems contemporary with the story), as well as giving an outline of the plot. Many of his early poems—poems such as 'La Fraisne' or 'Cino'—adopt an explicit 'persona': the emphasis is as much on the character of the narrator as on the anecdotes. (The same technique is used in Eliot's 'Journey of the Magi'.) Later ex-plicit 'personae', such as *Mauberley*, withdraw most of the narrative interest of the early ones and substitute for it an 'ideogrammic' interest. But Pound was a very good story-teller in verse, and he wanted to write long narrative passages where an explicit 'persona' would either be an intrusion or else be too slight to sustain the length of narrative that he wanted. On the other hand, he did not want to lose the advantages afforded by a 'persona' in providing an atmosphere. The solution was to use an implicit 'persona': to have the narrative told by a scarcely-named member of a party ('I'), or by the whole party ('we'). This is the technique adopted in many of the long narrative passages of the Cantos: in Canto I, the identity of the

---

[1] *Collected Poems*, p. 99. It was first published in *The New Republic*, LXXXV (1 Janu-ary 1936), p. 224.
[2] *Collected Poems*, p. 134.   [3] Ibid., p. 173.

narrator (Odysseus) is concealed for some time, and the emphasis is on the voyage and the preparation for the voyage; in Canto II, the narrator (Acoetes) does not tell his name for many lines, and the emphasis is on the action, not the narrator; in Canto III, the 'I' of line 1 is not revealed as Ruy Diaz for a considerable time, and the emphasis is on the scene and atmosphere. In passages like this, the important thing for Pound was the action, the setting, and the atmosphere. These were conveyed in a loose syntactical construction, the sentences consisting largely of a series of vivid sensuous details, most of them containing a verb and hence advancing the story.

This kind of narrative was emulated by MacLeish in parts of *The Hamlet of A. MacLeish* (1923), though the result was considerably less incisive and compressed. Bleheris's narrative, for instance, runs thus:

> . . . and all that day
> Seaward and down from ridge to ridge and the
> Pines oak and the oaks birch and the birch trees
> Pine again rooting in coarse sand, the horse track
> Swallowed behind, the jays ahead of me screaming,
> And I by the ridge rode on: and the wind changed with
> Flaws from westward, cold in the sun, and a sound
> Echoing surf from the leaves: and the steep land
> Fell and I saw the sea.
> And by the sea was a ship but no man in her.
> And sail was set on the ship and I led the beast by a
> Rock's bridge and I cut rope and the wind was
> Off shore smelling at first of the furze root,
> Afterward cold: and the boom jibed over and
> She moved, wind in the sail top, rolling to the long
> Swell, the land against the wind, the skystain
> Spilling from trough to trough of the dead waves. . . .[1]

There is even a resemblance between this passage and the opening of Canto 1 in the abbreviated syntax that Pound seems to have thought especially suitable for narratives of sea-faring: Pound's 'Set keel to breakers' and 'we went over sea' correspond to MacLeish's 'I cut rope'; and his 'day's end' corresponds to MacLeish's 'Rock's bridge'.

The same kind of resemblance is found in MacLeish's longest

[1] *Collected Poems*, p. 202.

poem, *Conquistador* (1932). It has been characterized by Robert
McAlmon as 'Eliot's tired old man in April trying to utilize the
technique of Pound's Cantos in a poem on the conquest of Mexico',[1]
and there is some truth in this. The 'persona' adopted for the narration is something like that of *Gerontion*, or perhaps more accurately
of 'Journey of the Magi'; and the technique does owe a good deal to
the technique of narration in the Cantos, though not to the ideogrammic method. The narrative technique is very similar to that in
The Hamlet; The Second Book, for instance, begins:

> . . . So
> Sailed we out from the Island to Cozumél:
> Winter it was and wind and a swell rolling
>
> And the stain of the foam on the long flank of the swells:
> And they gave us the signals for night with the swung lanterns
> And the chains came in: foul with the tatters of kelp:
>
> And the bow fell off from the wind and the sails slatted:
> Shaking aloft: filling the bunt: the sea furrow
> Following under the drawn keel . . . .[2]

In this passage the alliteration of some of the lines and the inversions of 'Sailed we out' and 'Winter it was' are reminiscent of the
special narrative style of 'The Seafarer'. In other parts of the poem
there are lines where the pattern of alliteration is quite similar to
that of 'The Seafarer'; later in The Second Book, for instance,
there are the lines:

> the sea-glare and the sunward glass:
> And we stood west on the wind and the seventh morning
> Wore ship to a shuffle of air and she slacked and the
> Sea was brown and the bog-root on the water;[3]

The Fifth Book has 'Hurt and the halt and the traitors at heart and
their corpses!'[4] and The Sixth Book:

> Meagerest burden of beggars our backs had:
> And we ate of the grain of the grass for our mouths' meat.[5]

Conquistador also essays Pound's epistolary style of narration.

---

[1] Robert McAlmon, *Being Geniuses Together: An Autobiography*, p 339.
[2] *Collected Poems*, p. 253.   [3] Ibid., p. 259.   [4] Ibid., p. 275.   [5] Ibid., p. 279.

Large sections of the Cantos, especially those dealing with Renaissance or early American material, are made up of real or imaginary letters. In *Conquistador*, MacLeish quotes in a very similar manner:

> And Velásquez wrote to the said towns and he warned them

> Blaming us all: and as for that shameless man
> Let them arrest the son-of-a-bitch for a traitor
> Shipping him down with the oats or. . . .
>   'given my hand this

> 'Tenth day of December Fifteen Eighteen':
> And they came with the writ in their belts and their mouths dumb:
> And Cortés was an eloquent man: skilled in orations:

> And even the Governor's messenger signed up:
> And the town clerk had a quill in the ink for Velásquez—
> 'That the hare was still as the tuft of a turf till you jumped him:

> 'And the boar a suckling till you bruised his back:
> 'And as for the Captain Cortés—Your Honor's obedient
> 'True man and a loyal tongue and irascible:

> 'And better armed than the Constable's guard or the Veedor
> 'And peaceful at heart: and they feared he would burn the town!'
> And they sent that off by a nigger for God speed . . . .[1]

MacLeish's adopted form, perhaps intended to be a very free adaptation of *terza rima*, prevents him from giving the same appearance of a letter as Pound achieves, but all the formalities of a letter are given in the one quoted from Velásquez, and the letter is linked to the narrative by Pound's typical introductory 'And'.

Frescoes for Mr. Rockefeller's City, written in the following year, that is, soon after the first of Pound's Jefferson-Adams Cantos were available, also uses the epistolary form:

> 'To Thos. Jefferson Esq. his obd't serv't
> Mr. Lewis: captain: detached:
>   Sir:

> Having in mind your repeated commands in this matter,
> And the worst half of it done and the streams mapped . . . .[2]

---

[1] *Collected Poems*, p. 252.   [2] Ibid., p. 74.

In this example MacLeish has even used the abbreviations that are almost the trade-mark of Pound's letters. As T. C. Wilson said at the time, 'This is simply an obvious imitation of a device which Pound has used brilliantly in portions of the *Cantos*, and Mr. Mac-Leish ought to be ashamed.'[1]

One would expect that a long poem written by a poet so much under the influence of Pound and Eliot as MacLeish would make use of the ideogrammic method. In fact, however, *Conquistador* and MacLeish's other long poems have either a narrative or a 'philosophic' structure. MacLeish was content with borrowing material (in the Eliot pastiches; in *Frescoes for Mr. Rockefeller's City*; and in *Elpenor*, which uses some of Pound's Odysseus material) and the more easily learnt tricks of style. He is, in fact, one of the least intelligent of Pound's imitators, and an excellent example of the conflation of Pound's influence with Eliot's.

It may seem strange that in discussing five poets who have all been at least slightly influenced by Pound's Imagism, I have said little about the third point of the Imagist Manifesto, 'As regarding rhythm: to compose in sequence of the musical phrase, not in sequence of a metronome.' It may seem especially strange in view of Eliot's statement that 'I cannot think of any one writing verse, of our generation and the next, whose verse (if any good) has not been improved by the study of Pound's'[2]—a statement made immediately before a comparison of Whitman's 'ear' with Pound's; or William Carlos Williams's statement that 'It is impossible to praise Pound's line. The terms for such praise are lacking.'[3] The difficulty is, however, that so much attention has been paid by modern poets to the question of rhythm and verse-structure, so much study of previous models has been done, that it is virtually impossible to disentangle Pound's influence from that of others. In what is probably the major element of rhythmical innovation this century, the movement away from the iambic, many influences have been joined. From the last century there are Whitman, Clough, and Swinburne, from early in

---

[1] 'The Pamphlet Poets', *Poetry*, XLIII, 4 (January 1933), p. 228.

[2] 'Isolated Superiority', *The Dial*, LXXXIV, 1 (January 1928), p. 5.

[3] Letter to James Laughlin, 25 September 1940; *The Selected Letters of William Carlos Williams*, p. 191.

this century Hardy and Bridges, and then, contemporaneous with Pound, there are the influences of Hopkins, Lawrence, Yeats, Eliot, and all those who have learnt from them. It may be possible to isolate Pound's influence from the others', but it is not a task for which I feel competent.

8. THE FRINGES OF INFLUENCE

THE influence of Pound on Yeats and Eliot has been studied in considerable detail; his influence on the poets dealt with in the last chapter in less detail. This chapter attempts to trace the ripples of influence to the point where they are lost in the general turbulence of twentieth-century poetry. At this point there is less advantage to be gained by dealing with poets one by one. What I intend to do instead is to take some of the chief forms of influence that have been noticed in the previous chapters and to show that they also apply to other, generally less important, modern poets.

The most obvious, and perhaps the most important, kind of relationship between Pound and other writers, namely his friendship and his efforts to get their work published, has had its major manifestations described in the early chapters. Many more minor manifestations have, naturally, had to be omitted from this description, and it may be worthwhile to mention one of them now, to underline the extent of Pound's friendship with literary people. The example I have in mind is a minor one because it was confined in time to a period when Pound was having little influence on the London literary scene and was becoming increasingly disgruntled about the fact. This was the period between the end of the First World War and Pound's permanent residence in Paris. Sir Osbert Sitwell recalls dining regularly with Pound, Eliot, Herbert Read, and Wyndham Lewis, and he remarks that Pound's 'kindness was very great to many young authors and artists, but he seldom allowed it to be suspected by its recipients.'[1] Sir Osbert's account of this period suggests, however, that if there was one of the group who made a greater impression than the others, it was not Pound, but Eliot. In his autobiography, Herbert Read gives the same impression: after speaking of the writers that he came to know during the period, he goes on to single out Eliot, who, he says, 'has certainly had a considerable effect on my intellectual development',[2] for more detailed

[1] *Laughter in the Next Room* (London: Macmillan, 1949), p. 32.
[2] *Annals of Innocence and Experience* (London: Faber & Faber, 1940), p. 101.

comment. Read's implicit assessment of the relative influence on him of Pound and Eliot as personal friends is particularly interesting in view of the fact that before he met either of them he seems to have thought more highly of Pound's work than of Eliot's. In speaking of this earlier period in his autobiography he refers to Pound as ' "il miglior fabbro" of us all'.[1] The other main point that Sir Osbert makes about Pound, his unobtrusive kindness to '*les jeunes*', is testified to by another writer who came to know him at this time: Edwin Muir. Muir had come to London in 1919, and seems to have met Pound in the following year while working as assistant to A. R. Orage on *The New Age*. '*The New Age*,' he says, 'had passed its brilliant peak when I joined it. Ezra Pound was still writing for it; I did not see very much of him, but enough to share his spontaneous kindness to writers.'[2]

The poetry of Read and Muir shows traces of the most common kind of literary influence exerted by Pound, namely Imagism. Imagism is a term that must have been applied, by one critic or another, to the youthful productions of almost all twentieth-century poets. In many instances it has been misapplied, most notably, perhaps, to Amy Lowell, D. H. Lawrence, Conrad Aiken, and Wallace Stevens. It is easy to mistake a facility for clear, precise description of natural scenes for Imagism; Imagism certainly includes this facility, but it must be applied to a particular object, not to a scene. Again it is easy to describe as imagistic a poem that begins with an Imagist description of a natural object, but then goes on to speculation or rumination about the significance of the object. Most of the so-called imagist poems of Amy Lowell, Lawrence, Aiken, and Stevens are, in fact, of one of these two closely related types rather than of the true Imagist type.

In Amy Lowell's work the true Imagist type is best represented by a poem called 'The Pond':

> Cold, wet leaves
> Floating on moss-coloured water,
> And the croaking of frogs—
> Cracked bell-notes in the twilight.[3]

---

[1] *Annals of Innocence and Experience*, p. 96.
[2] *An Autobiography* (London: The Hogarth Press, 1954), p. 174.
[3] *The Egoist*, III, 3 (1 March 1916), p. 37.

This is obviously based in structure on poems written earlier by Pound, such as 'April'. But this type of poem is rare in Amy Lowell's work. It is doubtful whether she ever consciously understood Pound's Imagist principles; as Pound said, she 'wants to weaken the whole use of the term imagist, by making it mean *any* writing of vers libre'.[1] But in so far as she approached Imagism she did so because of Pound's mentorship; Eliot even went so far as to say that 'Miss Lowell appears to have nothing that she has not borrowed from Mr. Pound or from Mr. Fletcher.'[2] Because of Pound's mentorship, she began many of her poems with clear, sharp, unotiose descriptions. It is these descriptions that have resulted in her being so frequently classified as an Imagist poet.

Lawrence, who was published by Amy Lowell in *Some Imagist Poets*, was, according to Pound, 'never an Imagist. He was an AMYgist'.[3] Like Lowell, however, he had caught from Pound and from other contemporaries the knack of clear, sharp description, especially as a means of opening a poem.

Aiken was one of the most vociferous critics of the Imagists, writing several condemnatory articles for *The New Republic* and *Poetry*.[4] But he knew many of the Imagists well, wrote most of his poems with the Pre-Raphaelite decoration and languor that appear in some of Pound's early poems, and borrowed a few images and a few conversational idioms from T. S. Eliot. These features have been sufficient for some critics to attach the name 'Imagist' to him. In fact, however, the closest he comes to Imagism is probably in the sharp descriptions of landscape found in parts of his 1931 volume, *Preludes for Memnon*.

Wallace Stevens is another poet who, although only briefly touched by Imagism during its life as a movement, occasionally falls back into an imagistic mode. Like Aiken, too, he frequently has his early verse erroneously classified by critics as imagistic. Marius Bewley, for instance, introduces part of 'Six Significant Landscapes' as 'a charming little Imagist piece hardly beyond Amy Lowell's prowess:

[1] Letter to Harriet Monroe, January 1915; *Letters*, p. 90.
[2] 'London Letter', *The Dial*, LXXII (1922), p. 513.
[3] Letter to Glenn Hughes, 26 September 1927; *Letters*, p. 288.
[4] E.g., 'The Place of Imagism', *The New Republic*, III (22 May 1915), pp. 75–6; 'Limits to Imagism', *The New Republic*, III (26 June 1915), pp. 204–5; see also Harriet Monroe, *A Poet's Life*, p. 307.

> Rationalists, wearing square hats,
> Think, in square rooms,
> Looking at the floor,
> Looking at the ceiling,
> They confine themselves
> To right-angled triangles.
> If they tried rhomboids,
> Cones, waving lines, ellipses—
> As, for example, the ellipse of the half-moon—
> Rationalists would wear sombreros.'[1]

It is ludicrous to classify this witty, ironic poem as imagistic, but one can understand how Bewley made the mistake. There has been a tradition in American criticism that Stevens began his adult poetic career as an Imagist. This is, in fact, true, but the evidence is not where one would expect to find it, that is, in Stevens's first volume, *Harmonium*, or in the *Collected Poems*. Stevens went to some trouble to suppress his Imagist origins by omitting from *Harmonium* the early poems, mostly printed in *Poetry*, that had caused him to be regarded as an Imagist. But critics who are aware of the tradition— having heard it, quite likely from unimpeachable sources—have been prone to seize on the poems of *Harmonium*, which was for several years Stevens's only volume, as offering evidence for his Imagism.

The real evidence was not reprinted until *Opus Posthumous* appeared (New York: Alfred A. Knopf, 1957). Here were published the poems that had originally appealed to Harriet Monroe as the work of a new Imagist. Her judgement was obviously based on such passages as

> There's a cab-horse at the corner,
> There's rain. The season grieves.
> It was silver once,
> And green with leaves;

and

> The vaguest line of smoke (a year ago)
> Wavered in evening air, above the roof . . . .[2]

---

[1] 'The Poetry of Wallace Stevens', in *The Complex Fate: Hawthorne, Henry James and Some Other American Writers* (London: Chatto & Windus, 1952), p. 172. Bernard Heringman says much the same in his doctoral dissertation, 'Wallace Stevens: The Reality of Poetry' (Columbia, 1955), pp. 76–7.

[2] *Opus Posthumous*, ed. Samuel French Morse (New York: Alfred A. Knopf, 1957), pp. 3, 5.

Both of these extracts are from 'Phases', of which Miss Monroe printed four parts (not including the second extract) in the November 1914 issue of *Poetry*. Other poems in an imagistic style appeared in *Poetry* and other periodicals shortly afterwards, and they too were omitted from *Harmonium* and the *Collected Poems*. From the work of subsequent years, the poem that probably comes closest to pure Imagism is one printed in the October 1919 issue of *Poetry*, 'The Indigo Glass in the Grass':

> Which is real—
> This bottle of indigo glass in the grass,
> Or the bench with the pot of geraniums, the stained
>   mattress and the washed overalls drying in
>   the sun?
> Which of these truly contains the world?
> Neither one, nor the two together.[1]

This poem also was omitted from *Harmonium* and the *Collected Poems*. Even much later than this Stevens would occasionally fall back into the Imagist style in order to achieve a clearness and hardness of detailed description. Perhaps the best example occurs at the beginning of 'The Poems of Our Climate':

> Clear water in a brilliant bowl,
> Pink and white carnations. The light
> In the room more like snowy air,
> Reflecting snow. A newly-fallen snow
> At the end of winter when afternoons return.
> Pink and white carnations—one desires
> So much more than that. The day itself
> Is simplified: a bowl of white,
> Cold, a cold porcelain, low and round,
> With nothing more than the carnations there.[2]

On the whole, however, Stevens rejected the principles of Imagism in favour of an abstract, metaphysical approach quite opposed to Imagism.

The two great practitioners of pure Imagism have, of course, been H.D. and Richard Aldington. As Pound discovered them writing poems that he described as examples of 'Imagisme', there might

---

[1] Ibid., p. 22.
[2] From *Parts of a World* (1942); *The Collected Poems of Wallace Stevens* (London: Faber & Faber, 1955), p. 193.

seem to be not much point in considering their work as being influenced by him. Yet it should be remembered that Pound had
given H.D. some help as an author before she wrote her imagistic
poems. He was, nevertheless, rather surprised—'worked up', as
Aldington puts it,[1] when he first saw these poems. This excitement
was due partly, of course, to Pound's normal interest in good work;
but it was also due partly, I suggest, to astonishment at a coincidence. The coincidence was that H.D. and Aldington, working
together, had arrived at the same technique for conveying the impression of classical poetry as he had, working independently. This
conjecture of Pound's astonishment at a coincidence is not easy to
substantiate, but there is some evidence for it. In the first place,
Pound's excitement undoubtedly had something to do with the
'classical' quality of H.D.'s verse; in sending the poems to Harriet
Monroe, he wrote:

I've had luck again, and am sending you some *modern* stuff by an
American, I say modern, for it is in the laconic speech of the Imagistes,
even if the subject is classic. At least H.D. has lived with these things
since childhood, and knew them before she had any book-knowledge of
them.

This is the sort of American stuff that I can show here and in Paris
without its being ridiculed. Objective—no slither; direct—no excessive
use of adjectives, no metaphors that won't permit examination. It's
straight talk, straight as the Greek! And it was only by persistence that
I got to see it at all.[2]

In the second place, Aldington and H.D. were writing in a very
similar style. When he wrote the letter just quoted, Pound had
already sent to *Poetry* three poems of Aldington's, 'Choricos', 'To
a Greek Marble', and 'Au Vieux Jardin', which were published
in the November 1912 number.[3] Between these and the first poems
of H.D. to be printed in *Poetry* there are unmistakable similarities.
Both poets have chosen Greek subjects, both write in free verse,
both use strong visual images, and both use oratorical constructions
and archaic diction. These features can be seen in an extract from
Aldington's 'To a Greek Marble':

[1] 'Farewell to Europe', *The Atlantic Monthly*, CLXVI (1940), p. 527.
[2] October 1912; *Letters*, p. 45.
[3] See Harriet Monroe, *A Poet's Life*, p. 262.

I have whispered thee in thy solitudes
Of our loves in Phrygia,
The far ecstasy of burning noons
When the fragile pipes
Ceased in the cypress shade,
And the brown fingers of the shepherd
Moved over slim shoulders;
And only the cicada sang.

I have told thee of the hills
And the lisp of reeds
And the sun upon thy breasts,

And thou hearest me not,
Potnia, Potnia,
Thou hearest me not.[1]

H.D.'s 'Priapus: Keeper-of-Orchards' has the same features:

O rough-hewn
God of the orchard,
I bring thee an offering;
Do thou, alone unbeautiful
(Son of the god),
Spare us from loveliness.

The fallen hazel-nuts,
Stripped late of their green sheaths,
The grapes, red-purple,
Their berries
Dripping with wine,
Pomegranates already broken,
And shrunken fig,
And quinces untouched,
I bring thee an offering.[2]

There are differences between the two poets, of course. H.D. is
more fecund than Aldington in the production of images, and her
images are harder and clearer; her tone (at least in comparison with
his softness and romanticism) is at times almost brutal; and her use
of the refrain or response is a less obvious device than his repetition
of syntax and phrase. But the similarities are more striking than the
differences, and this fact must have been observed by Pound. The

[1] *Poetry*, I, 2 (November 1912), p. 42.   [2] *Poetry*, I, 4 (January 1913), pp. 121–2.

third piece of evidence for Pound's hypothetical astonishment is the marked similarity between the style of Aldington's and H.D.'s Greek poems on the one hand, and his own most recent Greek style on the other. Pound's Greek style is best exemplified by 'The Return', which was published in the 1912 volume, *Ripostes*. Its combination of jewelled and prosaic words, and something of its delicacy and variety of rhythm are paralleled in the work of H.D., and, to a lesser degree, of Aldington. H.D.'s 'Hermes of the Ways', for instance, forms a close parallel to 'The Return'; it reads:

> But more than the many-foamed ways
> Of the sea,
> I know him
> Of the triple path-ways,
> Hermes,
> Who awaiteth.
>
> Dubious,
> Facing both ways,
> Welcoming wayfarers,
> He whom the sea orchard
> Shelters from the west,
> From the east
> Weathers sea-wind;
> Fronts the great dunes.
>
> Wind rushes
> Over the dunes,
> And the coarse, salt-crusted grass
> Answers.
>
> Heu,
> It whips around my ankles![1]

In this poem there are smaller details, too, that correspond to Pound's style. There are the compound adjectives, for instance: H.D.'s 'many-foamed', 'Of the triple path-ways', and 'salt-crusted' correspond to Pound's use in 'The Return' of ' "Wing'd-with-Awe" ', 'swift to harry', and 'keen-scented'. Or again, the placement of 'Dubious' corresponds to Pound's placement of 'Inviolable'.

The resemblances between the work of H.D. and Aldington on the one hand, and Pound on the other are surprising, particularly if,

[1] *Poetry*, I,4 (January 1913), pp. 118–19.

as Pound apparently believed, they were achieved without cross-influence. It is possible, of course, that H.D. and Aldington had learnt from Pound's published work without telling him about it, and without admitting it subsequently in their memoirs. One cannot be certain of this. But what one can be certain of is that Pound inaugurated or revived a school of Imagism in order to gain attention for their work, and that his efforts in organization, publicity, and publication caused them to concentrate for virtually the rest of their productive lives on the elements of Imagism that he pointed out in their early work. Aldington became, perhaps, the staunchest advocate that the doctrine of Imagism had, and both he and H.D. began deliberately to write pure Imagist poems.

H.D.'s 'Storm' is one of the best examples of a pure Imagist poem. It is full of clear, vivid images devoted to a single subject.

I

You crash over the trees
you crack the live branch:
the branch is white,
the green crushed,
each leaf is rent like split wood.

II

You burden the trees
with black drops,
you swirl and crash:
you have broken off a weighted leaf
in the wind—
it is hurled out,
whirls up and sings,
a green stone.[1]

In a typical Imagist manner, the subject of the storm is reduced to individual vivid details, which are set down without comment, and the poem ends with the familiar superimposed image ('a green stone') so commonly found in Pound's Imagist poems.

Aldington has written a good many poems simply labelled 'Images'. These include examples of all the familiar types of Imagist poem. I shall quote just one example, an example on the model of

o   [1] *Poetry*, V, 6 (March 1915), p. 266.

Pound's poem, 'The Bath Tub'. Aldington's poem, it will be noticed, represents a considerable debasement of the model:

> The blue smoke leaps
> Like swirling clouds of birds vanishing.
> So my love leaps forth towards you,
> Vanishes and is renewed.[1]

It was the somewhat limited forms and themes represented by 'The Storm' and 'Images' that Pound's influence brought to the forefront of H.D's and Aldington's work. His interposition directed their attention to what had been one of several notable features of their early work, and caused them to concentrate on that feature almost to the exclusion of the others. His influence on the direction of their work could be considered good or bad, depending on one's opinions about the worth of Imagism as a principle for writing poetry.

Aldington and H.D. form, with Eliot and Williams, and such minor poets as F. S. Flint and Skipwith Cannéll, the first generation of Poundian Imagists. Later, when Imagism as a movement was dead, poets who came to know Pound often tried their hand at Imagism. Occasionally, at the time of *The Exile* or *Active Anthology* for instance, they almost formed a group, but these collective demonstrations of neo-Imagism are generally less interesting than isolated examples in individual poets.

One poet who was a few years too late to join in the original Imagist movement was Herbert Read. He has acknowledged the lasting impression made on him by Imagist doctrines. During the years 1913 to 1917, he says, 'I quickly evolved what I would have called my philosophy of composition',[2] one that was based on the six points of the preface to *Some Imagist Poets*. Some idea of the strength of this 'philosophy of composition' can be gained from Read's statement that

The years to follow held such surprises as Rimbaud and Apollinaire, Hölderlin and Rilke, but though such poets have deepened my conception of the content of poetry, they have not altered the attitude to the problems of technique which I formed under the influence of the Imagists.[3]

---

[1] *Poetry*, VII, 1 (October 1915), p. 23.
[2] *Annals of Innocence and Experience* (London: Faber & Faber, 1940), p. 97.
[3] Ibid., p. 94.

The earliest of his poems written under this influence were dated
1915. In that year, he says,

I was already writing in the imagist manner, and from the Front I sent to
the *Gryphon*, the students' magazine at Leeds, various contributions of
which the earliest must have been written within the first few weeks of
my war experience. They are, as imagist poems should be, coldly objective. The following is an impression of Ypres:

> With a chill and hazy light
>   the sun of a winter noon
>   swills
>   thy ruins.
>
> Thy ruins etched
>   in silver silhouettes
>   against a turquoise sky.
>
> Lank poles leap to the infinite
>   their broken wires
>   tossed like the rat-locks of Maenades.
>
> And Desolation broods over all
>   gathering to her lap
>   her leprous children.
>
> The sparrows whimper
>   amid the broken arches.[1]

This example is not sufficiently concentrated on the image and is
too abstract to be regarded as pure Imagism. In later poems Read
managed to achieve the fashionable concentration on the image,
but I doubt whether he ever entirely rid himself of his fondness for
abstract thought. Even a poem that looks very much like a Japanese
haiku (and is in fact remarkably similar to one of Amy Lowell's
poems quoted earlier in this chapter) ends with a non-Imagistic
line:

THE POND

> Shrill green weeds
> float on the black pond.

---

[1] Ibid., p. 154.

> A rising fish
> ripples the still water
>
> And disturbs my soul.[1]

When Read's poems do not have an overt abstraction like this, they present some other feature that is non-Imagistic. 'Woodlands', for instance, has traces of symbolism and of ninetyish diction:

> Pine needles cover the silent ground:
> pine trees chancel the woodland ways.
>
> We penetrate into the dark depths
> where only garlic and hemlock grow
> Till we meet the blue stream
> cleaving the green
> twilight like a rhythmic sword.[2]

After the initial phase of Imagism in his work, the phase represented by the 'Eclogues' of 1914–1918, Read turned increasingly towards symbolism and the possibilities of musical form. T. S. Eliot's images and rhythms were generally of more use to him than Pound's. Eliot, who remained in London, became a much closer friend than Pound, who went to Paris and Rapallo and who, in any case, probably felt that Read had never taken enough trouble to apprentice himself to the craft of poetry.

From Aldington and H.D., original members of Pound's Imagist movement who remained basically loyal to the creed for most of their lives, through a second-generation Imagist like Read, who remained not quite so loyal, the Imagist tradition descended to the unimportant extremists that Pound encouraged during his years at Rapallo,[3] and to several poets who make occasional use of the technique. To illustrate the occasional use of the technique, I wish to cite six poets in all, three American, two British, and one Australian.

The oldest of the three Americans is Robinson Jeffers, who has had little personal contact with other writers, being almost a recluse for all his writing life. His rustic isolation has sharpened his appreciation of natural detail, which finds its way into many of his poems. The result is something that is virtually Imagism, though it may

---

[1] Read, *Collected Poems* (London: Faber & Faber, 1946), p. 18.   [2] Ibid., p. 16.
[3] See Chapter 4.

have been arrived at independently of any influence. His poem, 'Night', for instance, opens with a stanza of Imagism:

> The ebb slips from the rock, the sunken
> Tide-rocks lift streaming shoulders
> Out of the slack, the slow west
> Sombering its torch; a ship's light
> Shows faintly, far out,
> Over the weight of the prone ocean
> On the low cloud.[1]

Like most poets who are not convinced Imagists, however, Jeffers goes on to evaluate the experience that he has described.

The publication of Charles Olson's poetry has been almost contemporaneous with the revival of interest in Pound after the Second World War. In doctrine, as the promoter of what he calls 'Projective Verse', Olson is very much in the tradition of Imagism and Objectivism.[2] Some parts of his doctrine are even more obscurely expressed than Objectivism, but it is clear that he believes in something like 'Vorticism', the doctrine of the moving image. In a letter he states:

Image, therefore, is vector. It carries the trinity via the double to the single form which one makes oneself able, if so, to issue from the 'content' (multiplicity: originally, and repetitively, chaos—Tiamat: wot the Hindo-Europeans knocked out by giving the Old Man (Juice himself) all the lightning.[3]

The best example of the image appearing in his work is probably his set of 'Variations done for Gerald Van de Wiele', which begins with a series of images:

> dogwood flakes
> what is green
>
> the petals
> from the apple
> blow on the road

---

[1] *Roan Stallion, Tamar, and Other Poems* (New York: The Modern Library, 1935), p. 84.

[2] See his 'Projective Verse', *Poetry New York*, No. 3 (1950), pp. 13 ff. Reprinted in *The New American Poetry 1945–1960*, ed. Donald M. Allen (New York: Grove Press; London: Evergreen Books, 1960), pp. 386–97, together with a letter offering further elucidation, pp. 397–400.

[3] *The New American Poetry*, p. 399.

mourning doves
mark the sway
of the afternoon, bees
dig the plum blossoms

the morning
stands up straight, the night
is blue from the full of the April moon

iris and lilac, birds
birds, yellow flowers
white flowers, the Diesel
does not let up dragging
the plow

               as the whippoorwill,
the night's tractor, grinds
his song . . . .[1]

This is set down in the manner of Olson's chief model, William
Carlos Williams, rather than in the fashionable style of classical
Imagism, but it could obviously be rearranged in the Imagist
style; the last three lines quoted, for example, could be set down as

The whippoorwill grinds his song:
The night's tractor.

Edward Dorn, a younger American poet, who came under Olson's
influence at Black Mountain College, also uses a technique approaching Imagism. His 'Vaquero' is, in fact, pure Imagism:

The cowboy stands beneath
a brick-orange moon. The top
of his oblong head is blue, the sheath
of his hips
is too.

In the dark brown night
your delicate cowboy stands quite still.
His plain hands are crossed.
His wrists are embossed white.

[1] *The New American Poetry*, pp. 34–5.

> In the background night is a house,
> has a blue chimney top,
> Yi Yi, the cowboy's eyes
> are blue. The top of the sky
> is too.[1]

Probably the only reason this poem would not be mistaken for a first-generation Imagist poem is that it is trying to do a little more than the early Imagist poems: 'plain', for instance, is obviously used with an awareness of Empson.

The first of the British writers of Imagist poems that I want to mention is the Scottish poet William Soutar. He has written many short poems labelled 'Epigrams' which are almost always Imagist in form and in arrangement on the page. When these poems are sensory in content, the result is pure Imagism, as in 'Whiteness', 'Immanency', 'Summer Snow', 'The Quiet Return', and 'The Butterfly'.[2] 'Immanency' and 'The Butterfly' give a good indication of his style:

IMMANENCY

> Under
> A clouded sky
> The radiance of the sun
> Brightens from earth in the still flame
> Of flowers.

THE BUTTERFLY

> Full sail
> The butterfly,
> With hurrying unhaste,
> Lightly surmounts the silent surge
> Of air.

Soutar was bed-ridden for most of his productive life, and so is unlikely to have met many Imagists. He was befriended, however, by Hugh MacDiarmid, who knew and approved of a good deal of Pound's work.[3]

---

[1] Ibid., p. 98.

[2] *Collected Poems*, ed. with introductory essay by Hugh MacDiarmid (London: Andrew Dakers, 1948), pp. 316, 319, 323, 325, 326.

[3] MacDiarmid himself wrote a few Imagist poems; see, for instance, 'Cattle Show' and 'The Skeleton of the Future', selected by Yeats for *The Oxford Book of Modern Verse* (Oxford: Clarendon Press, 1936), p. 325.

The Welsh poet, R. S. Thomas, has a similar eye for natural detail, which he incorporates occasionally in a brief Imagist poem, such as 'January':

> The fox drags its wounded belly
> Over the snow, the crimson seeds
> Of blood burst with a mild explosion,
> Soft as excrement, bold as roses.
>
> Over the snow that feels no pity,
> Whose white hands can give no healing,
> The fox drags its wounded belly.[1]

Finally in this brief discussion of latter-day Imagism I want to mention one Australian poet, Ronald McCuaig, whose *Vaudeville* (Sydney: privately printed, 1938) showed that he had read Pound and Eliot very carefully. What might otherwise have been Imagism in his poetry is conflated with a diluted form of Eliot's Laforguian irony. 'The Razor' and 'The Cheque' come fairly close to the type of poem written by T. E. Hulme:

THE RAZOR

> Edged with incuriosity
> Whom it cuts, or if, or why,
> Her beauty is a lazy razor
> Drawn across the brain that has her;
> Death so alive is mere illusion
> So is her beauty, which, being gone,
> Stays as a razor, cold and jagged,
> Lazily over the brain is dragg'd.[2]

There is obviously in this poem more of Laforgue than of Imagism, but I doubt whether at the time he wrote it McCuaig was aware that he was assimilating two very different traditions from Pound and Eliot. It is a good poem with which to finish this survey of Imagism, for it shows Imagism losing its character under the influence of one of the other forces in twentieth-century poetry.

Pound's notion of ideogrammic form has been far less widely received than his notion of Imagism. It requires a poem of some length for its application, and poems of some length are popularly

---

[1] *The New Poetry*, ed. with introd. A. Alvarez (Harmondsworth, Middlesex: Penguin, 1962), p. 58.

[2] *Quod Ronald McCuaig* (Sydney: Angus & Robertson, 1946), p. 28.

supposed to have been avoided by twentieth-century poets. Yet the most influential poem of the twentieth century, *The Waste Land*, is long enough to have employed the technique, and many poems of similar length have been written. But although there seems to have been widespread dissatisfaction with the traditional techniques for the long poem—the narrative, the dramatic, and the philosophic— few poets have attempted to follow Pound's method. Many poets, including Aiken and Auden, have written sequences of poems, each with different material, but all linked by a common theme; the individual poems have, however, been intelligible (and antholo-gizable) on their own, and they have not been preoccupied with presenting data, and setting it alongside data from radically different fields. The experiments with musical form made by Aiken, Herbert Read, and others are non-ideogrammic for similar reasons: the poems written have been too lyrical and not factual enough. Some poets have written long poems that have been either continuous, or separable only into a few long sections; these, however, have generally been narrative or philosophic in structure, with references backward and forward between the sections: Wallace Stevens's 'Credences of Summer', for instance, presents a complex of thought through the very simple basic structure of a landscape poem.[1]

Basil Bunting is one of the few poets who have genuinely tried to use the ideogrammic technique. In long poems such as 'Chomei at Toyama', Bunting sets down data from various sources, without comment and without transition passages, in the hope that an 'ideogram' will result. In Pound's hands, this technique is able to incorporate the quick poetic flash side by side with the matter-of-fact piece of data, but Bunting does not often succeed with the quick poetic flash. Louis Zukofsky's long poem, *A*, written over almost as long a time as Pound's Cantos, is also largely constructed according to Pound's notion of the ideogram. Some of the contemporary American poets, particularly those who are influenced by William Carlos Williams and Zukofsky, seem to be moving in the direction of the ideogrammic method. Charles Olson, in 'The King-fishers'[2] for

---

[1] A few other examples of non-ideogrammic long poems are Louis MacNeice's *Eclogue from Iceland*, and *Autumn Journal*; Charles Williams's *Taliessin through Logres*, and *The Region of the Summer Stars*; and David Jones's *In Parenthesis* and *The Ana-themata*.

[2] *The New American Poetry*, pp. 2–8.

P

instance, presents a good deal of data from different fields, but some of it is linked together by being made part of a single dramatic monologue. Robert Lowell, a friend of Pound's, sometimes makes tentative use of the method, as in the insertion of the 'Our Lady of Walsingham' section into 'The Quaker Graveyard in Nantucket'.[1]

The type of stanza used by Gautier is, like the technique of Imagism, much more easily assimilable than the ideogrammic method: it requires little practice and little concentration. This stanza form has been used for satire by a few poets who seem to have learnt from Pound. Osbert Sitwell made a good deal of use of it from the time just after the First World War when he and Pound were members of a weekly dinner-party. It is true that he had used the stanza form at least as early as January 1916,[2] when he had little or no acquaintance with Pound, but it was not until after the war that he came to use it with the astringent levity of Pound and Eliot. At the end of the war he seems deliberately to have adopted a spare, satiric mode of writing; in a passage from his Armistice poem, 'How shall we rise to greet the dawn?', a passage that in phraseology is highly reminiscent of T. E. Hulme, he resolves:

> Let us prune the tree of language
> Of its dead fruit
> Let us melt up the clichés
> Into molten metal;
> Fashion weapons that will scald and flay;
> Let us curb this eternal humour
> And become witty.[3]

The result of this resolution was a number of stanzaic poems introducing Mrs. Freudenthal and Mrs. Kinfoot, worthy companions of Eliot's Burbank, Bleistein, and Mr. Apollinax. Sitwell's early Gautier-like poems are as strict as Eliot's: the number of syllables to the line varies very little from a standard eight, and the four lines of the quatrain almost fall into a single couplet; Sitwell even retains the double rhyme. These qualities can be illustrated from the last three stanzas of the first of the Gautier-like poems, 'Nursery Rhyme':

[1] Robert Lowell, *Poems: 1938–1949* (London: Faber & Faber, 1950), pp. 18–24.
[2] See ' "Therefore is the Name of it Called Babel" ', *Collected Satires and Poems of Osbert Sitwell* (London: Duckworth, 1931), pp. 9–10.
[3] Ibid., pp. 37–8.

> Girls who cannot act with grace
> Should learn behaviour; stay at home;
> A convent is the proper place.
> Why not join the Church of Rome?
>
> A waiter nearly drops the tray
> —Twenty tea-cups in one hand.
> Now the band joins in the fray,
> Fighting for the Promised Land.
>
> Mrs. Freudenthal resents
> The scene; and slowly rustles out,
> But the orchestra relents,
> Waking from its fever bout.[1]

The machinery of tea-parties, waiters, and religious imagery appearing in these quoted stanzas, a machinery highly reminiscent of Eliot, is used quite frequently by Sitwell. Later Gautier-like poems relax the strictness of the form by the use of stanzas of long lines; unlike Pound, however, Sitwell does not usually vary the length of line within the stanza, but only from one stanza to the next—this can be illustrated from the last two stanzas of 'Introducing', where there is a sudden change from an eight-syllabled to a ten-syllabled line between the stanzas:

> The arrogant yet gluttonous camel
> Never shows satiety;
> Would rather rest in asphodel
> Than figure in Society,
>
> But Mrs. Kinfoot, spotting a new head
> To add to her collection—grasps her hand,
> And Mrs. Freudenthal is gently led
> Within the portals of the Promised Land.[2]

No other poet has, I think, made such extensive use of Gautier's type of stanza as Sitwell, and his use of it owes more to Eliot than to Pound. It is, however, occasionally used by other poets who have read Eliot, or Pound, or both. John Peale Bishop makes use of it in a form that seems to be borrowed from Eliot, though the subject touches on Pound's political material:

[1] Ibid., p. 40.   [2] Ibid., p. 62.

He squats in Quincy Adams' seat
Dishonourable hulk of hair and bone.
Amazed the planets hear his bleat
Across the spacious microphone.[1]

Ronald Bottrall makes occasional use of a stanza apparently modelled
on Pound's adaptation of Gautier, but his sense of rhythm is too
flaccid, his addiction to 'verse as speech' too ingrained, and his wit
of too discursive a kind to find this form congenial.[2]

There is one other form that has experienced something of a
revival in modern poetry, possibly as a result of Pound's example:
the sestina. After the experiments of Spenser, Sidney, and Drummond of Hawthornden, the sestina was almost a forgotten form in
English until late in the nineteenth century, when Swinburne,
Gosse, and Kipling revived it. Early in his career, Pound was attracted to the form, perhaps because it was invented by Arnaut Daniel,
whom he greatly admired, perhaps because it was enjoying a vogue
at the time. Pound's 'Sestina: Altaforte' may have been partly responsible for suggesting the form to Auden, Eliot, and Bottrall, and
to such minor American writers as John Ashbery, Donald Hall,
Donald Justice, and Richmond Lattimore. Hall's 'Sestina' uses the
same rugged Browning-like tone as Pound's Canto II: 'Hang it all,
Ezra Pound, there is only the one sestina!'[3]

Pound, as has been noticed in the previous chapter, has had some
influence in bringing certain subjects into poetry. The political and
historical material from the early years of the American Constitu-
tion is one of these. Another is economics, especially of the Social
Credit variety; Pound seems to have had some part in infecting
Edwin Muir and Hugh MacDiarmid, and even Osbert Sitwell, with
it. But perhaps the most interesting material that Pound has helped
to make fashionable is the sea and sea-voyaging. His first poem on

---

[1] 'New England III: The Wonders of Science', *Selected Poems*, introd. Allen Tate
(London: Chatto & Windus, 1960), p. 73.

[2] See, for instance, 'Un Bel Homme du Temps Jadis', in *The Collected Poems of
Ronald Bottrall* (London: Sidgwick & Jackson, 1961), pp. 124–6.

[3] See Auden, 'Kairos and Logos', in *Collected Shorter Poems: 1930–1944* (London:
Faber & Faber, 1960), pp. 25–30; Eliot, 'The Dry Salvages', II; Bottrall, ' "For Our
Time" ', and 'Ritornello', in ed. cit., pp. 87–8, 145–6; Ashbery, *Some Trees* (Yale
Series of Younger Poets; New Haven, Conn.: Yale University Press, ?1955); Hall,
'Sestina', in *The New Poets of England and America*, pp. 96–7; Justice, 'Sestina', ibid.,
pp. 147–8; Lattimore, 'Sestina for a Far-off Summer', in a book of the same title (Ann
Arbor: The University of Michigan Press, 1962), pp. 89–90.

the subject was the highly experimental 'The Seafarer'; then there were the river poems of *Cathay*, and the sea images and references of *Mauberley*; and later the recurring theme of the Odyssean voyage in the Cantos.

Pound's accuracy in sea-faring matters was praised by Hugh MacDiarmid in his autobiography, *Lucky Poet*. After commenting on the unfamiliarity with the sea displayed by most English authors, he wrote:

> This is what Ezra Pound means when he says rightly (in that most admirable book, *How to Read*, which should be required reading for every youth, male and female): 'After Chaucer we have Gavin Douglas' *Eneados*, better than the original, *as Douglas had heard the sea*!' (Italics and exclamation mark mine.)

. . . .

> I would be like Homer, who, while composing Books IX–XI of the *Odyssey*, worked (according to the late M. Victor Berard, 'ce poète de la geographie', as Albert Thibaudet called him in his *La Resurrection d'Homere: Au Temps des Heros* (1930), with a *periplous* or navigation guide for Phoenician sailors before him . . . .[1]

The concept of periplous is one that comes into Pound's Cantos several times, being defined on the first occasion as

> periplum, not as land looks on a map
> but as sea bord seen by men sailing.[2]

It is a concept that, according to MacDiarmid, MacLeish embodied very successfully in the nautical descriptions of *Conquistador*. Mac-Diarmid's own desire to 'be like Homer' has resulted in a fair amount of poetry and prose about the sea. What he probably had in mind when he wrote the words in *Lucky Poet* was his prose commentary to *The Islands of Scotland: Hebrides, Orkneys, and Shetlands* (London: Batsford, 1939), published a few years before. Poetry from all stages of his career has imagery of the sea in it,[3] but in only one early poem can any trace of Pound's influence be seen;

---

[1] *Lucky Poet: A Self-Study in Literature and Political Ideas* being the autobiography of Hugh MacDiarmid (Christopher Murray Grieve) (London: Methuen, 1943), pp. 57–8.

[2] Canto LIX, Faber editions, p. 339.

[3] Examples may be found in *Collected Poems of Hugh MacDiarmid* (C. M. Grieve) (Edinburgh and London: Oliver & Boyd, 1962), pp. 14 ('The Man in the Moon'), 75–6 ('Ebb and Flow'), 225–30 ('Shetland Lyrics'), 393–9 ('The Wreck of the *Swan*').

this is ' "U Samago Moria" ',[1] the alliteration and caesuras of which suggest very slightly 'The Seafarer'.

Robert Lowell is another poet who seems to have been impressed by Pound's descriptions of the sea and sea-faring. No doubt the sea imagery of 'The Quaker Graveyard in Nantucket', 'Buttercups', 'In Memory of Arthur Winslow', 'Salem', or 'Mother Marie Therese'[2] is only to be expected of a poet whose father was a naval officer, but what is not to be expected as the result of such a cause is the similarity to the metre of 'The Seafarer', in 'The Quaker Grave-yard', in 'Salem', and in poems about subjects other than the sea, such as 'Christmas Eve under Hooker's Statue', and 'Between the Porch and the Altar', Part I.[3] This similarity is partly a matter of using ten-syllabled alliterative lines—lines such as

> When the drowned sailor clutched the drag-net. Light
> Flashed from his matted head and marble feet

or

> Off 'Sconset, where the yawing S-boats splash

in 'The Quaker Graveyard'; or

> In Salem seasick spindrift drifts or skips

or

> There sewage sickens the rebellious seas

in 'Salem'; or

> A cannon and a cairn of cannon balls

or

> His stocking is full of stones. Santa in red

in 'Christmas Eve'; or

> Meeting his mother makes him lose ten years,
> Or is it twenty? Time, no doubt, has ears

in 'Between the Porch and the Altar'. By themselves, however, such lines indicate only a minor influence from Pound, for they do not occur very often, they lack strong caesuras, and their pattern of

---

[1] *Selected Poems of Hugh MacDiarmid*, ed. Oliver Brown (Glasgow: William Maclel-lan for The Scottish Secretariat, 1954), p. 16.

[2] *Poems: 1938–1949* (London: Faber & Faber, 1950), pp. 18–24, 28, 29–32, 36, 87–90.

[3] Ibid., pp. 27, 51.

alliteration is not very strict. But in 'The Quaker Graveyard' there are two other features that seem to have been borrowed from Pound. The first is the occasional short line; the quotation given above, for instance, goes on

> When the drowned sailor clutched the drag-net. Light
> Flashed from his matted head and marble feet,
> He grappled at the net
> With the coiled, hurdling muscles of his thighs:
> The corpse was bloodless, a botch of reds and whites,
> Its open, staring eyes
> Were lustreless dead-lights . . . .

The second is the use of kennings of the same type as Pound's 'whale's acre' and 'whale-path'; Lowell uses 'earth-shaker' and 'whaleroad'. ('Earth-shaker' is obviously a kenning for 'whale'; but 'whaleroad', which ought, if Anglo-Saxon principles were followed, to mean 'sea', in fact seems to mean the 'road' or life of the whale in the phrase 'the end of the whaleroad'.)

Because it is known that Lowell was aware of Pound's work,[1] one can suggest influence by Pound with some probability. With W. H. Auden and with Cecil Day Lewis there cannot be the same probability. Auden's 'Doom is dark and deeper than any sea-dingle' and most of *The Age of Anxiety* are written in imitation of the Anglo-Saxon metre, as are Day Lewis's Poem 12 in *From Feathers to Iron* and 'A Time to Dance'.[2] Both poets may have arrived at this metre without drawing on Pound's example at all, but if so it is strange that Auden should resemble Pound in using so many hyphenated nonce words—such as 'sea-dingle', 'day-wishing', 'cloud-soft', and so on, corresponding to examples in Pound's work like 'breast-cares' and 'sea-surge'—and in using occasional short non-alliterating lines; and it is also strange that both Auden and Day Lewis should resemble Pound in their condensed and inverted syntax, and in the 'disembodied' quality of their sensuous detail.

Eliot, Lowell, Auden, and Day Lewis indicate the type of influence exerted on twentieth-century poetry, directly or indirectly, through 'The Seafarer'. A few other poets have been influenced in

[1] See *The Selected Letters of William Carlos Williams*, p. 324.
[2] See W. H. Auden, *Collected Shorter Poems*, pp. 49–50; *The Age of Anxiety: A Baroque Eclogue* (London: Faber & Faber, 1948), p. 20; *Collected Poems of C. Day Lewis* (London: Jonathan Cape with The Hogarth Press, 1954), pp. 61, 141–57.

their original verse by the Anglo-Saxon metres, sometimes, but by
no means always, through Pound. The American poet, W. S. Merwin, who has other affinities with Pound, uses most of Pound's 'Seafarer' devices in his 'Leviathan'. In the lines quoted below, one can
see a fairly strict ten-syllabled alliterative form with strong caesuras;
loosely connected syntax that contains condensation and inversion;
and a frequent use of kennings:

> This is the black sea-brute bulling through wave-wrack,
> Ancient as ocean's shifting hills, who in sea-toils
> Travelling, who furrowing the salt acres
> Heavily, his wake hoary behind him, ...
>
> .   .   .   .
>
> First created he was of all creatures,
> He has held Jonah three days and nights,
> He is that curling serpent that in ocean is, ...[1]

Merwin was probably influenced by Pound, whereas Kingsley
Amis, who uses in his 'Beowulf'[2] some of the alliterative devices
and terminological clichés of Anglo-Saxon verse, was probably not.

A more obvious and more pervasive kind of influence stemming
from several sources, including Pound, is the allusiveness, and the
frequency of quotation found in much twentieth-century poetry.
Some examples show little advance on the use made of these devices
by Browning. Carl Sandburg, for instance, commonly uses quotations from newspaper reports that are so typical and self-explanatory
that no reference to the source need be given: his method of using
quotation is similar to Browning's, but rather more extensive; he
begins one poem, for instance, with

> 'The kindest and gentlest here are the
>   murderers,' said the penitentiary warden.
> 'I killed the man because I loved him,'
>   said the woman the police took yesterday.
> 'I had such a good time,' said the woman leaving a
>   movie theater with tears in her eyes. 'It was a swell picture.'
> 'A divorced man goes and marries the same kind of
>   a woman he is just rid of,' said the lawyer.[3]

[1] *The New Poets of England and America*, ed. Donald Hall, Robert Pack, and Louis
Simpson (New York: Meridian Books, 1957), pp. 220–1.

[2] *The New Poetry*, ed. A. Alvarez, p. 85.

[3] Sandburg, *The People, Yes* (New York: Harcourt, Brace, 1936), Poem 23, p. 42.

At the other extreme, Hugh MacDiarmid's use of both allusion and quotation is very far in advance of Browning's use, and owes a good deal to the example of Pound. MacDiarmid's own account of his method is that 'I began to write very long poems, abounding in phrases from many foreign languages and packed with literary and scientific allusions of all kinds.'[1] The poem to which these words form part of the introduction is a very long one about words and languages, and about MacDiarmid's personal experiences with them. It comes closest to Pound in passages like the following, with its learnedness and its (perhaps irrelevant) aside:

> All poetry lost in the *guorguolacadas*,
> As Dom João de Castro might have written,
> Of some fantastic Ogpufbi world of Basic Grunters
> (What threatens ethnography we agree
> Is to be darkly stifled
> Under a clotted jumble of facts
> Like sociology in America
> Where a horrible mixture of 'applied sociology'
> And its theoretical justification
> Has utterly buried the meagre theory,
> Giving birth to a malignant tumour
> Of half-educated people. Our ideal ethnological method
> May be fairly called the ecological one.)[2]

Somewhere between the extreme belligerence of MacDiarmid and the conventionality of Sandburg lies the usage of poets like the American, Philip Whalen. His poem, 'Sourdough Mountain Lookout', offers examples not much more advanced than Sandburg, like

> Mr. Edward Wyman (63)
> Steams along the trail ahead of us all
> Moaning, 'My poor old feet ache, my back
> Is tired and I've got a stiff prick'
> Uprooting alder shoots in the rain[3]

But for the '(63)' and the actual content of what 'Mr. Edward Wyman' says, this could almost be Browning. But the poem also offers examples of the suddenly inserted quotation existing in an

---

[1] *In Memoriam James Joyce: From A Vision of World Language* (Glasgow: William Maclellan, 1955), pp. 11, 15.

[2] Ibid., pp. 60–1.

[3] *The New American Poetry*, ed. Donald M. Allen, p. 284.

isolated fashion as data within the poem. Such are, for instance, the quotations from Heraclitus and from Dr. Johnson:

> HERACLITUS: 'The waking have one common world
> But the sleeping turn aside
> Each into a world of his own.'
>
> .   .   .   .
>
> From Duns Scotus to this page
> A thousand years
>   ('. . . a dog walking on his hind legs—
> not that he does it well but that he
> Does it at all.')[1]

It is possible, of course, that Whalen has never read any of Pound's poetry, but the point being made is not that Whalen was directly influenced, but that his technique of quotation was made possible for twentieth-century poetry chiefly by Pound. At the primary level of influence, Pound's use of brief, pointed, often ironic, quotations in *Mauberley* became a prominent feature of Marianne Moore's verse. Then, later, several other poets seem to have been influenced in this matter by Pound, or Moore, or both. Among them are the Americans, Donald Finkel and Donald Hall. The uncompromisingly direct, low tone of Finkel's 'An Esthetic of Imitation' is reminiscent of Pound, and it may be that the technique of quotation in the poem was derived from Pound too; the poem begins:

> Preferring 'resemblance to beauty,'
> There were some who found more
> Truth in Philoktetes' rotten legs
> Than in the smooth buttocks
> Of a hundred Venuses. . . .[2]

Hall's tone is closer to Moore's, as can be seen in this extract from 'Munch's Scream', where he uses as a quotation a variation on the title of one of Yeats's poems:

>   Mayn't
>
> we say that time cannot represent
> space in art? 'The fascination of
> what's impossible' may be present,
> motivating the artist to move.[3]

---

[1] *The New American Poetry*, p. 285.
[2] *The New Poets of England and America*, p. 65.   [3] Ibid., pp. 98–9.

The technique of quotation, like all the techniques so far discussed in this chapter, is one that is obvious, and of fairly limited application; it is something that can be isolated in the work of a poet, and that can be studied in relation to Pound's usage of the same technique. What is perhaps the major influence exerted by Pound is, however, not of this neat, specific kind: it is something that is of such a general nature that specific manifestations in the work of those influenced may be quite different from the specific manifestations in Pound's work, and it is something that has become popular as a mode only partly through the influence of Pound. I am referring to the prosaic, matter-of-fact mode in which so much twentieth-century verse is written. It is a mode that is formed partly by rhythm, partly by the length of line, partly by syntax, and partly by diction: it avoids the iambic, it varies the length of line (either through the use of long and short lines coming together, or through the looseness with which a uniform length of line is adhered to), it uses conversational, uninverted syntax, and it avoids poetic diction in favour of the colloquial, the businesslike, and the erudite. Obviously Pound has been only one of the influences at work in making this mode popular: Browning, Whitman, Clough, and Hardy, and, more recently, Yeats and Eliot have also played a part. It would perhaps be invidious to single one of these out as the major influence, but Pound would have a good claim to pre-eminence. His early admiration for Browning, an admiration which he tried throughout his life to share with the young poets who came to him for help; his dictum that, in Ford Madox Ford's words, 'Poetry must be as well written as prose'; and his unremitting attempt in the Cantos to accommodate blocks of data in verse have provided theoretical and practical backing for the work of other poets.

At the simplest and most obvious level he has, with Browning's help, taught such poets as MacLeish, Herbert Read, Edwin Muir, Louis Zukofsky, and Basil Bunting to write straightforward and exciting narrative. Muir's 'Troy' provides a good example; it begins:

> He all that time among the sewers of Troy
> Scouring for scraps. A man so venerable
> He might have been Priam's self, but Priam was dead,
> Troy taken. His arms grew meagre as a boy's,
> And all that flourished in that hollow famine

> Was his long, white, round beard. Oh, sturdily
> He swung his staff and sent the bold rats skipping
> Across the scurfy hills and worm-wet valleys,
> Crying 'Achilles, Ajax, turn and fight!
> Stop cowards!' Till his cries, dazed and confounded,
> Flew back at him with: 'Coward, turn and fight!'
> And the wild Greeks yelled round him.
> Yet he withstood them, a brave, mad old man,
> And fought the rats for Troy.[1]

This example contains a number of features of Pound's typical narrative as used in 'Near Périgord', *Homage to Sextus Propertius*, and the Cantos: there is the plunging *in medias res* at the beginning; the anticipation of the subject with 'He'; the omission of the verb; the staccato movement of 'Troy taken'; and the loose syntactical linkages, especially the 'Ands'. Pound treats almost the same subject at the beginning of Canto IV, and it is interesting to notice that his account has most of these features too.

This adaptable and relaxed form of narrative has become so common in twentieth-century poetry that anything like the more formal style of Tennyson, Morris, or early Yeats is now unthinkable. Even a poet who is somewhat dubious about Pound's and Eliot's innovations, the Australian R. D. FitzGerald, has praised Pound's early work, and modelled his own narrative on Pound's line;[2] his 'Heemskerck Shoals', for instance, begins in a very relaxed, colloquial style:

> Too many councils and committees, too many
> making decisions beforehand—that was no way
> to run an expedition. Still that catch-penny
> assembly in Batavia had last say
> and first say too; and there it was all set down
> what had to be done . . . .[3]

The narrative use of the prosaic mode is, however, only one of its many uses, and is perhaps somewhat atypical. What is more typical is its use for the presentation of data, comment, and criticism: it is, indeed, the concentration on these that distinguishes twentieth-century poetry from any other period of poetry in English. It has

---

[1] *Collected Poems: 1921-1958* (London: Faber & Faber, 1960), p. 71.

[2] See Robert D. FitzGerald, 'An Attitude to Modern Poetry', *Southerly*, IX, 3 (1948), pp. 148-55.

[3] *Voyager Poems*, ed. Douglas Stewart (Brisbane: Jacaranda Press, 1960), p. 25.

often been remarked that this is an age of criticism, but what is generally meant by this statement is that the twentieth century has produced vast amounts of literary criticism. The statement would also be true, however, if it were applied not only to the criticism of poetry, but also to the poetry of criticism: the twentieth century has produced not only vast amounts of prose criticism of poetry, but also vast amounts of poetry that is criticism—criticism of modern conduct, aspirations, taste, and literature. These matters have been criticized in earlier poetry, of course, but with nothing like the same intensity. Poetry written about the writing of poetry has been commonplace in the Romantic and Victorian periods, for instance, but it has almost always dealt with the problems faced by the individual author in his work. Modern poetry about the writing of poetry has, however, not limited itself to this; it has discussed the whole critical problem as it applies to all poets, and it has done so not in general terms but in detailed examples. Kenneth Koch, for instance, writes:

> Supposing that one walks out into the air
> On a fresh spring day and has the misfortune
> To encounter an article on modern poetry
> In *New World Writing*, or has the misfortune
> To see some examples of some of the poetry
> Written by the men with their eyes on the myth
> And the Missus and the midterms, in the *Hudson Review*,
> Or, if one is abroad, in *Botteghe Oscure*,
> Or indeed in *Encounter*, what is one to do
> With the rest of one's day that lies blasted to ruins
> All bluely about one, what is one to do?
> O surely one cannot complain to the President,
> Nor even to the deans of Columbia College,
> Nor to T. S. Eliot, nor to Ezra Pound,
> And supposing one writes to the Princess Caetani,
> 'Your poets are awful!' what good would it do?
> And supposing one goes to the *Hudson Review*
> With a package of matches and sets fire to the building?
> One ends up in prison with trial subscriptions
> To the *Partisan*, *Sewanee*, and *Kenyon Review*![1]

This poem is in a line of descent from *Mauberley*, through some of Wallace Stevens's poetry, through *Four Quartets*, and through

[1] 'Fresh Air', *The New American Poetry*, p. 233.

Paterson. It might be difficult to find another passage of similar directness and pungency on the question of literature—apart from passages where poets such as Eliot and Bottrall discuss their own poetry—but countless passages could be found in twentieth-century poetry on other questions. The prosaic mode seems to have been adopted partly because so many poets wanted to introduce data, comment, and criticism into their work.

The earliest examples of the mode, including Pound's and Eliot's, frequently preserve a semi-dramatic form as a vehicle for these elements. Examples such as Pound's 'Portrait d'une femme', 'The Bellaires', and 'The Social Order', or Eliot's *Prufrock* and 'Portrait of a Lady' will be familiar. But the same sort of thing was being done by lesser men. One of them was that staunch upholder of the prose tradition in poetry, Ford Madox Ford, the author of 'On Heaven', which includes the lines:

> Well, you see, in England
> She had a husband. And four families—
> His, hers, mine, and another woman's too—
> Would have gone crazy. And, with all the rest,
> Eight parents, and the children, seven aunts
> And sixteen uncles and a grandmother.
> There were, besides, our names, a few real friends,
> And the decencies of life. A monstrous heap!
> They made a monstrous heap. I've lain awake
> Whole aching nights to tot the figures up![1]

In poems written a few years later by John Peale Bishop, the semi-dramatic form is less obvious; his 'In the Dordogne', for instance, contains the lines:

> And each day one died or another
> died: each week we sent out thousands
> that returned by hundreds
> wounded or gassed. And those that died
> we buried close to the old wall
> .within a stone's throw of Perigord
> under the tower of the troubadours.[2]

Sandburg, too, has some barely dramatic poems with a similar casual, colloquial tone.

[1] *Poetry*, IV, 3 (June 1914); quoted in a review of that number of *Poetry* by Richard Aldington in *The Egoist*, I, 13 (1 July 1914), p. 237.
[2] *Selected Poems of John Peale Bishop*, p. 26.

This mode was taken up by Auden and other poets prominent in the nineteen-thirties: in its worst manifestations (in some of the work of Day Lewis, Bunting, and Zukofsky, for instance), it produces a result very like journalism. Most current American poets seem to adopt it as one of their primary means of expression. Charles Olson, one of the acknowledged leaders of contemporary American poetry, begins his 'The Death of Europe' with the lines:

Rainer,
the man who was about to celebrate his 52nd birthday
the day I learned of your death at 28, said:
'I lie out on Dionysius' tongue'!

the sort of language you talked, and I did,
correctingly—
        as I heard this other German wrongly,
from his accent, and because I was thinking of you,
talking of how much you gave us all hearing
in Germany (as I watch a salamander on the end of a dead pine branch
snagging flies), what I heard this man almost twice your age say was,
'I lie on a dinosaur's tongue'![1]

This conversational mode was cultivated as a means of getting facts into verse by contributors to *The Black Mountain Review*, most of whom accepted the tenets of Olson's 'Projective Verse' and admired the work of William Carlos Williams and Louis Zukofsky. The review ran from 1954 to 1957, printing the work of these poets and of Robert Creeley (the editor), Robert Duncan, Paul Blackburn, Denise Levertov, and Edward Dorn. The Black Mountain poets were rather self-consciously aware of their inheritance of a tradition coming from Whitman though Pound and Williams, and many of them felt a sense of mission to oppose the tendencies typified by Eliot, and the New Critics. The use of the colloquial mode was, however, something that could not be confined to any one American group, and there are as many instances of it in the work of, for instance, Reed Whittemore, Howard Nemerov, W. S. Merwin, and Donald Finkel as in the work of the Black Mountain poets.

An esoteric form of the colloquial mode occurs in the poetry of the Beat Generation; in this poetry the diction and syntax are so much the preserve of a coterie that it is difficult for the outsider to

[1] *The New American Poetry*, p. 16.

know whether they are truly colloquial or not. The difficulty is increased by the intention these poets have of imitating the rhythms of jazz music. One might expect that this intention would interfere with the colloquialism of diction and syntax. The experiments of Hart Crane and E. E. Cummings in these fields seem, however, to have shown that it is possible to reconcile the two, and it is probable that the best work of Jack Kerouac and Allen Ginsberg, at least, has successfully followed their example. Kerouac's '221st Chorus' from 'Mexico City Blues', for instance, seems successful.[1]

Contemporary British poets—David Jones being a notable exception—are not nearly so experimental or so turbulent. Stanza form is much commoner in their work than it is in the work of the Americans; as a result, their poems probably look, to American eyes, as if they belong to the generation of John Crowe Ransom or John Peale Bishop. But the colloquial mode persists in their work too, though it is not so common, nor, when it does occur, so strident. Philip Larkin, for instance, writes:

> That Whitsun, I was late getting away:
>   Not till about
> One-twenty on the sunlit Saturday
> Did my three-quarters-empty train pull out,
> All windows down, all cushions hot, all sense
> Of being in a hurry gone. We ran
> Behind the backs of houses, crossed a street
> Of blinding windscreens, smelt the fish-dock; thence
> The river's level drifting breadth began,
> Where sky and Lincolnshire and water meet.[2]

Or Christopher Middleton begins a poem with:

> Since last September I've been trying to describe
> two moonstone hills,
> and an ochre mountain, by candlelight, behind.
> But a lizard has been sick into the ink,
> a cat keeps clawing at me, you should see my face,
> I'm too intent to dodge.[3]

Charles Tomlinson, who, largely because of his professed interest in William Carlos Williams, Louis Zukofsky, Basil Bunting, and the

---

[1] See *The New American Poetry*, p. 174.
[2] 'The Whitsun Weddings', *The New Poetry*, p. 81.
[3] 'Edward Lear in February', ibid., p. 116.

Black Mountain poets, is often credited with being an experimental writer, adopts quite often a slack, discursive form of the colloquial mode, though he laces it with off-handed quotations in foreign languages. Keith Douglas, too, deserves mention: he was incorporating more and more of the prosaic and colloquial in his verse up to the time of his death during the Second World War.

I do not suggest, of course, that the poets who use the colloquial mode have all been directly influenced by Pound. But it is being asserted that Pound has had a good deal to do with the popularity of this mode among twentieth-century poets. Where the mode is used for the presentation of data, comment, and criticism, his part in innovation and leadership is a very great one. The greater popularity of the colloquial mode in America is, furthermore, an index of the geographical distribution of Pound's influence in other matters as well. His influence—and his rather vague, indirect influence through such poets as Williams—has been far greater in America than in Britain. In Britain, the major influences of the twentieth century have been Yeats and Eliot, and their work contains, as has been suggested in earlier chapters, much that owes nothing to Pound.

R

CONCLUSION

POUND as an unselfish publicist for other writers' work is an engaging figure. His concern to secure publication for struggling writers; his appreciation of a wide variety of verse and prose, even if quite unlike his own; and his incessant campaign to educate the public have been, no matter how one attempts to explain them in terms of his personality, valuable and praiseworthy. His concern for the material welfare of writers, even if occasionally resented, has undoubtedly made life a good deal easier for scores of his friends and acquaintances. The awareness and solicitude of a Boswell, a John Newton, and a Watts-Dunton were highly developed in Pound, and directed by him towards several major, and a host of minor, writers.

This sort of interest in writers might, of course, have been exercised by a person of no literary talent whatever, though such a person would have needed prodigious luck to select so many good writers as Pound did. Pound's literary talent, which manifested itself in his judgement of other writers, was also the quality that made his interest in them of literary, rather than merely biographical, importance. He felt that he could help them with their writing as well as with their day-to-day existence. Some, such as Richard Aldington, Robert Frost, and Conrad Aiken, found his literary help oppressive; others, such as T. S. Eliot and Ernest Hemingway, found it sympathetic to their own intentions. All were impressed by his enormous enthusiasm for writing, and some, such as Yeats and Eliot, were encouraged in times of disappointment to turn back to their work.

What Pound passed on to his friends, acquaintances, and imitators was sometimes style, sometimes a tone, sometimes subject-matter, sometimes a form of construction. The more superficial tricks of style—the startling new image in the last line of an Imagist poem, the omission of articles, the insertion of letters into narrative —could be learnt by quite unintelligent and minor poets, or by major poets as a passing phase. The less superficial aspects of style, such as the handling of colloquial rhythms and the use of brief anecdote to illustrate a point, were less teachable, and few poets made the intense study of Pound's work necessary to learn them; one who did, with limited success, was Basil Bunting. A tone of hearty jauntiness, or of straight-faced levity, or of exasperation could not be learnt without being transmuted to some extent by the personality of the learner, and so one finds that William Carlos Williams, or T. S. Eliot, or Archibald MacLeish, for instance, never wrote, and perhaps never wanted to write, a poem with exactly the same tone as Pound. Subject-matter and the writer's attitude to it are again rather personal matters, and Pound's interests have been almost as esoteric as Yeats's; he has, however, maintained and passed on the typical Romantic interest in the sea, and in travel. The invention or promotion of a form of construction is a much rarer kind of influence, yet Pound has promoted both the Imagist poem and the ideogrammic method. As both of these forms are capable of indefinite modification, it could be expected that Pound's influence with them is likely to continue.

With all his efforts, however, Pound has probably had no more influence than Hopkins, Yeats, or Eliot, and little more than Dylan Thomas or William Carlos Williams. His influence has differed from theirs, however, in that, to a degree unparalleled in English literature, it has been a deliberate influence, a conscious attempt to set up the equivalent of a Berlitz or extra-mural course in poetics. This earnest interest in the propagation of efficient 'know-how' may partially account for the fact that, throughout his career, his theorizing and his practice have made more appeal to American poets than to those of the country where he has been living. He has un-doubtedly influenced more American poets, and more good American poets, than anyone else this century. But his influence has always been mingled with and diluted by the influence of others; at any particular time he has been overshadowed as a popular source of inspiration by other writers—Yeats during his time in England, Eliot during the twenties, Hopkins during the thirties, Dylan Thomas during the forties and early fifties, Williams since then. One can account for these changing patterns of popularity in terms of publication dates; one can note that the influence of Hopkins, Eliot, and Dylan Thomas has waned since they have had no new

poems to offer; one can point to Pound's greatest periods of popularity as occurring during the early days of his publications in *Poetry*
and *The Little Review*, the flurry of periodical publications in the
thirties, and the notoriety surrounding his trial and the award of
the Bollingen Prize to the *Pisan Cantos*. It would seem as if the
constant (and occasionally spectacular) effect of Pound on other
writers has been due partly to the persistence of his publishing programme, the unceasing attempts to 'make it new'. It is possible
that when he has nothing new to offer, his influence will decline like
those of Hopkins, Eliot and Dylan Thomas. They offered either
superficial tricks of style, or lessons too hard to assimilate, or
methods that they invented and exhausted. But some other influences have managed to persist well after any novelty has worn off,
and it may be that Pound's influence will be as steady as Yeats's.
Yeats offered a tone of aristocratic assurance, a subject-matter
drawn from the poet's own life, and a conservative modernization
of traditional style. Pound's habitual tone and his favourite subject-
matter are less useful to other poets; and he has some meretricious
tricks of style that might repel rather than attract. But his handling
of colloquial language, whether of speech or comment, and his
advocacy of certain forms may still prove attractive and useful to
important poets.

INDEX

Abbey Theatre, Dublin, 75n., 86, 98, 99
Abercrombie, Lascelles, 39
Active Anthology, 57, 58, 59n., 138, 157, 194
Agenda, 72
Aiken, Conrad, and Imagism, 18, 19, 167, 186, 187; commissioned as editor, 69–70; and T. S. Eliot, 106, 107, 113n.; theory of 'poetic tones', 111; and *persona*, 132n.; experiments with musical form, 201; and Ezra Pound, 218.
  Works of: 'Counterpoint and Implication', 111; *The Jig of Forslin*, 19; 'Limits to Imagism', 187n.; 'The Place of Imagism', 19n., 187n.; *Preludes for Memnon*, 187; *Ushant: An Essay*, quoted, 18, 19
Alden, Raymond, M., 38
Aldington, Richard, 189–94; and Imagism, 9, 10–13, 30, 133–4, 196; and Ezra Pound, 15, 23, 36, 38, 42, 140, 218; runs *The New Freewoman*, 24; and *Blast*, 30; and Gourmont, 35, 140; helps promote 'Bel Esprit' scheme, 42; and Hemingway, 47; verses in *The Exile*, 52; review of *Poetry*, 214n.
  Works of: 'Au Vieux Jardin', 190; 'Choricos', 190; 'Farewell to Europe', quoted, 10, 15, 190; 'Images', 193–4; 'Le Latin Mystique', 35; *Literary Studies and Reviews*, 35; 'Modern Poetry and the Imagists', quoted, 12, 13, 133; 'Natal Verses for the Birth of a New Review', 52–53; 'To a Greek Marble', 190–1.
Amis, Kingsley, 208; 'Beowulf', 208
'Amygism', 14, 115, 187
Anderson, Margaret, 27, 40, 41, 46n., 164
Anderson, N. D., 37; *The Voice of the Infinite and Other Poems*, 37
Antheil, George, 40, 41, 48
Anthology of Famous English and American Poetry, An, 69
Aragon, Louis, 57
Arnold, Matthew, 132
Ashbery, John, 204; *Some Trees*, 204n.
Athenaeum, The, 39, 131n.
Atlantic Monthly, The, quoted from, 10, 190

Auden, W. H., 58, 64, 65, 70, 71, 159, 167, 201, 204, 207, 215; works of: *The Age of Anxiety*, 207; *Collected Shorter Poems: 1930–1944*, 204n., 207n.; 'Doom is dark and deeper than any sea-dingle', 207; 'Kairos and Logos', 204n.
Ayscough, Florence, 33; 'Chinese Written Wall Pictures', 33n.

Barnard, Mary, 54, 58, 59
Barnes, Djuna, 46
Barney, Natalie Clifford, 49
Barrett, William, 71; 'A Prize for Ezra Pound', 71n.
Barry, Iris, 23, 39, 115, 140
Bates, Margaret, 73; *Cinco Poesías*, 73
Baudelaire, Charles, 114–15, 135
Beach, Sylvia, 41, 49
Beardsley, Mabel, 90n.
'Bel Esprit', 42, 43, 45, 157
Berryman, John, 76; 'The Poetry of Ezra Pound', quoted, 76
Bewley, Marius, 187–8; 'The Poetry of Wallace Stevens', quoted, 187
Binyon, Laurence, 59–63, 64; works of: *The Adventures of Ulysses*, 61; trans. of Dante's *Inferno*, 59, 60, 61, 64; trans. of Dante's *Purgatorio*, 60, 61
Bird, William, 43, 44
Bishop, John Peale, 203, 214, 216; works of: 'In the Dordogne', 214; 'New England III: The Wonders of Science', 204; *Selected Poems*, 214n.
Black Mountain Review, The, 215
Blackburn, Paul, 215
Blackmur, R. P., 70, 132n.
Blast, 19, 25, 30, 36, 65, 174
Blast Group, the, 29
Blish, James, 69; 'Rituals on Ezra Pound', quoted, 69
Bogan, Louise, 70
Bollingen Prize for Poetry, 70, 71, 220
Bottome, Phyllis, 3–4, 9, 44; *From the Life*, quoted, 3
Bottrall, Ronald, 58, 59, 204, 214; works of: 'Un Bel Homme du Temps Jadis', 204n.; *Collected Poems*, 204n.; ' "For Our Time" ', 204n.; 'Ritornello', 204n.